WOMEN OF SPIRIT

For my mother, a woman of indomitable spirit

Published in 2019 by SilverWood Books

SilverWood Books Ltd
14 Small Street, Bristol, BS1 1DE, United Kingdom

www.silverwoodbooks.co.uk

ISBN 978-1-78132-838-5 (paperback)
ISBN 978-1-78132-839-2 (ebook)

British Library Cataloguing in Publication Data
A CIP catalogue record for this book is available from the British Library

Page design and typesetting by SilverWood Books
Printed on responsibly sourced paper

Women of Spirit

Volume Two

Compiled and photographed by

Susie Mackie

SilverWood

Contents

Contents continued...

Foreword by Arti Halai

When Susie Mackie asked me to write the foreword to this book, after reading a single chapter, I agreed in a heartbeat. What an honour and privilege to share some words about the tremendous achievements of the extraordinary women here. I'm humbled and grateful for having had the opportunity to experience the powerful and transformational stories that unite and show humankind at its best.

Everyone has a story.

These stories belong to *Women of Spirit*. Beautiful. Courageous. Selfless.

I admit I cried when reading some of the stories, but I also felt relief, uplifted and pride.

Every woman has relived and exposed her past, always difficult, sometimes traumatic or disturbing and with searing honesty. Their experience is so powerfully articulated we find ourselves imagining their 'real' situation. To call it an emotional rollercoaster is an understatement and yet it is testament to their strength, their courage, their generosity and desire to help others that shines through the most for me. Incredibly, the women even managed to weave some humour into their experiences – a lovely touch and as a reader, I am sure something for which everyone will be grateful. It is the elixir that replenishes after the storm. It is clear that all the women are now embracing, enjoying and living their lives as they chose to do. How empowering is that!

There are many common themes that emerge throughout the book, which includes women from different backgrounds, ages and stages in life. The mind and body connection is a powerful reminder of the effect and impact one makes on the other. Stories including the start and loss of life, illness, physical and emotional abuse, challenges and difficulties, yet through resilience, focus, self-belief and love their success is resplendent.

Every story stands as tall as a lighthouse, steering ships away from the rocks in depths of darkness, towards calmer waters and the rays of light.

Earlier this year, I was asked at an international conference 'what makes me who I am?'

My answer was "life, learning and love."

Life – because we are all on a journey, but it pays to stop, reflect and look back at how far we have come and what we have taken on board.

Learning – because as humans we are always growing, developing and sharing our knowledge, insight, and experiences.

Love - because the more you love yourself the more love you have to give to others.

All of the above are reflected in the pages of this book. In sharing their stories, these women allow us all to do the same: make a difference.

A final word has to go to Susie Mackie. As founder of *Women of Spirit*, Susie is on a mission. She is passionate, driven and leaves a lasting and memorable impression. She is the bedrock of this book and without her it simply wouldn't have been written and the images would never have come to life.

Women of Spirit, you make us proud.

With love, respect and gratitude,

Arti Halai

Biography

Arti Halai is a public speaker and executive coach on personal effectiveness, profile raising and creating positive mindsets that empower and lead to results. She specialises in presentation, media and communication skills working with clients around the world. She is co-founder of three businesses under the Fleet Street Group. (www.fleetstreetgroup.com)

Arti honed her skills during a successful fifteen-year career as a television presenter, reporter and producer working for the UK's leading media organisations including ITV, the BBC, ITN and Carlton. In addition, she authored 'Positivity' which was published in 2009.

Arti supports several charities and helps to raise the aspirations of under achieving teenagers and those coming from disadvantaged backgrounds.

Arti lives in London with her husband and daughter, with whom she credits giving her "a whole new learning opportunity."

One

The Road to Self-Love

The most beautiful people we have known are those who have known defeat, known
suffering, known struggle, known loss, and have found their way out of the depths.
These persons have an appreciation, a sensitivity and an understanding of life that fills
them with compassion, gentleness, and a deep loving concern.
Beautiful people do not just happen.

Elizabeth Kubler-Ross

Heidi Clutterbuck

What struck me first about Heidi are her twinkling eyes, out of which shine love and warmth in equal measure. When you learn of the events of her childhood and later, how she fought for justice and to regain her power, her joyful personality and determination to make changes for the vulnerable is all the more admirable.

I AM A HAPPILY MARRIED MUM to five amazing children. My husband and I own a successful Tool and Plant Hire company with three branches and over thirty dedicated and loyal staff. My life is busy, chaotic and at times stressful, but we work hard and appreciate the rewards this can bring. Throughout my day I wear many labels: wife, mother, colleague, friend and finally the one I wear as a victim of child sexual abuse.

For a long time, I hid this label, scared of so many things attached to it, all negative, all destructive and attached to great personal pain and fear. But when that pain finally overwhelmed me and my fear for other victims became too much, I decided to report my abuse.

Desperation and fear are great motivators, and at that time, they proved to be for me. For some four years, I have existed in a world of emails and reports about myself, all in various guises; victim, complainant, survivor and the most recent label 'Mrs A' – a person talked about, reported about and upon whom decisions were made. Such a situation became for me a dark murky world where I was often lost as a person and unable to express my thoughts in a way that they would be heard.

Rarely are survivors depicted as strong, capable and calm, not normal people, individuals, with families and friends, all living within the heart of everyday communities. The chances are you already know someone like me: you probably just don't know it. The profile of a perpetrator's power is to pass all the guilt, shame and fear to their victims. However, I decided to take back my power, give up my anonymity and be seen in full view as a survivor of childhood sexual abuse.

So here I am in full view: the anonymous Mrs A, but you may call me Heidi.

There are moments in our lives that can define us, change us forever. Some are good, some are bad. But whether good or bad they have the potential to propel us to be a totally different person. These are my 'three moments'.

Moment One

I wrote this the day I wrote my police statement at the age of forty-one years old to report my childhood sexual abuse.

"As I climbed into my car I can feel the rise of acid-filled sick in my throat. It catches me by surprise and I swallow hard to try and 'will-it' back into its rightful place. Inhaling deeply, I sit motionless gripping my steering wheel. Although I am not moving, my mind is racing at supersonic speed. Am I really going to do this? Is this the right thing to do? What about everyone I care about? What if I'm not strong enough? What if no one believes me?

Then I did something I had never done; I remember, I go back to that time, I remember all those long ignored but not forgotten memories.

Then I start the car. On autopilot I take a familiar route used for carefree shopping trips and coffee with friends. Except this journey will not be fun, no laughter or purchases to hide. I will come back from this trip different. This journey will change me forever. Again, the doubts and fears become louder in my head, louder and louder. I grab at the radio desperate to hear a new noise. But the chatter is too loud, too prominent. Ok, who can I phone? Who of all my friends will chatter with little input from me? Jane. I quickly hit dial on my hands free and after a few rings she is chattering happily with tales of rugby matches, nits and a very unusual rash. I have never been so pleased to hear of normal humdrum in my life. I listen intently trying to focus on every word, occasionally umming and agreeing with her where necessary.

But then hot, nervous, angry tears prick my eyes. I blink hard, willing them away. But more come making my nose fill. I sniff, trying to gain my composure. "Are you ok?" comes the question into the car space surrounding me. Are you ok? No I'm not. I'm scared and frightened, I feel sick, I don't want to do this but I know I have to. I want so badly right now to share this with you but I can't and I just want to turn around and pretend this isn't happening. I want to go home but I can't I just can't.

Startled, I can't think of what to say. After an awkward silence I said "Oh I think I'm coming down with something." My heart is now nearly beating out of my chest. But in true Jane style she then happily launches into a rundown of the various bugs and viruses doing the rounds at playgroup and school and safely back to that mysterious rash. A feeling of guilt washes over me. Jane is one of my closest friends; a friendship steeped in history and shared experiences. She knows me inside out and yet today she has no idea. This journey, this destination will change me forever and she doesn't have a clue. But that isn't because I don't love or trust her. In fact it is because I love her so much. I am protecting her and that is the way it needs to stay. No good will come of sharing this, not with people I love of that I am sure. As Jane launches into an intricate description of the rash, I arrive at the police station.

I am here. Now I need to move before I lose my nerve. "Jane I have to go. I'm in town and need to pop and get shopping before the school run, I'll call tonight to check on how things are with the rash! (Pause.) Love you." I press end call. Shit! Shit! Shit! A lie. Jane had done her job in distracting me but now I felt guilty and sad. Reasoning this isn't about anyone else but me and wanting to protect her, I rationalise my small white lie as an act of kindness. As I step out of the car I am met with icy cold sleet and a piercing wind. I stand lifting my head to the grey bleak sky. Closing my eyes, I just breathe in and out, slowly forgetting all the noise and chaos in my mind. It is time. I walk head down determined and set on my path. Strangely, a sense of calm increases with every step.

I walk boldly up the steps of the police station and stride confidently to the desk. I don't want anyone to pick up on my fear. I want to appear in control. I am not scared. I am not a victim. I am in control. The receptionist smiles as I approach her. "I'm here to see Inspector Adams, he is expecting me: Heidi Clutterbuck." I sit in the welcoming atmosphere of grey walls and posters in every language about domestic violence. I begin to fidget and can feel a rising sense of panic. God, please don't leave me here for long. I then randomly decide to play a bizarre game of guess the crime of the people who enter the reception. Inspector Adams appears. After pleasantries are exchanged I follow him into an interview room. It is a small grey box of a room with a small desk in the corner, a chair either side and old fashioned recorder on the desk. Inside the grey box we begin. Inspector Adams has left me in the capable hands of Sergeant Carol Evans, a professional-looking woman who is heavily pregnant. She looks a kindly soul. After small talk we settle down to business.

We begin with basic details of who I am: date of birth, personal details, my family, all easy, safe territory. Then she speaks the words I have dreaded since I entered the grey box of a room. "Can you tell me in your own words about your abuse?" I suddenly feel startled, my mouth is dry and the nausea is rising again in my throat. I dig my fingernails into the side of my leg to try and push myself to speak and my brain jolts into action. I travel back in time to those long ignored but not forgotten memories. Autopilot kicks in and I repeat the details. As I do so I stare intently at the wall opposite, trying to trick my brain into speaking without feeling the horror of the details. All the time talking but not listening to my own words. But then something jolts me back into the room – a memory which I have no power to ignore.

It is of a little girl. It is snowing and she can't wait to play outside. She scurries around getting all wrapped up and waits excitedly by the front door. But then a teenage man appears to take her out to play. This won't be fun. She doesn't want to go, but her parents usher her out of the door. Where they live there are communal garages and he leads her away from the direction of the park to a garage with a green door. As they walk she looks at their footprints in the deep snow. I can hear what she is thinking…perhaps this is the day, perhaps today he will get caught. People will see the footprints. They will see them and come and find us…whilst inside and he is doing those awful things to her tiny body, she lays face down waiting for someone to come. She hears voices and footsteps and he is startled. He stops, pauses, but then the footsteps walk away into the distance so he continues. As he lifts the garage door and her eyes adjust to the light she searches desperately on the ground for their footprints. But they are gone as new snow has settled. No one can see, that's why they didn't come. She feels so sad. No one is ever going to come. She doesn't want to play in the snow anymore. She wants to hide in her room. She's sore from what he's done and just wants to hide.

Suddenly I feel her in that grey box of a room. I can feel her sadness hanging in the air around me: it almost feels like I am having an out of body experience. She is crouched on the floor curled into a tiny ball in the corner of the room. Hugging her knees she is bent forward. I cannot see her face. Although she makes no sound I can tell she is crying. (I remember those silent tears. Tears full of pain and fear but which make no noise. You try so hard to keep them in but they push and push until you feel like your head will explode. So, eventually your body betrays you and they begin to flow. In a last act of defiance you stay silent trying not to be part of this involuntary process.) For a brief moment I study her. I recognise those clothes, hair even the smell of her. I know what she is thinking I can tell without her saying a word…

You left me.

You left me here and you never came.

I needed you and you never came.

I've waited so long, why did you leave me here alone?

I want to crouch down. I want to scoop her up in my arms and hold her close. Kiss her hair and comfort her like I would my own children. Make her feel safe. I am here, you are safe, I came back for you, I'm sorry it's been so long but I'm here now. But then she is gone. All I can hear is my own breathing.

A voice breaks the silence "Are you ok?" asks Sergeant Evans. "I just need a minute, can I pop to the toilet? " I respond. Without thinking I stand and reach for the door. It's locked and it makes me panic. I wasn't expecting that. It hits home where I am: in a police station. This is a dangerous place. The doors are locked to either keep people in or out. It just depends which side of the door you are. A perfect place, I reflect, to share those memories. Lock the door and throw away the key.

I'm now stood in the toilet feeling startled and numb. What just happened? Am I really doing this? I lean over the sink and splash cold water on my face. That feels lovely. I concentrate on this pleasant sensation as I try to settle myself again. Come on, you can do this. The hard part is over. Just go back in and finish what you came to do. Then the secrets aren't yours anymore. Someone else can carry them. Someone else can worry. Someone else can make decisions. This is your chance to be free. From this moment you can be free. I step back inside the 'box' with my calm exterior restored. I search for a new part of the wall. This technique works and there are only small parts where I falter and the tears threaten. I dig deep and will myself forward.

We then busy ourselves with the paperwork. As she re-reads my statement, I watch her hand wrap protectively around her tummy probably to protect her baby from hearing the horrid details and my mind wanders, thinking of her unborn baby: I hope you are always safe, always loved and lead a happy life.

Outside it is snowing heavily and once again I am comforted by the coolness on my face. I walk slowly back to the car trying to catch up with my own thoughts before I return home. Tears come unexpectedly in a wave of relief and real physical pain. I ache all over in every bone, every muscle; I must have been tensing every part of myself without realising it. Here comes the acid sick again but this time I can't hold it in, it pours out of my mouth and onto my shoes and I am powerless to stop it. I am now bent over trying to catch my breath. My two worst nightmares; being sick and crying in public! Can this day really get any worse? Then my phone rings in my pocket and I answer without thinking. It's James asking me to pick up some milk on my way home. Now I'm back in my life, back to normal; things are the same as before, life is still here going on, nothing has changed. It's all as it was. But am I? I give myself no time to answer; I walk back to the car and go home. Enough, enough for today. Think no more. Tomorrow can wait.

And so an investigation began, but little did I know back then it would be a further two years before it would become an independent investigation with the former Independent Police Complaints Commission.

The trust required to vocalise and repeat childhood sexual abuse for a police statement is huge. But for me it was given freely, openly and honestly. Yes, I was scared, yes I had fears but these were around finally saying aloud my innermost thoughts and letting the words hit the air. Never did I fear the trust I had placed in Gloucestershire Police…not back then anyway.

Then I got used to its existence – as the investigation progressed I would see emails in which my case was discussed, referred to, or I would give permission for it to be shared. This was scary, but a necessary evil to assist the officers as they went forward with my case. I got used to it being there, tucked safely away in their world, away from mine. I had no fear: they were all professional and mindful of the need for privacy, sensitivity and my trust in them.

Moment Two

Then out of the blue – a passing conversation with a friend in which they repeated my case details I had shared in no other place than in my statement: personal, intimate, heart-breaking details. I had shared these with no one; not my husband, not a trusted friend, just the police in those private moments when giving my statement. Her source? That led back to the officer being investigated, back to Gloucestershire Police. I always knew there would be a consequence to me telling my story. This was, to me, the last manipulation to keep me silent. It brought me instantly to my knees; I struggled for breath.

The policeman who leaked detail was my brother. He knew that while everyone was watching he could not be seen to intimidate or attack me. So, in a very clever way, which left no trace, he publicly shared my most horrific moments. 'Operation Elder' which investigated the leak could not prove this and said it was due to Gloucestershire's Police lack of an archive and auditing system. The emails were permanently deleted. It did however find details of poor data practices, training, auditing and lack of appropriate conflict of interest policy. It was recommended to buy an archive and auditing system, but they chose to only buy an auditing system – which means officers can still permanently delete data.

It felt like an assault had taken place but because I was not dripping in blood, or had broken bones to fix, stitches to have, 'all was well'. If there had been a physical version of the internal assault I would be in intensive care on a ventilator. I really was fighting for my life. Mind racing, my first thoughts are for my family, what if someone tells them? Who else knows? No, this isn't fair. No, this shouldn't happen. No, this isn't what was promised. Anonymity for life, that's what they said, that's what they promised; a cloak of protection to be able to share your darkest, weakest, most horrific moments.

I was forced to make some heart-breaking decisions. Share the details with those I loved or run the risk of others telling them? It was the cruelest of choices. Just for the record, I had chosen not to share the details as I didn't want that horrific stuff in their minds. I had made a conscious decision to protect them.

There are three common responses a victim of trauma can use. Fight. Flight. Flop. In my childhood, because of the imbalance of power both physically and emotionally, I had always used flop. Remain still, silent, comply; essentially play dead until he is done with you. My brain had become wired to consider this to be the most effective response. Its success rate was one hundred percent: I was still alive so why consider another way? Because although yes, I had survived, I knew this time that same response wasn't going to work. If I didn't fight, didn't get up and quickly, this would kill me. I needed to find my power to fight.

Emotionally against the wall, the only valid option was to choose the one I feared the most: to share, in order to protect them. This was a pivotal moment for me because in those horrific moments it forced me to consider taking control. To take ownership of my past and then no one could ever hurt me or those I loved with it again. I also knew I couldn't do this alone, that I needed to be open and honest about my experiences and let those people who loved me support me and hold me whilst I felt so weak and vulnerable and wounded.

I felt like a thief in the night stealing back my power whilst no one was looking. That thought grew from a tiny seed: maybe I can do this, maybe I can take control, maybe I can speak up, maybe I can be brave. Maybe, just maybe I, Heidi Clutterbuck, could be a survivor.

Courage is not the absence of fear, its feeling the fear and doing it anyway.

Then it's like a floodgate; when you start to consider you can do anything you set your mind to, you can. First it began slowly, surely. I began a petition, started a blog on this topic, attended the IICSA (Independent Inquiry into Child Sexual Abuse) Truth Project and spoke my truth in the hope of learning and change. I joined their forum and attended with others to discuss and look for solutions. I sat on the IICSA panel to have a voice in the issues, impact and systems that survivors can face. All this was in the midst of a long complicated investigation. Then as the investigation started to conclude I had a voice in recommendations of Operation Larkspur. I had a radio interview on BBC Radio 5 Live with Adrian Chiles to share the recommendations and to create dialogue.

Then the conclusion: 'Officer One' was found to have a case to answer for gross misconduct, yet allowed to retire during the process of the investigation. 'Officer Two' was found to have a case to answer for misconduct and put on management action whilst sitting on

Glospol (Gloucestershire Constabulary) Senior Command Team. They re-employed the officer who had been allowed to retire, as technically he never went through a conduct hearing, so 'all was well'…?! Anyone who has read Operation Larkspur and the statements of other victims may form a very different view. However it is a protected document so that view is not represented in public.

The changes in our society here and now regarding CSA (Child Sexual Abuse), CSE (Child Sexual Exploitation) and sexual crime/harassment will define a generation. Like no other time before we are attempting to take ownership of the failings of the past and learn lessons to protect the victims of the future. The IICSA Inquiry and Truth Project was formed to create understanding, learning and enable change; a pledge to listen to the voices of victims without fear or favour, promising care, respect and to value all that is shared. It was to be a safe space where victims can feel supported to speak freely, honestly and openly.

Society has responded with an overwhelming roar of support and fellowship as with the '#MeToo' campaign, a very public call to action. Women and men from every race or social group are standing together for progress and change. People are feeling supported and empowered to take ownership of their past and stand firm in their right to justice. They find strength with love and support from friends, strangers and communities alike, from all who do not judge or blame nor turn away, but stand firm in solidarity. When people are empowered they can choose how to heal themselves. They can have open, honest discussions about all the issues to look for resolution and change. Together people are so powerful.

Moment Three

Suddenly I felt I had inherited a super power and I was determined to use it for good. I decided more needed to be done to share, implement and create dialogue to help victims and officers alike. I wrote to Chief Constables with an interest on this topic and offered to write a presentation to help create the dialogue I believe is needed. Little secret here…I never write a shopping list let alone something like this. Oh, and the public speaking thing – not done that before either! Yet here I was making these offers and if I received a "yes" I knew I would make this happen because I have the knowledge they need, the impact, the experience to be able to say "this is how this feels", let's talk and perhaps find another way. After days of writing I had a very raw, but valid document. In its unshapen state I could see the potential of something great. I shared it with my now increasing contacts of friends, other survivors and professionals met along the way. Feedback was overwhelmingly amazing with helpful suggestions and points to consider – but not one person wanted to change its words, its essence. Then came surprising offers of help to polish my presentation and a crash course on public speaking, all within a tiny timeframe. I was overwhelmed with the offers of people's time, skills and knowledge. Within days I had a presentation to be proud of and enough naivety, courage and basic speaking skills to will me on.

On Thursday the fourteenth of June 2018 I stood in front of a room full of police officers and shared my journey to help create what we both need: progress and change. My voice faltered a little but I stood firm and strong. I will never let anyone silence me ever again. I will speak, but I will also listen.

In the words of Eminem, "You can do anything you set your mind to".

Looking back with hindsight and knowledge there are always things you wish were different. Chances missed, moments where you so wanted to be brave and speak up but you were paralysed by fear, shame and guilt, believing that somehow all of this was your fault and so you remained silent. I began to wonder about what someone could have said to me to help me in my younger days. So I've decided to write all the things I would have said in the hope that it could potentially reach just one person…

"This is not your fault. None of it. I know you are confused, scared and believe you are trapped. He says not to tell, to keep the secret and then things will be fine. But they are not fine are they? He does terrible things to you when no one is looking. It hurts and it makes you feel scared. What he does is not right. No adult no matter how much you love or trust them has the right to do those things. I know you cry every night wishing this was over; silent sobs that you hold in your chest so no one can hear. He tells you no one will believe you, they will call you a liar. I will, I believe you and others will too. There are people who want to help you, who can make you feel safe and not alone. They will help you face what has been happening and deal with it. No one is going to force you to do anything you don't want. You are in control. Most of all, more than anything I want you to know that if you can be brave you will be listened to and believed. You are not alone."

As an adult who finally made this step I can say it has been the most freeing, healing and positive thing I have ever done for myself. One tiny step can lead to a very different future...

Biography

Heidi Clutterbuck is the complainant who refused to give up. In a quest for justice and closure she reported her childhood sexual abuse and naively entered a four-year process culminating in an independent inquiry with the now IOPC (Independent Office for Police Conduct). A journey which would test her to the limits of human endurance. A process hampered by data breeches, leaks and Gloucestershire Police's refusal to accept the wrongdoing of their officers.

Sexual crime is based on power and the loss of it. Heidi decided to be like a thief in the night and steal it back while no one was looking. To use her power for good to help create change and learning in a system stacked unfavorably against those who may be vulnerable due to their circumstance or trauma.

In September 2017 'Operation Larkspur' made a number of recommendations: to highlight it's learning for how Professional Standards Departments engage and look after those with certain vulnerabilities. Seeing more was needed to be done to implement, create dialogue and share this vital learning, Heidi created her own presentation to assist the police. In July 2018 this work was endorsed by Chief Constable Martin Jelley and Heidi is currently visiting a number of Police Forces to present 'Larkspur'.

Described as inconvenient, stubborn and relentless, Heidi takes all those labels as a compliment.

A defining thought…

"One doesn't have to operate with great malice to do great harm. The absence of empathy and understanding are sufficient…"

Charles M. Blow

www.rapecrisis.org.uk
www.theglade.org.uk
www.truthproject.org.uk/i-will-be-heard
www.barnardos.org.uk
www.nspcc.org.uk
www.napac.org.uk

Bertie Ekperigin

Looking at Bertie's portrait you might be surprised to know that for decades she dreaded being the centre of attention and suffered a crippling fear of speaking in public. Events which happen in our childhood can have a negative impact on our lives, even if we don't remember them. Overcoming that fear is exciting and empowering for Bertie, and she now helps others do the same.

How two minutes can change your life.

What you are about to read is a true story from my early life, and I tell it because I want to awaken your mind to the possibility that, just like I once was, you might be locked down in some incomprehensible way, unable to live to your full potential or live your dream life.

As you read my story, I'd like you to consider two very important questions. Of what would you like to finally understand and let go? What could be stopping you from living your best life?

The reason I ask these questions will soon become very clear, but for now, let me tell you something about the life I have led. A former fashion model and personal trainer, it would be very easy to look at me and assume that I am supremely confident, and that everything about my life is perfect.

In reality, ever since I was young, I have dreaded being the centre of attention. My life was severely restricted as a result, and for over forty years I suffered from a crippling fear of speaking in public. I was frightened to be seen and heard…to have everybody's eyes on me.

There are many memories I can recount that illustrate this. When I was twenty, I was invited to a group interview to become an air stewardess. The interview involved around sixteen of us sitting in a circle, and we were taking it in turns to talk about ourselves to the rest of the group. All I can remember about that interview is the horribly familiar feeling of intense fear. My heart rate was pumping, my head was spinning, and I felt utterly sick with terror. I couldn't hide how uncomfortable I was, and I wanted the ground to swallow me whole. Yet the feeling didn't make any sense to me; I wasn't shy, and I knew I was good enough to do the job.

Despite how terrified I had been, to my amazement I *did* get the job, and I went on to love my early career as a stewardess. Either I hadn't been that bad in my interview, or my other qualities shone through more brightly – I will never know, but that interview had taught me something. I must avoid embarrassing myself like that ever again.

Later, at the age of twenty-one, I went to live in London to try out fashion modeling. It was a tough gig, which surprised me because I thought modeling would be easy. How wrong was I? When I joined an agency, it didn't occur to me that I would have anything to be afraid of, after all, models don't have to speak, and I believed that my fear was to do with speaking in public, not being seen.

But modeling is, I think, a tough life for young girls. They come up to London feeling confident about how they look, only to get torn down by multiple criticisms about their appearance. As you might imagine, it is very hard to feel 'good enough' when you are constantly being criticised. After receiving a fair bit of rejection myself, I started to feel less attractive, and I didn't really enjoy modeling.

However, the real shock was that while I was happy to have my photo taken, actually taking part in a fashion show was very stressful. I could hardly bear to walk down the runway and have so many pairs of eyes focused on me, watching as I walked. Every time I was booked for a show (which wasn't often, because I had trouble hiding my fear) I dreaded the experience. Yet as with my air stewardess interview experience, I couldn't understand where this powerful terror had come from.

This terrible phobia meant I had to turn down many people and opportunities throughout my life, because I felt I had to hide what I believed was my 'inadequacy' from the world. When I was twenty-nine, I was asked to be godmother to my friend's little girl. I was thrilled and of course said yes, but only on the proviso that I wouldn't have to make a speech, at the Christening or any other event! Even such a joyous occasion was spoiled for me, because of my fear.

Years later, my fear was still dictating my choices. I became a personal trainer in my late thirties, because I loved exercise and wanted to motivate other people to get fit. l enjoyed working with one or two clients at a time, but I couldn't add 'aerobics instructor' to my skill set, because I never wanted to stand at the front of the room and be seen by a class of students.

Over the years, I learned to hide my self-doubt and my fears well. I stayed within my comfort zones as often as I could, and I never over-extended myself for fear of being discovered. While occasionally I would let my guard down and talk to others about my fear, it seemed that most people I knew were afraid of presenting, so in that respect everything felt normal. What was wrong with me?

Nobody else (including me, if truth be told!) could understand or accept that I lacked confidence or self-belief. It's a total misconception held by many that attractive people must be confident – a classic example of judging a book by its cover. When they met me, people automatically expected me to be a certain way, and I just wasn't.

But I still didn't understand *why*.

If you have this kind of fear, you'll understand just how frustrating and limiting it can be. I never gave up trying to solve it, because I knew I'd never be happy with myself if I didn't. That fear hung over me like the sword of Damocles, and I so wanted to be rid of it.

I did my best to banish the fear for good. I was determined. The terrified way I felt was so at odds with my personality – I'm a complete extravert who loves being around people, so I made myself give a speech at a friend's hen party, I forced myself to read out a poem at a fortieth birthday celebration, and I was even the compere for a 'This Is Your Life' book at another friend's party! I kept pushing hard against my teaching fears, and I started to teach group Pilates to eight students at a time; also holding circuit training for groups of six.

"You'll be brilliant, Bertie!" my friends would say, and I so *wanted* to be brilliant, that I kept on pushing. I found that a glass of wine or two would take the edge off my nerves, and if all I had to do was read some lines, I could pull it off without being discovered.

I was making progress, but it was too slow.

I then jumped at the opportunity to join a very well known public speaking group, called 'Toastmasters'. While I learned a lot, and had some high moments during which I seemingly broke free from fear, in reality I was still trapped. I finally left the organisation on a low, after humiliating myself at a contest. I could hardly believe it: two years of constant, dedicated practice, and I would still freeze mid-speech and get myself completely tongue-tied.

As you may imagine, it felt like a hopeless quest! Others I spoke to either admired my perseverance, or they would tell me I had no need to overcome my fear at all. I would hear comments such as, "I would never put myself through what you are doing at Toastmasters", and I even wondered if some people felt I was making up the fear. But still, I knew something was wrong: this was a genuine fear, and it was one I desperately wanted to conquer.

It wasn't until I met the acclaimed therapist Marisa Peer in my gym one day that I finally made the breakthrough I had been waiting for. After talking with her, Marisa offered to help me overcome my fears through hypnotherapy. While at first it all sounded too good to be true, she helped me far more than I could ever have imagined. When Marisa regressed me back to my childhood, I realised that a two-minute event, one that had taken place way back in my childhood, had quite literally changed the course of my personality.

This moment had kept me trapped in fear for the next forty years of my life, and I'm going to take you back there now, so you can understand how my fear of being visible to the world really began.

I was seven years old, sitting obediently at my primary school desk in 1969. My fearsome teacher, a tall and imposing woman, was clearly having a challenging day. Our class was trying her patience, so she had banished us to total silence. She chalked the word 'SILENCE' onto the blackboard in big, bold white letters, and our task was simple: we were to work quietly and not move from our chairs or disturb her for the rest of the lesson.

I can picture myself like it was only yesterday, sat at my desk in the classroom with another eight children, my little green exercise book and my pencil set out neatly in front of me. All the traditional brown wooden desks were facing inwards to form one large table, so we could all see each other. But I wasn't looking at anybody. I had my head down and my mind focused.

Then the nightmare began. My pencil broke and I had no pencil sharpener. There was a communal sharpener bolted down to a nearby table, but our teacher had told us not to move! I sat for a while, silently debating my choices. Do I write nothing, put up my hand and draw attention to myself from my angry teacher, or…perhaps I could borrow my friend's sharpener?

I decided to go for option three. I started whispering to get my friend's attention, mouthing, "Can I use your sharpener?"

You could hear a pin drop in that hushed classroom, so it wasn't easy to stay quiet. Finally, my friend looked up and saw me – but she wasn't the only one whose attention I had caught. My teacher had clearly been disobeyed, and she wanted everybody to know that there would be consequences. She demonstrated the full force of her anger as she bellowed for me to get up and approach her desk. I was literally shaking with fear as I made my way to the front of the classroom. My head hung down with guilt and shame, not daring to look up and see her red, angry face, or the terrified eyes of my classmates.

When I reached my teacher's side, she really let me have it. "You stupid girl. How dare you talk, when I have told you to be silent! You will be punished for speaking." With these booming words, she slapped me hard around my leg and buttocks. In sheer terror, I remember looking down at the floor and seeing my white socks and blue shoes suddenly dripping wet. I was so frightened that I had actually wet myself, in front of the entire class. Of course, my teacher saw this too, and it just about tipped her right over the edge. "You are a *disgusting* child!" she scolded, her face twisted with rage, before she hastily grabbed my elbow and dragged me to the school office. Shaking uncontrollably by now, I could hardly breathe through my uncontrollable sobbing; it felt like the tears would never, ever stop. Once I reached the school office, the secretary took me to her side and held me there until I calmed down. She then found me a pair of dry white underpants, ones that would only fit with the aid of a large safety pin.

The rest of the memories I have about this childhood incident are foggy and unclear, though I remember my mother telling me about how angry she was with the school. However, nothing more happened.

If you were a child of the 1960's or 1970's, then you may remember how common it was for teachers to slap children – even caning them if they felt it necessary. My mother may have been angry, but she still could not have done very much about what happened that day. And so, as far as the school was concerned, the incident was closed. I had been dealt with, and that was that. But I was still feeling the knock-on effects from that one incident years later, without even knowing it. When I revisited that horrific incident in the classroom during my session with Marisa, I reviewed every second of it as though I was watching a movie. That moment made me cry all over again, but this time it was such a wonderful release. I finally understood why, when and how I had developed so many limiting and self-defeating beliefs. I had lived my life hiding because of a fear of shame and humiliation, and because I had never felt good enough. Marisa healed my 'inner child', and then she re-programmed my brain to love speaking in public.

Did you know that a two-minute event in your childhood can literally change your personality? Or that a small incident, like the one

I experienced at the age of seven, can have such a powerfully diminishing effect on you that you lose your self-esteem, and live your life afraid to shine or even be visible? Until that first session with Marisa, neither did I. After that session, and through listening to Marisa's recording for twenty-one days, I felt so different and began to take up every opportunity to speak and present to groups. When my daughter turned twenty-one, I actually jumped at the chance to speak to over eighty of her friends at her party – what an amazing feeling that was for me!

Years later, I knew that I wanted to become a hypnotherapist myself. I wanted to help other people find the kind of release and freedom I had experienced. I called Marisa to ask for a recommendation, and it turned out that she was about to start teaching her own method to others. I became one of her very first students, and since that moment I have never looked back.

I now believe that personality is created and formed from our own personal reality. As children we are like sponges, absorbing everything that we see and hear from our parents, siblings, relatives…and as I discovered, our teachers. We are unable to distinguish between truth and lies, and cannot form any kind of subjective opinions until we get to around ten years of age.

We simply absorb and believe, and these beliefs become our programming…until we break free from them. Now that I am free to be me (and like most of us, I am still discovering who that is), I want to share this awareness, and help others realise that they too can uncover negative programming from their past, which may be holding them back.

Today I help teach new graduates, and I fulfilled my dream by setting up my own hypnotherapy business. Perhaps it won't surprise you to learn that one of the subjects I specialise in is helping people break free from their fears!

I have no regrets about the past. I don't do 'if only's', because I believe that everything is as it is meant to be. There is no point looking back on what could have been, who I might have been, or what else might I have done with my life. It's the past and that's where it remains: I can choose to see it negatively, or to see it as a gift. To think otherwise is nothing but wasted energy.

To suffer fear, and then to genuinely overcome that fear, is empowering and exciting. It has given me a massive passion and a true desire to help other people, and while it might sound corny, I genuinely believe that my life's purpose is to make a difference.

I'm so happy to understand my journey and be over it. Now, when I speak, I remind myself that I am not seven years of age, and I have no need to be afraid. However it goes, nobody is going slap me, and I'm not going to wet myself!

As an epilogue to my story, when I was fifty-five I was asked to do a fashion show in Bath, wearing very elegant clothes designed for older women. I turned down the opportunity at first, but then I changed my mind. I hadn't been part of a fashion show for nearly thirty years, so it would be a real test. I wanted to see if I was finally over that fear too!

I was thrilled to discover that I was perfectly comfortable, and I even enjoyed being in the show. While I wouldn't take a turn on a catwalk again, because modeling is not what I do, it was truly wonderful to walk right into that old fear, and leave it behind me for good.

Biography

Bertie Ekperigin is a Rapid Transformational Therapist and coach. Her passion is to help people break free from self-sabotage, bad habits and negative thinking patterns, so that they can embrace more meaningful lives. Bertie works with the subconscious mind to discover exactly why her clients have their particular blocks and where their memorised, negative emotions have come from. She then installs new empowering thoughts and beliefs, which enables them to change first their personalities – and ultimately their lives – for the better.

Bertie loves working with fears, phobias, anxiety issues and lack of confidence, as well as excess weight and depression. She believes that everyone she sees is really seeking happiness and inner peace, which is why she created the 'Happiness Project' to help women overcome the blocks to self-love and self-acceptance.

She is passionate about making a difference to her clients' physical and mental wellbeing, having herself suffered from major lung surgery and anxiety. Using Rapid Transformational Therapy Bertie has overcome a debilitating fear of public speaking, and low self-esteem. She is a mother of three grown up children and loves skiing and dancing.

If you crave more balance, freedom and joy in your life, then you will be interested to discover more about Rapid Transformational Therapy and the Happiness First Programme on Bertie's website.

www.changedforgood.net

Gail Reynolds

With sheer determination and huge strength of character Gail has turned her life around in a way some would deem impossible. Her belief that you don't 'fail' but instead 'learn' from your experiences, however hard they are, has meant that her success has come hard won, but is truly deserved.

Home

Failure to me is just the negative version of the word 'learning'. I never 'fail' and neither do my kids, we just learn how not to do something, how not to treat people, how not to repeat the same mistake twice. Having this mindset can also set you free and it will teach you how to live a life without ever feeling like a failure again!

Having come from a huge (and I mean huge) family, we never had a lot of money, but we were rich in so many other ways. From an early age my grandmother, Nan, taught all of us the value of love, fun, laughter, hard work and independence. Being rich wasn't the amount of money you had to spend; being rich was far more precious than that. Being rich was about the amount of time you were able to spend with your family and loved ones, and how you made them feel. My childhood memories are filled with Nan's unconditional love, warmth, understanding and laughter. It took me to breaking point later in life until I realised how important her family values were and how they were going to not only save my life but enable me to help others build their lives too...

The air was muggy and thick with the smell of freshly cut grass. My handmade Bay City Roller trousers were flapping furiously in the wind as my heart raced as fast as my bare feet could run. Fun and laughter filled the air; the game was in full swing, with family (and a few neighborhood friends) scattered all around me. Running as fast as my skinny little legs could carry me, closer and closer I got to the tall proud oak tree we knew and loved. But so did grandad! Crouched down, trousers rolled up to his knees and arms outstretched he was either going to catch the ball or catch me; the rounders rules didn't apply to grandad. He missed the ball much to the dismay of half the family; cheers and boos came from the crowd as grandad grabbed me, there was no escape. My ribs hurt, and my heart raced even faster. I thought I was going to die of laughter there and then.

The smell of Nan's Sunday dinner began to waft up towards the field, "Right," she said looking at her watch. "Time to put the spuds on." She began to walk back to the wide-open front door where my aunty was sitting holding the baby and watching my smaller cousins playing with their bricks and toys. I stepped over them all and duly followed Nan inside.

In the kitchen the wireless was playing as it always did. Jim Reeves 'I love you because' had just begun and Nan burst into song. Grandad would often sing the words to her gently and hold her around the waist whilst they both waltzed around the kitchen. As little as I was I knew what love looked like, I knew what love felt like and I knew what effect love had on people.

The sounds, sights and smells of those precious moments and memories surround and fill my soul to this day. The happiness I feel engulfs me every time I think of my childhood and how I wanted to be just like her: my Nan was my world, she was my lighthouse on my darkest nights, my constant when I lost my way and my rock when I was weak.

Monday morning. Another day. Another feeling.

The plastic shoes made my feet sweat and it didn't help that I had to wear thick brown rubber bands around the tops of my long socks to keep them up all day at school. My tummy sank as the bell went. How can life be so rich in fun, laughter and love one day, and then be overshadowed with total despair and loneliness the next?

Standing in the dinner line with my free school meal ticket, my tummy rumbled with hunger pains when another sharp pain ran through my back: a boy's fist! This one boy who seemed to enjoy humiliating, hitting, shoving and shaming me on a daily basis had pushed in behind me. His scary, loud, bellowing voice began to scream out for everyone to hear: "Oh my God, look at those shoes, what a tramp! Don't stand next to me, get to the back of the queue Jonesy." Before I knew it, others were laughing and pushing me away from the dinner line. I walked with my head down to the back of the queue, hungry, humiliated, sad and lonely. Each day I would anxiously wait for the end of school bell to ring, so I could run home, get changed, make a butter and sugar sandwich and run across to Nanny's, aunty Lynn's or aunty Penny's, for that small dose of love I was starved of all day.

Mom was a hard worker. She held down several jobs just to make ends meet, but with four kids back then there wasn't much money for luxuries, especially for me. My idea of luxury from my mom would be a simple hug, or the whisper "I love you," but they never really came much after the age of seven. My brothers seemed to soak up all her affection, so there was never much left for me or my sister. It was and still is the hardest lesson to learn: how does a seven-year-old little girl, surrounded by love and warmth from her nan, inclusion and caring from her aunts and uncles and being surrounded by the love and connection they all have to their children, process what 'LOVE' is?

Surely this 'feeling' should come from your own mom, surely she should want to give it to her own daughter, surely that wasn't expecting too much?

For what felt like an eternity I tried to win her affections. But to this day nothing seems to work. I have grown to accept my mom for who she is, and what she has to offer as a parent and a grandparent, which today is pretty much non-existent.

I could feel a failure to these circumstances, that feeling of not being loved by the one person on the planet who should love you the most, and being bullied at school for many, many years. But I don't, in fact I feel as though I have learned so many lessons from my journey up to now. How could I have failed as a seven-year-old little girl? How could not feeling loved by your mom or accepted at school mean failure? It can't and it won't define me. Nan had taught me everything I needed to know about feeling rich in love: her family values were so priceless that no lack of love from my mom, or some kid who probably had problems of his own at home, was going to prevent those values from shaping the rest of my life.

Aged twenty-one I met with my first failure, or so I thought

I was eighteen and it was no surprise to anyone when I announced my due date: July fourth – Independence Day! – although Ashleigh had plans of his own and he arrived exactly a week later. I should have known back then that this was the start of things to come and that life as a mother was going to change the course of my life forever.

I couldn't hold down the relationship with Ashleigh's dad and we split up. I remained strong though, I remembered the unconditional love

I had from Nan and I showered Ashleigh with it every day. My son and I had a bond that no one could break; he knew his mom loved him and would protect and defend him no matter what!

I met someone else when I was twenty-three and I thought all my Christmas's had come at once. He took on Ashleigh like his own and before I knew it we were packed up and moving to Germany to be with him. We never married so couldn't live in the Army barracks: we rented privately from a lovely German lady who spoke little English.

Being four months pregnant I couldn't wait to arrive at our destination and into my unborn baby's dad's arms, especially after the grueling twenty-four hours on trains, buses and ferries. Ashleigh and I were excited and a little scared as we stepped onto the German platform, but deep down I knew we needn't be because when we were in England we had always been shown so much love and affection by this man.

In the car the atmosphere was cold. He was angry; we were late! I was confused. "Look at me when I'm talking to you," he screamed. I laughed nervously looking to the back of the car at Ashleigh. I couldn't believe what was happening; we were exhausted and hungry, and all he was worried about was the fact we were thirty minutes late. "No, you can't tell me what to do!" I retorted, trying to hold my own. "Look at me or I'll make you look at me," he spat back. I raised my eyebrows and slowly turned my head away towards the window and away from him. A cold, hard, blunt force ripped through my cheekbone and mouth as I went to look back at him. The pain was excruciating and within seconds the sheer shock of him hitting me set in. "Now you'll look at me," he whispered back coldly.

The next four months were horrific. He would often leave Ashleigh and me with little or no money for weeks at a time whilst he went away with his work. On several occasions I endured being pulled out of bed by my hair, so to get away I would cuddle up with Ashleigh in his small single bed. My son didn't know it, but he was my only connection to love, my only connection which gave me hope that love would get us through this. The final straw was when I was eight months pregnant and my partner locked me out in the snow in my dressing gown and slippers and told Ashleigh he wasn't allowed to let me back in. He did of course, so we were both thrown out into the snow. I remembered where a guy lived who I had been introduced to just a few times before and Ashleigh and I walked to his house, not really knowing what we were going to say or do once we arrived. We were wet, cold and clearly upset and he took us in. The next day he put two hundred pounds in my hand so Ashleigh and I could get back to England; within two weeks we were settled in a little two-bedroomed terraced house with a small courtyard. I was feeling relieved but nervous about bringing up two kids by myself, until there was a knock at the door...

Yes, it was him. And yes, I took him back.

Libby was six weeks old. I was sunning myself in the garden whilst the pie was cooking in the oven and the spuds were boiling in the pan along with some peas. The door opened and shut; he was home. Ashleigh was in his room playing computer games and Libby was beside me in her pram, fast asleep.

With a whirlwind of words and anger the next thing I remember is a pan of boiling peas being held over my face as I lay looking up at him, terrified. I managed to calm down the situation; the dinner was turned off and then Libby began to cry. He took her from her pram and walked upstairs with her. I didn't know what he was going to do next, so, following him up the stairs I pleaded with him to give her to me. He refused, swung her around and banged her head on the doorframe, then threw her on the bed and stood in the doorway to prevent me from getting to her.

The next few moments were a blur. A powerful mother's instinct kicked in; I don't know how, but I managed to overpower him. Eventually, sitting on the bed with Libby, soothing her as much as I could, I looked up at him and said, very calmly, "You need to get out, and never, ever come back." I never saw or heard of him again.

Aged twenty-five I met with my next failure – or so I thought

Here I was, battered and bruised and left holding the baby and a seven-year-old boy from two different fathers. I was living on income support, with no job, no self-esteem and no confidence. I looked in the mirror and didn't recognise myself. "I don't belong here," I remember saying to myself, "Who are you?" In that instant I remembered my nan: I hadn't seen her for many years since I had moved away years before, but I knew I wasn't living the life she had taught me all those years ago. I wasn't strong and independent, I wasn't hard working, I had lost all fun and laughter from my life and I hadn't put my kids first. There was only one thing to do, and that was to get my life back, to teach my kids the values and love my nan had taught me so many years ago.

I was never, ever again going to let anyone make me feel like I wasn't worthy or good enough. I was about to take charge of my own destiny, my own kids, and I knew that if I wanted things to change – I had to change.

It was a warm June morning; I walked Ashleigh to school as I always did, but this particular morning I took a different route back and Libby and I headed towards the local college. I arrived at the front desk nervous and worried. I needn't have been as the receptionist was just delightful. I asked her what I could study that would allow me to be at home with my kids. She asked me what I was good at during school, which wasn't much, but I was good at numbers. She looked through a few folders and files and came up with a few ideas. I left having signed up to a bookkeeping course that I could do from home. Six months later I passed the course and started a National Vocational Qualification in accounting. This time I was going into college one day a week for just a few hours and within the next year I passed that too. Over the next five years I began to build my self-confidence, my self-worth and my independence. Soon I found a part-time job and came off income support. The kids were happier than ever, both settled in good schools and I was growing in confidence every day.

When I was twenty-seven my younger sister gave me her old car; it needed a few hundred pound's worth of work doing to it to get it road worthy, so I began to save. Within a few months I had my little car on the road; I took just six driving lessons and put in for my test. I passed! That same week, I packed up our little car with the kids and took them to Butlins on their first ever holiday.

Nan's values were now mine:

Hard work
Fun and laughter
Strength and independence
Family comes first

These were now part of my life, my purpose, my reason to keep growing.

Aged thirty-one and things really began to heat up!

I changed jobs, and I met Brian, my boss's boss. He was tall, dark and handsome, suited and booted and very well respected. He drove around in a posh new car and had his own house. Never wanting to marry or have kids, he wasn't going to be interested in someone like me. Or so I thought.

Within six months we moved in together. But remember this is my life we're talking about – nothing is that easy! We not only moved home, we moved towns too; we moved to be closer to his family so we could spend some quality time with them. It was the hardest thing I had done in a long time. No friends, lonely and depressed, after three months I wanted to move back home. I had a job, but I wasn't making friends or socialising. Brian still hadn't found a job and was also feeling depressed. I wasn't going to fail at this, so I waited for the 'Free Ads' paper to come through our door and went straight to the 'Opportunity' section: it wasn't another job I needed, just an opportunity to meet new people.

WOW…five words changed my life forever: 'Join Avon – meet new people'.

Little did I realise that in May 2002 my life was going to change forever. Every lesson I had learned and every failure I refused to accept had brought me to this point.

Within a day or so I was recruited into the business as a self-employed representative. All I wanted to do was meet new people, make new friends, and be at home for my kids. I was already working twenty hours a week, Monday to Friday, so I had to fit in this extra opportunity at weekends and evenings. I was earning one hundred pounds a week at my day job, which paid for my sixty pounds food bill, twenty pounds electric key and twenty pounds gas card. I couldn't afford to quit my job until I could cover those living expenses, so I set my first goal: to meet at least one hundred new people/friends and earn enough money to quit my job and be at home for the kids. I gave myself six months – I did it in five!

I couldn't believe it, I had found something that fulfilled every single value I had been raised with: I was hard working, was independent and having so much fun and laughter with the people I met every day. The time I was spending with my kids was priceless; no more paying a babysitter to watch them whilst I went to work, and it never really felt like I was actually working anyway, I was helping so many people fulfil their dreams, their goals, their desires. I loved every minute of it.

Brian and I got married in 2003. We didn't have a lot of money and we only had twelve people join us at the registry office to celebrate our vows. After we had signed on the dotted line we went across to the gardens outside our rented accommodation and had photos taken. By one o'clock we all made our way to the hotel on Hastings seafront: with large glass windows overlooking the sea I felt like a princess in her castle, with her prince by her side and her loved ones all around her. We sat and chatted through our three-course meal; everyone had contributed ten pounds towards the cost of the meal and no one seemed to mind. Debbie, Brian's' sister, baked the wedding cake so we all went back to the house to cut the cake and celebrate a little more. By four o'clock we were waving off our few guests and sped off to the airport to spend a week in Spain in the villa my ex-boss had lent us as a wedding gift.

"Rich in LOVE" I thought to myself. Rich in happiness, fun and laughter, rich in belonging and feeling like "this is it"; I had finally made it, I had finally made peace with my past and my own family was complete.

Or so I thought.

A year after being married, Brian joined my business. It was tough for the first few months but as the income grew and bills were settled things began to look good. That's when he dropped a bombshell on me. "I think I do want a baby," he announced!

"Oh, ok" I replied, thinking, "Crikey I'm not getting any younger, we need to get a shimmy on before I pass my sell by date!"

Rosie was born in Feb 2005. A six-pounds eight-ounce bundle of fluff. She was just beautiful; so delicate, with masses of dark brown hair and olive skin like her dad. I was in love as a parent for the third time.

We carried on building the business from home, and the years rolled by. It wasn't until our sixth year in business when the recognition and validation for our hard work began to pay off. In 2008 we won 'Team of the Year Award' and were one of the fastest growing networks within the company.

The next few years rolled by and in 2011 life challenged us once again

We were in Jamaica: first-class flights to a five-star all-inclusive three-week holiday. We were by the pool on day three when a call came in on Brian's phone. I answered it as he was in the apartment getting some goggles with

Rosie. It was his dad, Chris. The news he shared with me was devastating: Brian's sister, Debbie, had been killed in a suspicious fire leaving behind her teenage son and devastated parents. We had to get back to England to be there for family. The next few months reiterated what life was about; making the most of it, loving family, and enjoying the special moments we share with loved ones.

Another year passed; it was now January 2012. I was playing darts in a local pub when Brian called and told me to sit down. "Ok, you have my attention Brian, what's up" I asked. "Our savings, our investments we made with Uncle Simon," he said. "Yes? What about it?" I questioned. "It's all gone babe, he stole it, he gambled it; it's just all gone".

What I did next was a total blur: a few shots of neat vodka, lots of crying and shouting outside the pub and a taxi home. The next two days were no better. I drank more vodka, asked loads of questions and blamed everyone for this injustice. How could he do this to his own family? He stole, lied, cheated and gambled our life savings and our kid's future savings to the tune of fifty-nine thousand pounds.

Brian offered to divorce me there and then as it was his family member and his idea to invest and trust in his uncle. That wasn't an option. I had to calm down, think of who I was and what I knew was the right thing to do. Deep down, I searched my soul. I knew one thing: Simon had stolen our money, our life savings, but I wasn't going to let him steal our dreams, our future, our new life that we had been working towards for the past ten years.

On the third morning after the news I got up went to the girls and asked them: "If mommy and daddy could take you anywhere in the world, where would you want to go?" I had to bring it back to the true meaning and purpose of life and that was my kids and my family, not money! The girls settled on Lapland to meet the real Santa Claus. We set about making their dreams come true, and by December 2012 – just eleven months later – we all got to meet Santa, we started a new savings account and we paid off a credit card debt of over seventeen thousand pounds.

Failure is never an option for me, and it need not be for you either.

Life will throw so many challenges at you and choices that sometimes are out of your control, but it is how we deal with those changes and choices that make us the people we are today.

Don't allow your past to define you; allow it to shape you, build you and teach you to become the success you truly deserve to be.

Over the following years more triumphs and tragedies hit our lives

We renewed our vows in 2013, ten years after our wedding day. We had over one hundred and twenty family members there with a few friends – and unlike before, none of them had to pay the food bill. On the very same day, just moments after we said our vows, my little sister had a massive seizure in front of her two boys and all our guests. She was rushed to hospital and we carried on the day the best we could with her boys by our side. By November she was diagnosed with a brain tumor and by December she had it removed and was out of hospital the same day! Five years have passed, and she is as healthy as ever. Her family means the world to her and she doesn't allow her brush with death to define who she is, but to strengthen who she has become.

Our business now turns over more than seven million pounds a year and we have travelled the world. We live in our forever home which we are transforming every day into our kids' and grandkids' forever home too, extending and building a warm, loving environment with an open door to all our family.

I have written an award-winning book called 'Mum's the Word' and I have been on national television and radio several times over the past few years, sharing my story and my road to success.

In 2013 I won the Direct Selling Association's Direct Seller of the Year Award – just to put it into perspective there are almost half a million direct sellers in the United Kingdom alone. My company had never won the award before my achievement and hasn't won it since.

Speaking in Brussel's parliament for European entrepreneurial women was one of my most exciting and proudest moments. Sharing my work ethics and values as an at-home mom with members of parliament and discussing how I built a successful business in and around a family has been a privilege.

Two of my three children have suffered depression and I have suffered for many years battling chronic anxiety but we are strong, we know the value of life, we know the importance of not seeing anything as a failure but a lesson from which to learn.

We have lost several family members over the past few years to cancer and at eighty-four years old my beautiful dear Nan fought cancer and against all odds successfully beat the disease. But two years' later it returned and she finally lost the fight. Nan's last words as she lay in bed in her home, with her sons, daughters, grandkids and great grandkids surrounding her, were: "Home".

Thanks Nan, this chapter is for you. You shaped me into the mother and woman I am today. You always gave me unconditional love. You are the most successful woman I know. You are my hero.

Biography

From a single parent living in a council flat with two kids and claiming benefits, with no business background, no qualifications and no knowledge of the industry she entered, Gail built an empire of over two thousand five hundred team members. With a massive annual turnover of over six million pounds Gail has pioneered training programmes, developed niche coaching skills and mentored thousands of women who have also gone on to become successful entrepreneurs. Among her army of award-winning team members, of whom she is hugely proud, Gail has achieved the highest accolade there is within the Direct Selling industry: the United Kingdom's Direct Seller of the Year Award. Gail's book 'Mum's the Word' gained her another tribute as an award-winning author at the London Book Festival Awards.

Gail's leadership, coaching and mentoring skills are also proven by her material accomplishments: dream homes, expensive cars and luxury holidays. She has remained in the top one percent of highest earners for many years, having built one of the biggest networks within her company. She was a Keynote Speaker in Brussels Parliament and has represented European Entrepreneurial Women in Business.

Gail believes "Not everyone can be a successful entrepreneur. We are simply born with attitude, personality and passion and it's how we use these that will dictate whether we become successful or not. It isn't our education or class; it's our adaptability, our enthusiasm and our core values in life that will dictate our overall success."

Using her common sense, mothering instincts and solid family values

Gail is now one of the leading experts within the Direct Selling Industry. Her entrepreneurial spirit is now being transported into her motivational speaking, where she shares her inspiring journey which led her to become one of the few millionaires within her industry. Gail's open heart, honesty and enthusiasm gains her the full attention of her audiences, who can relate to Gail's story so much that the impact on them is often life-changing right there in the room with her.

www.gailreynolds.co.uk

www.gailsreps.co.uk

Karen Ramsey

When we 'keep on keeping on', when we forget to stop and take stock of our lives, where we are going, what is and isn't working, we risk losing the very happiness and fulfilment we seek. Karen's corporate career was, on the surface, successful. However a culture of fear and negativity at work had impact on every area of her life, including her health. Learning to 'let go' brought about much needed transformation and healing for Karen, and a joyful return to her authentic, radiant self.

Primary school fool

When I was six years old at primary school I was taught by nuns. Each week my class was asked to recite the times table: I hated math's! I liked drawing and colouring-in, reading and creativity, picking and drawing wildflowers, catching butterflies and reviving little birds. I loved to just 'be' on my own, outside with nature.

I was a quiet child who never said 'boo to a goose', I had been brought up to be quiet: quiet and good. A good girl for my parents. My father did not know how to communicate with his girls. He was a good father but showed no emotion. This made me afraid to express myself in many ways, afraid to make a mistake…

But this week at school things were different. This week the head nun at school decided to make an appearance. Petrifying.

She asked us to stand up in front of the class – one by one. You can imagine when it got to my turn I was absolutely terrified of getting my times table wrong. As each child was called in turn, most got theirs correct; four times table, three times table… God I hope I get an easy one.

As I stood on my chair shaking and awaiting the instruction to begin, negative thoughts began spiraling around my mind. I was so scared of making a mistake. "Recite the seven times table," said the nun.

I could hear the sums in my mind: one times seven is seven, two times seven is fourteen, three times seven is twenty-one – then my mind froze. I realised everyone was looking at me and I made a mistake; the pressure got to me and I did get it all wrong.

As a punishment I was made to stand on my chair for the rest of that lesson, ashamed, in front of all my friends. No health and safety in those days! I was cross and ashamed that I didn't know something so simple. How could I not know? I wanted to speak out for the others. But I didn't. I suddenly felt trapped. After all, the teacher knew much more than me, right? My childlike spirit was crushed that day and I remember thinking I never wanted to be made a fool of ever again in front of others. I just wanted to feel free…

The peak of my career?

After years of pushing down my creativity, my visibility and my true values, and having no boundaries due to my relationships with men much like my father, I lived many years suffering severe anxiety with any challenge and feeling a failure, just like that little girl.

Fast forward to the age of thirty-six, my marriage had failed and I had just found out that my dad had a malignant brain tumour. I was devastated but felt a sudden sense of urgency to go out there and live and I fell into a new boundary-less relationship. With two young children, and the sole breadwinner, I was also faced with redundancy. Suddenly everything had begun to fall apart.

Six months later, after the loss of my dad, I decided that life was too short to stop and although I was in a lost state of mind, I found another job. By the age of forty-five I was drawn further into complications by finding myself as a senior higher education leader in a very difficult marketing and communications department with – guess what? – communication concerns and problems with boundaries: I had again attracted exactly the issues I was experiencing in my personal life.

I remember attending a week's mindfulness course to get away from the stress at work and I loved the feeling meditation gave me of just 'being' like I did as a child in nature. I left wondering if this was all there was to my life? Stress and worry to pay my bills?

Although I had risen to management quickly through my own determination to not fail, I was seriously struggling with my inner feelings and lack of boundaries. In my career, was leading communications which was ironic due to the complete lack of communication in my personal life.

I'd made it to the role that I saw at the time as the pinnacle of my career. However, less than eight months into my new role I started experiencing serious problems, and my worst nightmare then ensued: in this new role I had to be really visible and I required connection with my creativity – something I had loved from the day I was born, but that I had lost over the years. At first, I ignored the concerns I began to experience inside myself, telling myself that this was a new role and that I needed to find my feet. I found myself working many long hours as I was unable to say "no" to my boss, my colleagues and even my team. I was struggling while at the same time restructuring, recruiting and running strategy for the department.

Climbing my mountain

Soon, my already vague objectives went out of the window. I was fire-fighting not just my work role but my whole life. Back-to-back meetings and managing change both at work and at home with my family became an impossible mountain. My evenings were spent organising the following day and sifting through job applications when I was at home, exhausted. I was drowning.

Mostly I began to go inside myself. I started to notice the negativity around me much more, criticism between teams and departments – and at home. Instead of being a place of creativity it was a place of negativity. No one was having time for the creative process people were stressed which created a culture of fear. My own lack of boundaries and fear of failure was eating into my natural capabilities. I began to protect myself: after all that's what everyone else was doing. My behaviour had become protective and one of self-sabotage; I felt less confident in my job and my home and personal life fell to the wayside. I was scared of being visible; I was scared of being ME!

My goals and my ambitions of being an inspiring leader had become the last priority. I was last on the pile. Literally. My ultimate fear was facing me: my fear of being visible and making mistakes. My fear of failure!

This is when my behaviour changed. I was no longer feeling like I could tackle the world simply with my determination. My confidence took a nosedive, I started hiding from the meetings where I knew I'd be challenged and my self-esteem dropped to an all-time low. I spent most of my time where I knew I could be of the best support: with people and building relationships, helping them to be creative. My caring female side kicked in. It was tearing me apart that I was seeing other women also struggling to juggle not just a full-time job and home life but trying to be a woman with no inner boundaries. We women are natural carers; we see someone in need and we go to help, we look for solutions even if it's the hard way for us.

A sign for help

I didn't want to admit it but being in a such a senior post I didn't know how to ask for help, as so many were coming to ME to ask for help. I could feel my fear and emotions piling up and the bottle top was firmly on! I needed to talk about it, but instead I kept distracting myself with meetings and interviews, social media, a glass of wine here and there in the evenings, television, an argument with my family – anything but look at the answers inside myself! I was distracting myself from my true inner voice and creativity, my gut was screaming at me to look deeper inside myself for the answers and I was deliberately ignoring it.

And then the bottle top began to come loose. Out of the blue my ex-husband was put in prison for a crime we will never know if he committed. My role at work became even more stressful with workplace bullying and more responsibility on my shoulders, and my own relationships and my children began to struggle.

Eventually the lid came off after attending a Women's Leadership course for leaders who needed support stepping into their leadership skills. "Ahh, this will be the fix for me I thought!" How wrong I was! The content and deep coaching on the course broke me open and I spent most of the week in tears: that week I had what I believe to be the beginning of an emotional breakdown.

I remember my line-manager, a very senior female person in the organisation, asking me if I had been on a spa day. She was a difficult person with whom to negotiate and communicate on a deeper level and so I found myself in a similar role to that which I played with my dad: poor communication and fragile boundaries to say "no", for fear of failure.

I began to move into a serious period of emotional anxiety, stress and physical illness. By the Christmas of that year, I knew that my career was over and I had to take some time away. But the biggest changes were yet to come. This was the result of many years of not listening to myself: my true creative self was buried and the fears that I had allowed to remain in my life from my very foundations as a young child had taken over. My values and all my boundaries had been compromised: I was lost and I felt completely stuck.

Knight in shining armour!

After I came to terms that perhaps a knight in shining armour with lots of money would turn up or an overnight lottery win was highly unlikely, I had two choices: I could leave the career to which I had aspired for twenty-five years, or I could find the courage to do something about this feeling of deep unrest I had inside me. Whilst I was deciding I found myself looking for opportunities to learn.

My muscles ached from stress and my now regular panic attacks and migraines were stopping me from thinking clearly. I had been sabotaging myself, stopping myself from being visible and ultimately from being successful. I had become truly afraid of speaking out. I felt like I wasn't good enough and I was scared of criticism and was not giving myself time and space to communicate as my natural creative self. My relationships at home were also suffering. What was going on? I decided to look inside and listen to my inner feelings instead of hoping something or someone external to me would come along to save me.

The big leap

I came across a book called 'The Big Leap' by Gay Hendricks. The book talks about reaching inside ourselves to find the level of huge success we all have which will create true abundance and fulfilment in our lives. It explores our negative thought patterns and the fear that blocks us from getting to where we need to be.

I realised that this was exactly what I had done; I had created all these negative thoughts and fears about my job, my responsibilities and my life, that would completely stop me from where I needed to go. I had been keeping myself safe – back in the place I thought I was supposed to be when I was six - not good enough and as invisible as I could possibly make myself from standing on that chair!

It was a belief and fear that I had absorbed from that early age.

Hendricks also writes about finding your zone of genius. He says 'When we take the big leap from our zone of excellence and into our zone of genius the harmful part of the ego falls away and fear dissolves."

What on earth was my zone of genius? I thought it was marketing and communications I'd been working in that field for years. I had successful performance reviews from my peers and I had never received a complaint about any of my work. And what was an ego? I had worked really hard to get where I was!

Ahh, I read on – the zone of genius is something I am *naturally* good at. What do I like doing that I forget about the time passing? Getting so absorbed in that I'd do it for free? What gets results for me? I needed to explore this! So I stopped completely. I came to a standstill because of my health, something I had never really done before. I spent a lot of time being quiet on my own which was incredibly difficult for a busy working mum of two, which I had now been for over twenty years. I began by trying to do the things I loved doing as a child; walking in nature every day at my local fishing lakes, getting creative and writing by following the changes of the seasons. I found a mysterious calm solace in nature, a beautiful true feeling I remembered having all those years ago when chasing butterflies and drawing wildflowers as a six-year old. I was able to 'just be'; to just be and listen to my breathing, to be outside in nature. This cemented the feeling that I needed to go back to what I really cared about in my life. The feeling that I really valued my freedom, that I really valued creativity, that I wasn't allowing myself to be the truly creative person that I really was inside and notice the issues with communication because of the way I had experienced relationships. All of these amazing values that I possessed but had forgotten about because I hadn't listened in and connected with myself for so long. Little did I know that as a child I was practicing mindfulness in nature, I'd just lost this natural skill throughout the years. Extraordinarily in turn, even though for so many years I had been fearful of failing in my life and work, I did not see any of this as a failure. I felt a huge relief letting it all go! I finally let go of all of it!

Through counselling, emotional freedom technique and my meditation, my private inner world poured out while I was walking at the lakes through the seasons of a year. I simply let go. I began to realise that everything is connected and that nature is connected to us all. *We* are connected to nature. We *are* nature. We are all part of something so much bigger than ourselves.

My relationship with my dad, my failed marriage, my failed relationships with men, my lack of communication about my values, my career in the corporate world and most of all my fear of failure if I stopped 'doing' – I surrendered to it all. And instead of experiencing anxiety, it began to slowly feel GOOD. One day, through this surrendering, I heard a voice. A voice that told me there was more for me: this wasn't the end but a beginning of something incredible and so true that I would not question it. I wanted more of this voice and daily began to practice connecting with my intuition and inner knowing. My practice helped me to take a step back and observe what was happening in my life. How I'd ended up with no career, no marriage, and walking away from trying to achieve the impossible. My walks in nature helped me to notice and appreciate the present moment and how I was feeling inside throughout my body.

The communication that I craved was really the communication which needed to come from within me. The connection and freedom that I craved was really the connection and freedom that needed to come from within me, and the creativity that I craved was the creativity that needed to come from within me.

I sought other women who were also digging deeper inside to explore where they were going. I kept a journal of what was coming up for me on a daily basis. I started sharing my walks out in nature and my fears and emotions on 'Facebook live' and by practicing this care of myself by sharing my emotions, doing the things I loved dearly and openly sharing my blocks, this in turn helped me to gain clarity on what was really holding me back and my confidence began to return – slowly but surely.

The women I found online were also talking about their own stories of learning to overcome fear of failure, self-sabotage, limiting beliefs and fear of speaking out when they were struggling and following their inner voice to success. I took the plunge and hired a professional coach I had met and began to meditate every day to help me listen in deeper. My relationship with nature blossomed and my mindfulness practice to become quiet and listen in together grew part of my daily life. I fell in absolute love with being coached through this transformation and began coaching training myself.

I knew it was in me to rise above my own fears and stop blocking my own truth. I needed to explore what my values really were and what all this meant for me and what I was going to do with the inner knowing I had that there was more, so much more for me to come. I had denied who I really was for so long.

Watching other women rise to their challenges and being open and honest about their own fears was incredibly inspiring and it encouraged me to begin to share my own story. In doing this I realised I could help and support others in a much more open and free way than I was ever able to do in my corporate work. I realised that everyone experiences one or more of these challenges on some level or another. Why oh why don't we talk about this more in our lives? It is no wonder my teams and my relationships had been struggling – we weren't sharing our challenges or having space to be more transparent and creative with our work.

In these online groups I found time to be creative and free, I was voicing it all and challenging my own comfort zone. I was spending time doing something I was really enjoying and I was passing on my experiences of connecting with my inner voice transparently and with passion, which was encouraging others to step up and do the same. I was able to be myself, my TRUE self at last.

I plucked up the courage to start my own online support group. I made a commitment to share my own experience and help other women too. I created a world online I never knew could exist with other like-minded incredible women leaders. A world where we were beginning to peel back the layers of the outside world and become *radiant* leaders. Through sharing and helping other women release their blocks and succeed at becoming more creatively visible as their true selves made me feel amazing! I knew it! This was my gift!

I realised in that moment that I was in my zone of genius. Now I know what Hendricks meant in his book! With all of these things put together, I realised that this was my true purpose: to connect with myself: to create and to be FREE. To communicate and to become a channel for all of these things. I realised that all the parts of me that I had been able to express, for example helping and supporting people, that in all this I had a purpose that I hadn't been living all these years.

I love to support women to rise above their fears and actively make their own purpose come true by voicing and communicating their truth with others. My work truly fulfils me because it has been my own personal journey to becoming whole again, to becoming well again, to becoming the person I was always meant to be, the person I was born to be before life got in the way.

And so I am very proud to be, well to be ME! I am proud of my story, my journey and to have become the person I was meant to be and I am still becoming the beautiful, creative, sensitive, loving, heart-centred woman I truly am.

My mindfulness practice and my coaching is incredibly special to me and so now as an advanced transformational coach and mindfulness guide

I help to inspire women leaders to come from that place where they feel stuck, lost, having lived all their lives for everybody else and not for their own true values, to be able to connect with their full potential, their truth, their inner voice and help them express it all with healthy boundaries so that they can become radiant natural leaders who shine from within. Most of all I am proud of the women I support; they continue to inspire and lift others as they discover and express their own truth and purpose in the world.

Imagine a world where we are open about our fears that are stopping us from being truly naturally ourselves, a world where we openly address the barriers to true purpose and creativity! If we had more spaces to be open, creative and transparent with our emotions, we'd have the freedom to be our true selves and work in our zones of genius using our natural leadership and gifts. Part of the problem is that in certain careers, in certain situations, we are expected to switch off our emotions which can do more harm than good. Perhaps if we checked in with ourselves a bit more, monitored how we are feeling, we would begin to understand how our fears are affecting us. So many incredible women struggle like this on a day to day basis, leaving their natural born purpose and truth behind because of fear of failure and not living out their true values and purpose.

As I said at the beginning, my story is both ordinary and extraordinary – and so is YOURS.

Biography

Karen is a Transformational Coach, Mindfulness Teacher and Visibility Mentor.

Karen supports heart-centered entrepreneurs/business leaders to connect with their true selves and their core values, helping them to create their 'bigger picture' vision, embrace their powerful mission and become visible to share their message with the world. This in turn aligns them fully in order for them to attract the right people and opportunities into their life and work.

Karen provides accredited transformational coaching, mentoring and teaching which combines her skills of powerful coaching, mindfulness and meditation tools and techniques with strategic marketing to support anyone who feels lost or limited in their own life. She enables her clients to connect to the truth of who they really are, empowering them to trust and become aligned with their passion and mission in life and work, supporting them to carry out their true purpose mindfully and with courage and conviction.

www.biggerpicturecoaching.com

Mirjana Sajko

Like so many women, Mirjana towed the line, married a 'suitable' man and lived a 'good' life. It took a hostage situation to bring her absolute clarity about the choice she must make. Self-love, and the right to live the life you choose, is absolutely necessary if we wish to live life to our fullest capacity. Mirjana is now working to enable other women in her Croatian community to flourish and pass their teachings to future generations.

THERE ARE FEW THINGS IN LIFE that will give you greater clarity about who you are, what you've accomplished, and where you're heading, than looking into the barrel of a sawn-off shotgun during a full blown hostage situation, with the SWAT (Special Weapons and Tactics) team visibly slinking past the huge windows, rifles drawn. Clearly, I lived to tell about it and the ramifications of such an experience were life changing.

It was the last day of the month, the thirty-first of March and the credit union was always full of activity at this time. We were at the height of mortgage season and I had an afternoon full of appointments. I was on the late lunch schedule and as I glanced up at the clock, it was twelve-fifty pm, only ten minutes to my lunch after what seemed like a never-ending morning. I was looking forward to my lunch break just to get some alone time after all the upheaval I had experienced in my life over the last two weeks. All of a sudden I could hear the huge accordion door to the bank entrance being closed. I looked up and could see one of the supervisors walking quickly and pulling the door closed behind her. In banking terms, it was not a good sign and could only mean one thing: we were being ROBBED. My immediate silly thought about missing my much needed lunch break was replaced with a sudden instinct of survival. I looked up to glance quickly along the twelve teller wickets and could not see anyone suspicious and half wondered to myself why the supervisor was closing the door. But everyone was frozen still, so I kept scanning. We get specific training for this in management courses but you never really expect to encounter it and certainly not to the degree I was witnessing. At the head of the long line was a man standing with a rifle, pointing it directly at the teller ahead of him, who had her hands up in the air. My heart skipped a beat. Holy shit, now what? We are trained to NEVER set off the silent alarm as it is best to let the robber leave the premises rather than hurt anyone upon hearing police sirens. The credit union motto was it was always most important that no one gets hurt, besides which the money is insured against robbery, theft and embezzlement. Also, each cash drawer has marked bait money.

I loved my job. I had been with the credit union for nine years, working my way up from bank teller to my now coveted position of Account Manager. Suddenly, everything felt like a slow motion silent movie, a bad Arnold Schwarzenegger movie. How the hell did I get here? My entire life seemed to flash before my eyes and my heart filled with despair and regret over the unlived life I had yet to explore and of never again seeing my family or friends. I was sure that this was the end and I thought it was my punishment for what I had done.

Just two weeks earlier, I did the toughest thing I had ever had to do in my life. I left a seven-year marriage (twelve-year relationship). But the actual leaving part seemed to pale in comparison to having to go to my mom and dad's house and break the news to them. That was the tough part and I had to do it fast before word got out and someone else called them to see if it was true. The time had come in my life where I had been pushed to the brink and had to make this life-changing decision for the sake of my own sanity and happiness: I was dying inside and trying to 'fake it till I make it' on the outside. It's not like my husband was a bad person or there was any kind of abuse involved; he was a good person and came from a good family who emigrated from Croatia in the nineteen sixties. I also came from a good and hard working family.

My parents emigrated to Canada in the early 1970s when they were thirty years old and had three small children; starting new roots in a country where they did not know the language. I had started grade one in Croatia and my brother was in grade two, so upon arriving in Victoria, British Columbia, we both entered elementary school and learned English as we went along. At that time there was no such thing as separate schooling to learn the English language so we were in regular classes and fully immersed! I felt very uprooted coming to a new country and it took me at least twelve to fifteen years to adjust and integrate into what I perceived to be a Canadian life. There was a small Croatian community and, as is normal for any immigrants, we were a tight knit group and gathered regularly at church and social functions. From an early age there was the expectation that we would all marry Croatian and it was a very common pressure for the kids of the Croatian community. I feel like my parents did the best for us with what they knew and had and with their culture. Both had only had an elementary education because village life in Croatia (former communist Yugoslavia at that time) was hard and children had to do many farm chores before and after school. Sometimes, as in my dad's case, they missed a lot of school because of farm chores. Grandma was a widow with three small children and my dad was the 'man' of the house and had to help with all that he could. Often it meant that my grandma got a fine for not sending him to school. I had great parents and I was amazed and in awe of their courageous trek into the unknown with three small children in search of a better life for us all: they carved out a very nice middle class life. It always, always gave me the belief that anything in life is possible when you put your mind to it. They were very happy, worked hard, supported each other and had a good life in Canada. Both learned English while working at their jobs. My dad was a master builder/carpenter and my mom worked in a poultry processing plant. Who knew that growing up in a Croatian village and regularly slaughtering chickens would one day be her livelihood, providing her with a nice living and a good pension; the irony of it is kind of funny.

In the summer of 1992 I picked up the new issue of Cosmopolitan magazine; it was an occasional splurge. My husband and his friends believed that it was a taboo magazine that was just all about sex and teaching women to cheat, so it wasn't a magazine to be left around, NOT a magazine for a married woman to be reading! This particular issue featured model Claudia Schiffer and one of the articles caught my attention, 'How Important is Sexual Chemistry?' (I still have that magazine, tucked away, twenty-six years later.) I read the article as soon as I got home and took the little quiz at the end. My heart sank and instantly my world crumbled around me. I re-did the quiz just to make sure I was not being too harsh but the result was the same: of the four possible range of results I fell in the bottom of the ranking, something to the effect that my relationship was dead. I could never quite pin point what was lacking in the marriage, but there it was in black and white and I just couldn't deny it anymore. I sat in my big walk-in closet and cried. Deep down I knew that I didn't have the kind of love for this man that I should and that's why there was no sexual chemistry. On paper, we were a great couple! "We can't rationalize why our bodies feel a specific way. When we feel something instinctually, in the gut, in the heart, it's a feeling that manifests in the body, not in the brain. Don't ever shut it out". I was in shock and numb as I tried to process what this meant. This was still a time prior to the internet so the only way to get information was to go to the book store or library to read about such issues. I had absolutely no one I could talk to about this. Everyone thought my life was perfect; good man, beautiful home, lots of travel and in the garage were a Mercedes, a Porsche and a pick up truck. I wanted my life to be the façade that I had presented for years, but my true feelings were starting to bubble to the surface and I could no longer stuff them down.

Weeks passed and I suffered in silence, wondering what to do, how to do it. Then in November I received what I felt was a big and obvious sign. There was a knock on the door, and it was our neighbour who told us he had friends visiting from Taiwan. The friends really loved our house and were wondering if we would be willing to sell it. I really loved this house. It was a dream house that we designed and it had all the luxuries of the time: heated marble floors, built-in speakers and surround system, underground sprinklers, huge kitchen and bathrooms. We had only lived in it for six months and it was the downside to being married to a realtor/builder where if the price was right, the house is sold and once again we would be displaced and on the hunt for new land to build on. I was looking forward to having a vegetable garden and a flower garden and setting down some roots; we had only been married six years and this was our third home.

The Taiwanese couple had a tour of the home and they loved it! We said we would think about selling it. After some discussion, we decided to price it very high, at an unprecedented top end value of the market for that particular area. Their counter offer was only fifteen thousand dollars short of our asking price and, suddenly, all was a fait accompli – in more ways than one. Normally, closing dates on real estate fall on the first or the fifteenth of the month and rarely did anyone go outside those parameters. The closing date of this sale fell on a Wednesday in March, the seventeenth to be exact. *That was my birthday!* It was like the wheels had been set into motion and after that it just felt like there was no turning back.

Looking back and having the benefit of hindsight and 'life school', my first sign was the night of our wedding rehearsal dinner. It was September fifth, 1986. I am twenty-one years old and have just come home from my wedding rehearsal at the Italian Cultural Centre that would be filled with five hundred guests in twenty-four short hours. I pop into the kitchen to say hello to my mom and dad who are watching television; we chat for a bit about the rehearsal and the big day tomorrow. I say my goodnights and head to my room and to get ready for bed. It's nine pm and I have a big day ahead of me. It has been an amazing nine months of planning and sorting and doing. So much fun and excitement that it makes me think I should have been a party planner and not a banker. Then the reality of it hits home: "This is my last night in my home as I know it, living with mom and dad and my siblings; the last night in my room, my bed. Tomorrow I am getting married, becoming someone's wife and starting a new life." I cried. I had been so caught up in the fun and excitement of it all that I didn't once consider the reality of it. Only two days ago I had finished sewing the six dresses for my bridesmaids. We did not do the mandatory marriage preparation weekend course that all Catholic couples are required to attend. Our priest did not register us as he wanted to do the teachings with us privately, but he went to Europe for the summer so we never did have that private session. I have heard that it is very good and really tests your compatibility, although I was set on getting married and nothing could have changed my mind at that point. The expectations were far too great from both sides of the family and there was no possible way I could have changed my mind. I could not *bear* to hurt and disappoint my parents. They brought us to Canada for a better life. This is what they dreamed for me, to marry a nice Croatian boy and have a nice life. On paper, everything was so right and I just figured I could 'fake it until I make it'. After all, how hard would it be? Married to a nice guy with all the trappings and material things any young girl could ask for or dream of…

Time, maturity and evolving as a person would eventually open my eyes to reality.

The gunman has told all the tellers to get down on the floor. Sandra, the supervisor who had closed the doors, pleaded with the gunman to allow all the customers to leave; he agreed and shouted "But no one else!"

Sandra quickly hurried them all out of the door and locked it behind them: at that very moment, the two branch managers were returning from lunch only to have the door closed in their face. They went pale as they realized what was happening. My gut sank for them as they clearly realised that their branch was being robbed on a day when they broke the number one rule: both managers are never to be out of the branch at the same time. Stan was an excellent manager, not only in business but as a person. He was already in his sixties and always told it like it was. As they headed out for lunch, one of the account managers mentioned the rule to him and he said, "I'm not going to listen to those dorks from head office." That was his go-to word for all management at head office: dorks. He would call them dorks when they visited the branch. "Hey, the dorks from head office are here!" Those of us within earshot would always snicker. Political correctness was just starting to enter the banking world and we had all been sent to many courses on the subject. Head office knew that Stan would be a challenge as he had been with the credit union for over thirty years and was not about to change his ways.

The gunman made his way over to our desks, told us all to sit on the floor in the middle of the bank and instructed all of us to keep our eyes on the floor. He then sat on one of the swivel chairs and put his feet up on the desk, all the while pointing the shotgun at us. This was not a 'gunman'! He was a mere kid, all of seventeen or eighteen years old! He was wearing a baseball cap and big overcoat so initially it was hard to see him. My immediate thought was that this was a kid on drugs and was after drug money, making him more volatile and dangerous.

He randomly moved the gun from person to person as if playing some kind of Russian roulette game with us. I remember when it was pointing at me and thinking "This is it, the end for me." I probably reminded him of someone from his past who hurt, scolded or rejected him and he would pull the trigger any second now. I am twenty-eight years old and have a whole life ahead of me. I think of all the things I will miss; finding true love, travelling the world, having children, growing old. I accept the reality of the situation and if it is my time to go, it's my time to go. After all, what do I have to return to out there beyond the banks doors? I just self-destroyed my life, crushed my parents and am still absorbing the aftershock of it all. There are family and friends who

I thought would stand by my side but have abandoned me and are firmly rooted in supporting my soon to be ex-husband as if he were a helpless puppy. It felt like such a betrayal and it hurt deeply. After all, it was *my* life and I felt like I had the right to finally start living it on my own terms and according to what felt true for me and would make me happy. But everyone seemed to be so deeply vested in my life and all had their advice and opinions to share. Only one lifeline, one source of support shone through the darkness of all that upheaval and it was from my brother and his wife. "We will support you in whatever you decide and you can stay with us for as long as you need." I remember my sister-in-law saying to me. No questions asked, no advice or opinions given. I stood there in silence and shock. Up until then, I had been feeling like I was being ripped apart in a tornado and was suddenly given refuge and a safe place to be while I weathered the storm. They were the first ones who I thought would be against my decision and not likely to support me. My sister, to whom I had been so close all my life, would surely fully support me. How wrong I was, in both cases. Older brother, younger sister, we were like the three musketeers all through childhood and adolescence. Always there for each other. I so long to have that sisterly relationship again. My heart aches when I see sisters hanging out and laughing and just enjoying life. It's a double-edged sword that cuts really deeply as I was a twin at birth: we were born two months prematurely and spent the first ten days of life in incubators. My twin sister was the first-born and much stronger than I, so it was a shock for my parents when she died ten days later. It's a story I overheard them whispering to other people many times during my young life. "Mirjana was a twin at birth and we were so shocked when her twin died because she was the stronger one, born first; they were sure Mirjana would not make it beyond a day or two". I have felt the void of my twin my entire life and often wondered *why was I the one to survive*? Surely there was something big I had to do or at the very least live a big enough life for both of us. Now I feel the void of two sisters.

There was no talking allowed during the hostage situation, but I heard a couple of the ladies crying and whimpering. Shit, their crying is going to trigger him and get us all killed! Soon it became clear that the gunman was not going to pull the trigger on anyone just yet. As I sat on that floor, another thought came to mind: "What if?" What if there were only two choices on the table: the choice to live and go back to my husband and continue on with the life I had, or the choice to die? The answer was as clear as day, I didn't even have to think about it. If those were the only two choices, then I would rather die. My life out there was already a death sentence, I was dying inside and I just could not fake it anymore. No amount of glitz and glamour could make me happy and hide the pain when I simply was not happy in my heart.

Meanwhile, I could hear my cell phone ringing in my purse under my desk, another thing that I thought would trigger the gunman. Back in 1993, cell phones were still new, expensive and mostly carried by business people. Mine was the only one ringing and of course the landline at reception was also ringing off the hook. By now, the whole shopping centre would have been closed off and surely news crews were outside as things like this just did not happen in our quaint, quiet and charming city of Victoria, British Columbia. I had already seen the SWAT team in full gear, rifles drawn, slinking past the window. "Hey, get the hell out of view, are you trying to get us killed?" I thought to myself, as flashbacks of various movies scrolled through my head where the SWAT team would always slyly encircle the building, *out of view* to the gunman, not in full view! Real life plays out a little differently than any movie.

Eventually, it seemed like they cut all the phone lines but one, and that one line kept ringing and ringing and ringing. I suspected that it was the outside world trying to make contact. Someone convinced the gunman to pick it up. We had been sitting ducks for about an hour at that point and even the gunman seemed unsure of his next move. He finally picked up the phone. He certainly didn't have a demanding voice and it was hard to tell if he was shy or a quiet psycho on the verge of snapping. Our lives were in his hands and now it was up to the hostage negotiator on the other end and how convincing he could be to talk down the gunman. You could hear a pin drop in the bank and he could clearly be heard saying "No one is leaving, I'm not letting anyone go!" My heart sank and as I glanced around all I could see was fear in everyone's eyes. After a few minutes of grunts, yes and no answers he put the phone down and announced that nine people could go. Everyone was frozen and no one wanted to be the first to get up. I got up and started plucking people out, "Angela and Randy you go, you have small children. Sue, you go" (she was crying too much). A few people got up on their own and soon nine people were safely out. I stayed behind. I really felt like there was nothing out there to return to: my family, friends and a whole community of people were mad at me, upset or not talking to me so I figured I may as well just stay behind and see it to the end, good or bad, with the rest of the hostages.

It was a long day and the standoff dragged into the evening hours. At long last, we were all released and quickly ushered into a staff room at the grocery store in the complex. Head office officials and counsellors were all waiting for us there. They kept us there together for an hour just to make sure we were emotionally ok before being released.

The majority of us returned the next morning to work. The branch had forty employees and only four people took stress leave. The office was buzzing and many declarations were made but I remember Angela's the best: she said she was no longer waiting for her hot tub and told her husband when she got home "That's it! We're getting our hot tub and I don't care how much it costs or how much we have to finance!" I made a declaration to myself to live life on my terms and not to be swayed by others.

I had been among the millions glued to my television on July twenty-ninth, 1981 as Diana Spencer married Prince Charles. It was so beautiful, enchanting and magical and they seemed a perfect fit. It had been such a storybook romance and was now a fairy tale wedding. A few years later they hit stormy seas and in December of 1992 they announced their separation. It was shocking and sad. I felt relief in a way, and it seemed like a confirmation for my own intentions, because if a Princess couldn't find happiness with her Prince, what chance did the rest of us have?

Ahhhh, the ever evolving curves and sharp turns on the road to self-love. 'LOVE' is sold to us in all its many forms and guises but at the very heart, the greatest love of all is *self-love*. Something I had no idea about; millions have no idea about. What the heck is self-love? I wish it had been taught in school. It sounds so conceited and arrogant but, in fact, is neither of those. True self-love makes a person kind and gentle, self-assured with an irrefutable knowledge of their own self-worth. It's when you have that definitive line drawn in the sand of what is and is not acceptable in your life. All the years that I spent crossing that line and blurring who I was and what I stood for were the bricks in the foundation of who I am today.

I stand in the heart of who I am, without wavering and no longer concerned or affected by what anyone thinks of me. After all, what you think of me is none of my business! I can tell you, it's a refreshing and exhilarating place in which to be standing!

All roads lead to Rome; there are no wrong choices. All paths, seemingly right or wrong, gave me clarity and contrast as to what I did or did not want and therefore gave birth to a new desire. Desire is good, it propels one forward and you cannot connect the dots looking forward, *only looking back,* which means trusting in the Universe or higher power.

I was that person in high school who did not have a set plan or desire for four years of university to gain a degree and then spend thirty years in one career. Shudder the thought! I just did not love anything that much and figured I would just wing it with something. Banking intrigued me and there was a one-year programme for Bank and Teller Training. I love money and dealing with money all day would be ideal! I started out as a teller at the local credit union and worked my way up through all the positions and into management. That career lasted nine and a half years.

Simultaneously, I was a partner in a construction company. Later, I sold real estate and did some home staging and had my own clothing store. A customer at the store was an ex co-worker from the bank; we reconnected and I eventually covered her maternity leave as a finance manager at the local Ford dealership, which turned into a permanent position for me. That was a fun and lucrative career which lasted eleven years and from there stemmed my own marketing company which served all the various brands of dealerships. This was very successful, involved travel, socializing and gave me the freedom to schedule my own time. It seemed a perfect fit but somehow, it still was not filling the ever growing void inside me.

In 2013 I moved continents to follow love: both for the love of my birth country, Croatia, and for the man that I met there.

Today, I am following my heart down a path that I love completely in all its varied forms. It completely utilizes all my careers to date: banking, construction, real estate and marketing. But more importantly I am able to incorporate all my beloved hobbies: photography, home staging, antique hunting and thrift or consignment shop hunting. How much better can it get to wake up every morning than this? I don't know, but

I'm sure time will eventually unveil more for me!

I can only urge you to trust you heart, gut and instincts even if it doesn't make any sense at the time. Only you can truly know how you feel and what you feel is right for you. It's ok to want stuff, after all we are spiritual beings having a *material* experience and that involves all the material things that we could ever wish for to make us happy. It is our birthright and part of our growth and evolution as human beings. Desire keeps us moving forward for when you no longer desire, you are no longer living but merely existing. Life is for living and thriving!

Biography

Today I live in the small town of my roots and birth; Vivodina, Croatia, with the man who fills my life with love. I once said, NEVER will I be involved with a Croatian man again! HA! Never say never, for the minute you do, it will surely come true.

It is here that I have pioneered a project with many delicious layers. A multi-million dollar project to rebuild, restore and revive the town for future generations to enjoy. It involves preserving the culture and history and rebuilding the old homes, some of which will be preserved as museums showcasing the old way of village life. Other farmhouses will be converted into vacation homes, preserving their authentic charms but with modern conveniences. They key aspect of the project will focus on the many women in their 20's and 30's who have exceptional domestic skills, farm skills, a university education and some even have a master's degree. My goal is to turn them into entrepreneurs using their 'smarts and skills'. The very skills that have enabled women to run household for centuries, albeit it, without acknowledgement. Each will manage a restored family farmhouse and host vacationing guests and give them an authentic, village life, experience. It is a game-changing concept that will allow the women to flourish, grow the town and pass the teachings to the following generation. It will enrich their families and the entire community.

There are daily requests for ancestral information and we will focus on heritage and cultural tours to help those searching for their roots walk the earth of their grand and great-grandparents. This area is truly where heaven meets earth and some of Mother Nature's finest work! A nearly seven-hundred-year old wine region with rolling hills, vineyards and churches atop each hill: it is magical and rejuvenates my soul every day and has had the same effect on all those who have visited me.

I am also a trainer and speaker for 'Infinite Possibilities, the Heart of Creating Your Dreams, created by Mike Dooley, a New York Times best selling author. Soon, retreats will be offered encompassing this and other essential material for all those seeking the road to self-love and creating a life according to their own terms.

To see more, visit me at With Love, From Croatia.

www.withlovefromcroatia.com
www.vivodinacroatia.com
www.vivodinaproject.com

Shirley Billson

What struck me about Shirley was her innate intelligence, something which took her many years, in fact, decades, to tap into in a way which would finally fulfil her and create a life of purpose. She is a wonderful example of 'better late than never' and I love that she has created such a fabulous business in order to help young people avoid the pitfalls into which she fell.

The crying years

My story begins around 1975, not the year I was born as you might imagine, but the year I turned fifteen.

I recall spending many afternoons and evenings shut away in my bedroom, listening to music and drowning in tears, for no apparent reason. The tears and the music related to a strong sense of wanting to be loved, of feeling unlovable.

My older brothers were happy to feed this particular anxiety with name calling and telling me no one would marry me.

I'm not quite sure how long this continued, but even though my mother had the good sense to leave me alone, respecting my desire for privacy demonstrated by the closed door, she eventually recommended I visit the doctor with her.

An old-fashioned doctor, who belonged in the post-war era and understood neither young people nor women's liberation, duly prescribed anti-depressants. I was advised these would take a few weeks to kick in, but when they did I found my sense of being alive became shrouded in a fog of nothingness. No ups. No downs. Just a straight line, emotion free sea of nothingness.

I stopped taking the pills, preferring the mad combination of euphoric highs, stomach aching laughter, dramatic and angry outbursts and melancholy lows of my experience. These feelings seemed to be a part of me, of who I felt I was, rather than a sedated version of who I was supposed to be to conform to normality.

The crying years tailed off for quite a few decades, but the teenage angst continued and the highs and lows became punctuated by events, rather than seeming to emerge from nowhere. I started to be bullied for how I looked – I have a big chin. This was crushing at an age when how you looked was way more important than how you behaved; and the very act of writing it down makes me feel uncomfortable still. At seventeen, I attempted suicide over a first broken relationship. At twenty-five, I was in a physically and emotionally abusive relationship.

Proving my worth

Behind all this seeming melancholy was a fiery, fun-loving temperament and fierce ambition. I was good at faking confidence which drove me to prove I could make it; that I was worthy and that I needed no one to define me, though I'm not sure to whom I thought I was needing to prove anything.

At the time of the abusive relationship, I had only recently graduated and had landed an advertising job I loved and in which I wanted to go far. I believe this 'saved' me from the relationship I was in way sooner than if I had had an uninteresting job. With the gratifying support of colleagues and bosses, I left the abuser after just six months. My colleagues fielded calls from him for a while and even the police agreed to watch the entrance to the lane where my office was on the first day of leaving him

I wanted to become a board director by the time I was thirty. I made it by the time I was twenty-nine, not in the original agency, but I made it nonetheless.

And there it is again – the phrase, 'made it.'

Of course, I soon realised that I hadn't made anything. I hadn't a plan beyond getting to become a director. I started to doubt myself, especially when it came to managing people. Although I had huge confidence in my ability, in what I had achieved and what I was capable of, the managing people part of the job scared me. I could be tough with suppliers, firm with clients, but I was terrified of staff. I was afraid of what they were saying about me behind my back, what they thought of me. I was convinced they didn't like me and that was an echo of earlier times, of bullying, of being afraid to be me in case *me* was something people didn't like.

New chapters

Then my life took on a new chapter, as all lives do. I got married and within a year gave birth to a beautiful boy. Though I did return to work after three months off, the birth had coincided with a biting recession. A major client of the agency had defaulted, owing us a large sum of money. Suddenly we were in receivership and I was unemployed at home with a young baby in a marriage that was fuelled by argument and discord. My confidence was so rocked by the closure of the agency that I struggled to get new work at the level I was qualified and so, after three years in the career wilderness, I got funding to do a Master of Arts in Export Marketing, which I hoped would provide my route back. It didn't.

It seemed that I'd stepped off the career ladder the moment I'd had my son and the agency had folded. I now began alternating jobs and self-employment contracts for the next seventeen years. Some of it was good and some of it wasn't. In all honesty, the self-employment came about because I couldn't settle in any of the jobs I was being offered. They were all at lower salaries and lower responsibility levels than I'd had in my late twenties. It felt like no one took me seriously anymore and nobody valued the major contribution I felt I could make to their business.

In the twenty-odd years between the ages of thirty-five and fifty-six, I was fired three times. Only one of those times did it have anything to do with my ability to carry out the work, but *every* time contributed to my growing sense of unworthiness.

Like a zombie, I kept getting up again. Lurching on to the next drama, still striving for career success and recognition, and as the years ticked by, the desperation to also earn serious money kicked in. I had no pension and no savings. Yet I had become, it seemed, unemployable. I was unable consistently to make the kind of income that would build my pension pot or give me the security I needed, even though I tried and tried and tried.

Starting again

Rewind to 1999. It was 'dot com' bubble era and I was working in a small information technology company. They were pretty good at the techy stuff but not so good at recognising the marketing potential of the internet which was unfolding around us. As a marketer, I could and I started by trying to persuade them of the jewel in their crown – to no avail.

Then my father died and, in his honour, I decided to start a 'real' business. I realised I could apply my customer and marketing know-how to help people build websites that users actually wanted to visit and create enjoyable, effective experiences, rather than uninspiring and cumbersome storefronts. Hard to believe now that the internet world was *ever* this way!

Although I couldn't persuade any of the key technical wizards at the company that this was worth jumping ship for, thankfully there was another recently joined marketing manager who was as up for it as I was: we joined forces and created a new company: 'Workspeak'. Our intention was to help ordinary companies create user-friendly websites enabling them to create an edge over their competition. We sub-contracted technical wizardry and got ourselves some clients, going from a standing start to six-figure turnover and two additional part-time staff in two years – yet still I lacked the confidence in my ability. So, when my co-director became pregnant in the same year my marriage broke up and our sub-contracted technical geek went rogue, I lost interest and walked away from it all.

And again

I had a kind of youth-fuelled denial keeping me from worrying too much about future income. "There's always more time", I told myself and I embarked on a few years of doing whatever I wanted, including seven months living in Catalunya and immersing myself in the Spanish language before returning to a 'proper job' in marketing and communications for the local National Health Service.

Still driven to do whatever I wanted, I decided to re-train as a hypnotherapist. My only motivation at that time was to train for a 'portable' career which would not be too expensive to study, too time-consuming or too arduous (did I mention my lazy streak?) and that would allow me to leave this God-forsaken country (as I saw it then) and return to my beloved Catalunya.

However, I fell in love with this hypnotherapy thing and, around the same time, was blessed to also find the love of my life. Life was looking good. I started building my hypnotherapy practice part time around my National Health Service role and after a couple of years decided it was time to finally throw in the towel with employment and go full time as a hypnotherapy practitioner. Only this time, my ambition, rather than rescue me as it had in my late twenties, got in the way. In the back of my mind was the nagging knowledge that I had no pension pot. I had to find a way to create something bigger than a little hypnotherapy practice, something that could deliver passive income.

And again

And this is where everything began to unravel – in a way that made all previous challenges pale into insignificance. I realised, at forty-seven, that I was now closer to ninety than birth. Panic set in. I started investing in business coaches which turned out to be both a blessing and a curse.

I needed help turning my ambition into reality, turning vague ideas into action plans; and I found people I thought could help me. However, I'd spent nearly ten thousand pounds and made no positive progress before finding a coach whose teaching 'clicked' for me. I bought into one of her entry-level programmes, followed the steps to the letter and, hey presto, as if by magic, it worked. Suddenly I was getting coaching clients who were paying me from one thousand five hundred pounds to nine thousand dollars to work with me.

The trouble was that I wasn't particularly in love with coaching. So, from the outset, although I was achieving a level of success and financial freedom looked like it was just around the corner, I was feeling out of alignment, out of integrity. The feeling inside didn't seem to match what was happening on the outside – and my clients seemed to be people like me, scared and vulnerable and looking for nirvana; looking for rescue from their later life prospects and empty pension pots.

I didn't believe I had it to offer them. But now I was hooked on coaching, almost to the point of addiction. I was flying to America several times a year, investing in each higher level of programme offered and spending the higher fees I was earning in making other coaches better off, instead of contributing to my own pension pot. I convinced myself (because that's part of the coaching sales pitch) that all of these coaching programmes were 'an investment' in myself and would be repaid with massive interest by the increase in flow of clients and the income that would generate.

In July 2012 I had my first five-figure income month and was ecstatic. And then I stopped actively marketing and doing the things that had got me there. Instead, I wrote and published my first book (with the help of a book coach, of course!).

Debt and fear

By November 2012 I had no client income at all, but what I did have was around fourteen thousand pounds of accumulated credit card and overdraft debt from all those transatlantic flights, hotels and coaching programmes. I was scared. And scared made it hard to be confident which made it hard to get any new clients. This meant I had to come to terms with having absolutely no way to meet the monthly payments on the debt: this was terrifying. I searched the internet, found out about a thing called a Debt Management Programme and turned to the charity 'StepChange' to help me out of the hole I was in. They helped me manage the debt, which helped me feel a little more in control.

However, it didn't give me my confidence back nor did it quell the background anxiety I now secretly carried with me, which, with hindsight, was merely an echo of my earlier fears and inadequacies; neither did it calm the outright fear I had around money, poverty and worthlessness.

There was no way I believed I could return to coaching with my self-esteem crushed and carrying the weight of shame that I had let myself down, I had let my son down (and I so wanted to be a positive role model and a source of financial support for him) and I had let my beloved partner Lewis down. To add irony to the mix, I had Power of Attorney for my mother's financial affairs yet seemed like the worst qualified person in the world to be figuring out how best to take care of her money.

I was at rock bottom. I was broke. Correction: I had created a situation which meant WE were broke. Our combined income wasn't enough to fully carry the weight of my burden but it wasn't low enough for us to qualify for any kind of benefits. We were in our mid-fifties living in a two-bedroom flat up three narrow flights of stairs, with no outside space and nowhere to park our car and no means to change it. I realised I had to get a job, but my confidence was so low, there was no way it would be a decent paying job, or one which even came close to matching my level of expertise or experience.

I started doing admin work and though it felt good to be finding some way to at least meet the monthly payments of my debt management plan and contribute in part to household income, I still felt crushed. Inside I felt ashamed and helpless, a victim of the circumstances I had created. Sadly, coming to terms with being the architect of your own downfall doesn't make it any easier to overcome it. I was still anxious, afraid and ashamed and getting poorer. I became expert at living on very little. If I bought clothes at all, I bought them in charity shops when I felt 'flush.' I couldn't afford to pay for hairdressers, so I taught myself to cut my own hair. I isolated myself from friends because I couldn't even afford a coffee.

I really had hit rock bottom. I was having suicidal thoughts. After all, what value did I bring to anyone or anything, how could the future be any different when I'd tried so many years to make a difference yet I'd failed and failed and failed again? Only the thought of my son and Lewis and the pain it would cause them kept me from choosing suicide as an option.

Something had to change – and that something was me

I had no idea how. I had no grand plan. I had no coach and no formula.

I'd previously tried self-hypnosis to overcome my self-sabotaging behaviours, but it didn't work. I'd tried hypnotherapy with colleagues, but it didn't work. Whatever was blocking me was powerful and however much I thought I wanted change, the sabotage got me. Every time.

One day, by chance while Googling for who knows what, I came across David Lynch and his endorsement of transcendental meditation. I'd heard of it, who hadn't? It was synonymous for me with the Beatles' weird transformation from loveable chaps to drug taking weird people who no longer seemed to get on with another. From afar, it seemed like a cult with the Maharishi Mahesh Yogi at the heart of it. However, David Lynch got me curious and I'd remembered meeting a mentor who had talked of the power of meditation as the single most powerful key to happiness and fulfilment.

I booked on to a local class to find out more. Again, it cost money I didn't have and though this made me even more sceptical of it as a positive step, I had no other plan. I had to try something to bring myself back to me. I hadn't laughed or genuinely smiled in a long time. I spoke little and shared little. I honestly don't know how Lewis survived this period, never mind me.

I committed fully and as instructed began a twice daily meditation of twenty minutes. Nothing dramatic happened, I was still anxious and fearful but I did see glimpses of 'me' return. I became more likely to retreat from my self-imposed silences and engage in conversation with Lewis.

Most of all I valued these periods of meditation for the temporary respite they gave me from worry, anxiety and lack.

Whatever else happened in life, wherever I was and whoever I was with, I remained totally committed to twenty minutes of meditation twice daily. Some days it was hard: my mind and body interfered with runaway thoughts, discomfort and cramp. Still I stuck with it. I found the mantra difficult to persist with, but I stuck to the practice, twenty minutes twice daily.

I gave myself permission to change the 'rules' of what my mind was 'allowed' to focus on during the meditation. As long as I stuck to the twenty minutes, I figured it was important that this remained the one place and time where no one told me what to think or feel, not even me, through my inner critic. I started to experiment with letting go of control, discovering just how hard this was for me, but deciding it was vital. If I could free myself from controlling thoughts and feelings in a meditative state, there was a chance I could free myself in day-to-day life. But I put no expectation on it. I allowed it to be, all of which seemed to fit with the notion of what I believed mindfulness was, though I had never studied it.

I started to meditate on words that seemed to sum up what I most needed in that moment. I started to 'allow' thoughts and feelings to happen, getting slowly better at over-riding the impulse to control and direct those same thoughts and feelings. I let the words float and morph, staying constant or becoming what they wanted to become.

Two years later, something changed

Out of the blue, I was offered a job by a previous hypnotherapy client as a sales coach to her telephone sales team. It seemed like a gift, and it was, but not in the way I initially expected. I did a great job of transforming nervous, anxiety ridden and underperforming members of the team to coping, confident sales people who hit their targets. But my way of working or who I was (who knows?) didn't fit with what the young management team expected. They fired me with no reason and even agreed I had done a great job. Instead of this crushing my confidence once again, this time was different. Instead of allowing myself to step into the old role of victim, I stayed confident. I knew I had done a good job. I knew my worth. I didn't doubt it. I took that confidence and my energy into a much-wanted role that materialised with my favourite homeless charity. For the first time I was motivated by who I was, not who I thought I should be and not by a drive for income and status, but instead for happiness and fulfilment.

My meditation continued but it now seemed as if the slow incremental and almost unnoticeable improvement in my life, wellbeing and sense of self that had been happening over the preceding years was gathering momentum. I had always struggled with planning and goal setting and old age seemed to be rushing towards me, increasing panic in decision making.

Twenty-year plan

This time I resolved to look forward, to how my life could be twenty years from now. To do this, I began by taking note of all the changes and achievements that had occurred over each preceding twenty-year period in my life: degrees, homes, jobs, relationships, investments, languages, skills; there was a mountain to be proud of. This simple exercise increased my sense of potential and possibility. Finally, I was ready to contemplate the future in an exciting way.

I also started using strategies that I'd used with people in my consulting room, people who were stuck and couldn't imagine what a positive future looked like. I started physically and emotionally connecting to childhood joys and achievements, even where they made no sense, using them to re-ignite positive neural networks that had long been dormant and enabling my complex brain to make the connections with my present and my preferred future. For example, I started going to a crochet group because I was good at embroidery as a child – but had a sworn aversion to needlework or craft of any kind as an adult. I volunteered with the local Wildlife Trust to coppice a woodland because I remembered loving trees and nature and making mud pies!

When the contract for my marketing role in the charity came to an end, my confidence had grown still more and I determined to return to self-employment, to build a new company from scratch, one totally dedicated to what mattered to me, what was important to my view of the world without concern for whether I believed it would make me money or garner me prestige or status. All that mattered now was my fulfilment: finally, every cliché I had ever read or spoken made sense.

Doors to opportunity started to open

Guided by the active strengthening of my positive neural networks, I started to take steps forward in faith. When I took one step forward in faith, it led me to another.

It began to be exciting but at no point was I in the old giddy state of blind excitement that obscured me from the truth of what really mattered, what I really wanted and who I really was. I felt emboldened, yet level headed. I kept stepping forward, trusting in the outcome. I took every opportunity that came to me. I resolved only to follow paths that aligned with what really mattered to me and how I wanted to live my life.

The Mental Wealth Factory

The 'Mental Wealth Factory' and the idea of working specifically with young people aged fourteen to twenty-six came to me in a series of rapid stages.

I was not motivated by a sense of pure charity in which my self becomes subsumed to a cause, neither was I motivated by a sense of profit motive. I simply followed inner urgings without allowing my critical, logical brain to over-ride them. I began to see that the things transpiring in my life were ways to fulfilment, to inner confidence, to true self-esteem. I came to realise that I could unpick the journey on which I had come.

The techniques and strategies I had devised to help myself could be reconstructed and taught

I thought how different my life might have been had I understood how to follow this path when I was a teenager. I realised that this was not something you needed experience to acquire. This was something innate, that we all had and that, for most of us, life had over-ridden. If you were young enough, you could learn how this works and create a store of mental wealth that could change the path of your life for the better. At worst, it could simply make your path through life, especially late teens and early adulthood, less painful.

This is what drives me, this and the Mental Wealth Factory.

I feel my journey has just begun. Instead of fear of the future, I feel excitement.

Biography

Shirley Billson is the founder of The Mental Wealth Factory, dedicated to working with schools and universities to create mental wealth in young people between fourteen and twenty-six, so they can truly thrive.

www.TheMentalWealthFactory.co.uk

www.stepchange.org

Susie Rose

A sweet, sensitive child, Susie was an easy target for bullies and later, controlling men. Forging through life and career, with no self-care, created all manner of pain throughout Susie's body until she learned to start putting herself first. She began to understand how powerful her mind was in creating the world around her, and how as an empath she needed to protect her energy before using her sensitivities to help others.

I WAS BULLIED AT SCHOOL AND it's taken me a long time to reclaim my voice, self-worth and confidence. Bullying is talked about much more these days; mental health is a hot topic, but more and more children and adults are taking anti-depressants or worse, taking their own lives. There were over twenty-four thousand 'Childline' counselling sessions with children about bullying in 2016/2017; bullying and cyber-bullying is an issue that affects almost all children in some way and the after effects can ripple through their life causing chaos in every facet.

I was always a quiet, sensitive child, brought up in a normal home with two loving parents and one brother. I loved animals and enjoyed spending time by myself, reading and observing the world and people around me. I remember starting school; I didn't like going and didn't enjoy being in a big group of children with the constant noise and stimulation. That said I had a small group of friends and a best friend, Emma. Emma and I were very similar and we enjoyed playing and doing our own thing together; we were also quite rebellious and got into mischief. We both loved horses and went to the local riding school, which was my favourite place. In fact from about the age of seven I spent most weekends and school holidays at the riding school helping out and enjoying the countryside and the freedom. Horses are very intuitive creatures, they are very much attuned to our emotions and in their company I was able to be completely myself with no judgement.

It was secondary school that really brought challenges my way and where I was to experience my first taste of bullying. My best friend Emma went to another school and my other friends from primary school were in separate classes, so we only got to meet at break times and in a few lessons. Most children in my class had their friend from primary school, and I ended up making friends with the two other girls; one who was very shy and the other one was who was being picked on for coming from the caravan park and wearing 'milk bottle' glasses – very thick lenses. I hated seeing anyone feeling sad or being bullied and was always quick to stand up for anyone. We three girls became good friends, and for the first year or so school life was pretty good.

I can't remember when the bullying started; I just remember it being constant and getting much worse in my early teens. The bully was in my class; I hadn't had any problems with her, although she was often the one who made cruel comments. I had no idea at the time why she suddenly decided to pick on me. She was often in trouble for wearing makeup, dying her hair or smoking. It was clear that her home life wasn't all rosy and she never seemed happy. She hung around with a crowd of older kids from the care home; they were definitely known as the crowd not to be messed with.

She started to call me nasty names, which I ignored. This just seemed to infuriate her even more. It became more and more constant and the focus of her day! I won't go into all details, but the nastiness increased with threats and warnings to shut up and keep quiet, or else. At the height of the bullying she had threatened and scared the entire class into not speaking to me, including my two 'friends'. I found it fascinating to see them playing along with her, even laughing at her cruel remarks, but I could see through the charade and their need to feel 'safe' themselves. Still, that hurt and saddened me so much.

I could not understand how anyone could be so hurtful. I had no idea at that time why she chose me. I could though, feel the underlying anger and pain that she was in. For me, the effects were physical and mental. I was suppressing all the hurt and emotions; I didn't talk about it or even try to make sense of why she picked on me at that time. I lost a lot of weight as I often felt too sick to eat at school and as a result my periods stopped almost as quickly as they started. I had frequent headaches, stomach pain and chest pains, especially on Sunday evenings and recurrent tonsillitis which continued until my early twenties. I also had symptoms of asthma but after chest x-rays and tests, doctors could not find anything physically wrong. I now know that whatever is going on emotionally will eventually come out in the body as physical symptoms or disease, unless it is acknowledged, expressed and dealt with.

I was living a double life: half my school day was 'normal', when I spent time with my old friends during break and half my lessons and the other half was a nightmare. My friends knew what was going on, but we didn't talk about it, they just helped me forget, particularly Lucy and Sean. They were my sanctuary; as friends we really clicked and had a lot of fun, laughing until we cried. I will be forever grateful to them, probably more than they'll ever know. If you ever read this, you two, you seriously rocked. I try and remember those good times as how school is meant to be. I still spent most of my spare time with horses; they are exceptionally intuitive and healing animals.

Despite the bullying, academically I was doing ok at school; not as well as I could have been for sure, and I admit to bunking off a few times when I couldn't face the day. Any thoughts of staying on or going to college or university had vanished; I was dreaming of the day I could walk out and never return.

The bullying eventually came to a head one sunny day when we were all out at break. I'd found out that it had started all those years before because a certain boy had a crush on me, and the bully had a crush on him; I wasn't even aware and wasn't at all interested at that age. What I do remember is that I'd had enough and I found my voice that day. The bully strutted over to me and stood almost in my face; she said I had apparently called her a not-so-nice name, which I hadn't, and she told me I had to apologise and give her my lunch money or I'd be sorry. By this time quite a big crowd had gathered, including her posse and she was enjoying being centre of attention. I think I was probably quite numb by this time, tired of her and all her hatred; it couldn't really get much worse as far as I could see. I remember saying "So what if I did call you that, what are you going to do about it? Just do it!" Her mouth opened but no sound came out; I can vividly remember looking at her and feeling quite sorry for her, she seemed to shrink about a foot, and was fumbling for words as she looked around her while everyone stared. I can't remember who walked away first, but I do know that from then on the bullying stopped. Everyone wanted to be my friend, even those 'friends' who had so easily left me to be picked on – I was quite happy with the ones I already had.

I left school a few weeks before my sixteenth birthday. I was relieved to leave all the painful memories behind and start work. I was however still holding the trauma; I'd still not talked about it and didn't realise how it might impact me in the future both emotionally and physically.

It wasn't until years later that I heard the term, 'empath' and all my childhood and early adulthood challenges made complete sense. Empaths are deeply sensitive individuals who are highly attuned to the emotions and energy of others. They can easily take on the emotions of others as their own and are often called 'too emotional' or 'sensitive'. They also feel trauma much more deeply, be it something that has happened to them or something they've seen; it can affect their ability to function normally. Being so attuned to others can be a challenge, especially if the empath's boundaries aren't strong; they can end up absorbing the pain and stress of those around them, especially in crowds. Empaths are also sharply intuitive and are extremely good at reading people and situations beyond just surface-level impressions. They also want to help people, and hate seeing anyone suffer, often to their own detriment. Empaths are often introverts and can have challenges with relationships until they learn to create healthy boundaries and love themselves first, then they can turn what feels like a weakness into a strength. If you've been called out for being 'too sensitive' or 'too emotional' or you have a son or daughter who finds being around others challenging, read up on being an empath or highly sensitive person; you'll recognise yourself or them.

So, I was already hardwired to attract and try to fix hurt people. Over the next few years I had many challenging or toxic relationships with both friends and boyfriends: I gave too much, trying to help but not having strong enough boundaries to protect myself. My first serious boyfriend at eighteen was very controlling and manipulative. He became extremely jealous if I spoke to anyone, and slowly but surely cut me off from my friends. I was forgiving as I knew deep down he was a good person; his last girlfriend had cheated on him and I could feel his pain. I made lots of excuses for his bad behaviour but I wanted to prove I wasn't like his ex. Deep down I knew I couldn't 'fix' him, that he didn't really like himself, but I wasn't ready to trust my inner voice which was telling me to run! After I finally left him, I had a few more disastrous relationships and any nice boyfriends were turned away: "Sorry it was me not you." I wasn't sure why I did that but them being nice made me feel uneasy. I wanted someone to focus on or fix so that I could carry on ignoring my own needs. I was always prepared to stand up for others but the truth of it was I didn't love myself enough to believe I deserved to be treated well.

In my late twenties I married and had a gorgeous baby boy. I was working as a manager at a publishing company and after having my son I went back to work part-time. Like many mums, I began the exhausting juggle of work and motherhood: this was where my lack of boundaries and self-care caught up with me. I was expected to do my full-time job in part-time hours, then go home to look after a baby who wasn't sleeping. After twelve years in the company, my boss was suddenly monitoring my time keeping, even though I hardly stopped for a coffee break; I felt that I needed to prove myself and that I was doing my job well. I had frequent sinus infections, viral meningitis and I was so stressed and exhausted I could hardly drag myself to work. I was burnt out and self-care was nowhere to be seen.

It should have been no surprise that when trying to get pregnant with my second child, my body was having none of it. I had two miscarriages, which if you've experienced one, you'll know are heart breaking. I was referred for tests and was told that from the results it was likely I was having an early menopause; that it would impossible for me to have another baby, even IVF (in vitro fertilisation) wasn't an option. I was devastated. There wasn't really any support; I was directed to a website where endless heartbroken women discussed hormone levels and sad stories and I never went back on there again.

I hadn't told anyone the full story; only my husband knew and I made him promise not to discuss it. I didn't want people looking at me with pity in their eyes; I didn't want my two pregnant friends to feel bad or to stop discussing their growing babies. I had a wonderful son, whom I loved dearly and I felt so grateful for that. So I carried on, kept it all pretty much to myself and tried to cope with the grief. Everyone around me seemed to be pregnant and for what seemed like months I remember spending much of my journey to work sobbing. I developed chest pains again and such pain in my back I often had to lie down on the floor. I was sent for x-rays, put on a heart monitor and had an MRI scan (magnetic resonance imaging). They showed nothing.

It was then I stopped and began really listening to my own intuition. I knew, somewhere deep down that what my body needed was healing. I knew that these 'pains' in my body were trying to draw attention to something, to all the trauma I'd collected, both mine and other people's. I could no long keep giving from an empty vessel.

I threw myself into researching holistic healing, nutrition and law of attraction. I read every book I could get my hands on, looked up acupuncture points for fertility, took Chinese herbal medicine, used essential oils, meditation, reiki, yoga and Bowen therapy. Slowly but surely, I began to feel much better than I had done for a long time; I learned to start putting myself first; to fill my cup before giving to others.

I began to understand how powerful my mind was in creating the world around me; I started trusting the signs and feelings I got about people, rather than ignoring them. I started learning about the challenges of being an empath and how to look after my energy and to turn my sensitivities into a strength.

A year later, I fell pregnant with my daughter; I remember the shock on my doctor's face. I remember at first being terrified that I was going to miscarry again. I was in my late thirties but was given a clean bill of health and told that I was healthier than most pregnant mothers much younger than me. I continued to use essential oils, meditation and yoga to see me through until my daughter was born healthy and well.

After my maternity leave I took redundancy from my job and started working for myself alongside running a local magazine for working mums. I also carried on with the self-development and started reading about spirituality and other healing modalities. I began to see how my past experiences had shaped my life and how keeping up a good regime of self-love and care was important if I wanted to help others and stay healthy and well. I wanted to become a good role model for my children and became fascinated by the mind, body and spirit connection. It was also clear that there were many other women struggling to juggle motherhood and life and those dealing with the challenges of being an empath or raising a sensitive child.

I co-founded 'Networking Women'; business meetings to educate and support women in business, and continued my education and training in energy work, psychology, counselling and essential oils. I have met more like-minded people and I continue to learn more about myself and others through life experience, such as my divorce and becoming a single parent.

Now my passion is empowering women, although I often work with children and teens, to guide them in leaving past traumas behind, whether it's bullying, a bad relationship, or other trauma or negative belief, and teaching them the tools to change their lives for the better, to find and use the power they have within them. Journaling is one of the tools I encourage; writing things down can be amazingly healing!

I hope reading this encourages someone to listen to their inner voice and embrace their sensitivities, to give themselves some love and take control of their life. I know from my own experience, there aren't many things you can't overcome, there's nothing that has to hold you back forever, and when you let go of the past, your life can be changed for the better.

Biography

Susie lives in Witney with her two wonderful children; a nineteen-year old son and a twelve-year old daughter, and Angus the cat. She's known for her work with women business owners throughout Oxfordshire and Gloucestershire, supporting and empowering them to succeed.

Her other passion is her healing business, 'Breathe Rise Shine', mentoring women to overcome their past and the blocks and fears holding them back, so they can truly fulfil all their potential in life and in the process become more empowered, confident, peaceful, happy and be great role models for their children.

Susie is qualified in a range of holistic and mind/body modalities and uses a powerful combination of ancient energy work, essential oils and modern applied psychology to help identify and clear blocks from the past and achieve fast, effective and lasting change. She teaches the tools and principles of success and self-love, so you can be the VERY BEST version of you.

Susie also leads a team of health conscious women who want to educate themselves and others on the power of natural healing and essential oils for health and wellbeing.

www.networkingwomen.org.uk

www.susierose.co.uk

www.breatheriseshine.com

www.mydoterra.com/susierose

www.childline.org.uk

Angelika Breukers

When I met Angelika, I was struck by the strength she exudes, not a hard, masculine power, rather a warm, feminine yet no-nonsense strength. After the abuse she suffered as a child and the dark path down which that took her, it is testimony to her strength and emotional intelligence that she found a way to accept what happened, to learn not to pass judgement and to realise that she had *choices*. The choices she subsequently made led her towards a positive path of self-love and a deep desire to help others know that they need not live with shame.

WHAT I'M ABOUT TO SHARE WITH you I've only shared in talks, but I would now like to reach out to a wider audience, as it is my intention and passion to let you know that *there is hope*.

When I think back, it seemed that all was going well in my life until the age of five-and-a-half. I remember kindergarten well: the toys, the games we played, and the other children. It seemed to be a happy time, I can still smell and feel the leather bag I used for my packed lunch and the little packets of sweets we got for our birthdays. But then things changed. At that young age, my existence was taken to a different level; one of fear, hopelessness and despair. The twinkling star within me suddenly lost its sparkle.

My father could be very funny and had a caring side to him. He was a hardworking man. But, unfortunately, he was also an alcoholic. He drank from a very young age, and was still drinking when he met my mum. In fact, he never stopped. During his drinking sessions, his personality would change. He would become an unpredictable, nasty man, becoming aggressive and violent towards my mum and us (my brother, my sister and me). We'd constantly be treading on eggshells, trying not to upset him. Over time, he became spiteful even when he wasn't drinking.

The day he changed my life, I was five-and-a-half years old. It happened when I was trying on my new school dress, an exciting time for many girls at that age. My mother needed to make some alterations, so she stood me on top of the kitchen table to save her crouching. She left the room for a moment to get something, and as she walked out, my father walked in. He saw me standing there, walked towards me and started speaking to me in manner that made me feel very uncomfortable.

I was hoping that my mother would come back into the room any second, because from the way he was speaking to me and from what he was telling me, I knew something was wrong. There was nothing I could do. Then he touched me in a way he shouldn't have. I knew that what he'd done was wrong and, by this time, I was praying for my mother to come back. It all happened in a very short space of time. Not only did he touch me in that way, but he also managed to scare me into keeping what had happened from my mother.

That was the first turning point in my life. One moment, I was five-years old, excited about my new dress and looking forward to going to school, and the next I was on a completely different path: a path of abuse, shame, guilt and feelings of disconnection. In that moment, my innocence was destroyed and the sparkle I'd always had just disappeared.

My father started to 'groom' me and my life took a different turn. He made the abuse sound interesting and exciting, so he would get me to touch him and please him. It was a gradual process that didn't feel right to me, but since I was then only six years old, I had no alternative but to go along with it. He also threatened me and kept me in fear, so that I wouldn't say anything to my mother. In this way, he continued to manipulate me.

The abuse wasn't just physical, but emotional, too. I must have been about seven or eight-years old when my father told me that, when I grew up, I should be a prostitute. This, I think, was going to be more for his benefit than for mine. I was devastated. I was so scared and horrified, in disbelief that my father could say something like that. This only led to feeling even more worthless and shameful. I remember being very upset, and when my uncle asked me if anything was wrong, I started crying and told him what my father had said. With kind and gentle words, he told me not to worry, that it was not going to happen, that my father was probably drunk when he said it.

Drunk or not, it had been said, and the words were very powerful. However, over time, the thoughts and fears I had about what my father said fell to the back of my mind. Life carried on as normal (well, what seemed normal for me) and on the surface I forgot about it. Subconsciously, however, the seed was planted.

It was rooted deeply in my mind.

Six years passed until my dad's abuse was discovered by my mother. She caught him touching me in forbidden ways and all hell broke loose. Shortly after that, he left the house, though he still lived in the same town. At first, I felt scared every time I left the house. If I saw him, I'd hide in a shop across the road because I couldn't face seeing or speaking to him. This continued until one day, when I was about twelve or thirteen-years old, I asked myself whether I really wanted to be scared of him for the rest of my life. And the answer was NO! I realised at that very moment that I had a *choice*.

So, plucking up all of my courage, I decided to visit him. I knew that I was going to be safe, as he had a new partner, so I went to his house.

I can't remember what I said or what the conversation was about. All I know is that when I left his house, I felt truly liberated. I 'felt the fear and did it anyway'. In my opinion, that was the first step of accepting what had happened to me. Of course, that one action alone didn't unravel or heal the deeply traumatic emotional experiences and their effect on my belief system. The question is: how can anyone want to accept something so bad and wrong? However, later I learned to accept him for who he was by understanding his background. That helped me to eventually forgive him. Someone once told me that not forgiving is like wishing someone else dead, but drinking the poison yourself. The anger, the sadness, the negative feelings that you hold inside do not harm the other person: they harm YOU.

Looking back at those dark times, it felt as though the real me was disappearing. I knew that things were not the same for me as they were for other children, but because I'd never experienced a loving, happy life, I didn't know how much better other children's lives were. A child forms its belief system in the first six to seven years of its life, when the brain is like a sponge, taking in all the negative and positive messages. It forms beliefs about the 'self', about others and about the world. The beliefs that I was developing about myself and the world around me were not positive at all. I had to learn to accept my awful experiences and to take responsibility for what I was thinking and how I was interacting with the world.

Making changes from within takes time. It's a gradual process and I'm grateful for that. If the changes had happened faster, I think I would've gone mad; I wouldn't have had the time to process everything as I went through the stages of learning how to be more self-accepting. It would have been an explosion of emotions sending me over the edge, rather than a process of growth, reconnecting with who I really am. It's like gradually getting rid of the weeds in a dark, dead, unloved garden and putting the love and light back into it, allowing the flowers to grow. It has taken me a long time, but I am so grateful that I've managed to make changes within me and that I've been able to forgive both him and, most of all, myself, as what happened to me was not my fault.

Accepting what my father did and accepting my father for who he was started me on my journey to freedom. I began to recognise that I could be free to be me, free from the demons of thought that I was not worthy of love. In coming to understand that it was not my fault, I could then begin to change the terrible feelings of guilt and shame and, with it, accept that I'd been dwelling on the past.

Over the years, I have learned to accept and not to pass judgement on people, because I don't know what experiences they've had that have made them become who they are. I believe that no one who chooses to have a sense of self-worth would choose a path of self-destruction or choose to intentionally harm other people. For my father, it was almost as if the dark side had won him over. It can take time to overcome and accept what's happened to you and what's been said to you, but you have to keep trying and never give up.

I wish I could give clear instructions on how to gain acceptance, like a set of road directions: 'take a left turn, right over the roundabout up the hill and take another left and you are at your destination'. But it's not as simple as that: there are no instructions for how to reach acceptance. You create the experience of finding it and getting there yourself. It's an individual process of inner growth. To find acceptance you have to look at people and situations from a different perspective. You have to find the mental agility to bend and guide your thoughts to a different and more positive way of thinking. Allow yourself to look for the positives and learn from what has happened to you.

Our belief system defines how we feel about the world, and governs how we behave and interact with others. How we perceive ourselves has a lot to do with the beliefs we created from the experiences we had from the day we were born.

I grew up with a negative belief system about myself and suffered silently from the effect it had on me. Nobody knew how I really felt about myself, and I couldn't tell anyone. I felt upset and alone with my emotional pain. I think, even if I had found someone I could have talked to, I wouldn't have had the words to explain my feelings and thoughts at that time. As a result, I grew up with emotional insecurities. I was rebellious and I made some bad choices as I didn't know how to trust my instincts. I did all the normal kid stuff; staying out too late, exploring life. But I also started to express my anger and frustration and nobody knew why. It must have looked as if I didn't care about anyone or anything, even though I did. I simply felt that I was misunderstood by the people around me, since no one knew what had been going on pretty much all of my life. I wanted to be liked, loved and nurtured. I longed to feel safe and wanted, as I was not experiencing any of those feelings at the time. I knew that my mother loved me, but she didn't know what was happening. I couldn't tell her because my father had threatened me that if I told anyone, I was going to be put in a children's home. So, life continued and I kept on praying for a better one, praying for help, and for someone to come and rescue me.

I was never any good at school. I had to repeat a whole year at the age of eight, and in my school report they wrote: "Angelika tries very hard but she just doesn't seem to be able to do it."

What a soul-destroying message for a child, and a very negative one for my parents too. What my parents and I didn't know at the time was that I was dyslexic. I didn't get the support dyslexic children have today – in my time, dyslexia was not recognised, so children like me were just called 'stupid' and were made fun of. I was only diagnosed with dyslexia in 2002, and up until then I believed that I simply didn't have what it takes to learn and study like other people.

When I left school, I went to the job centre for careers advice and instead of leaving full of hope and courage, I felt that I'd had another doomed day. The advisor remembered my brother, who had done very well in school, and said something like, "What has happened to you? Your brother has done really well. Why haven't you done well, too?" I felt my heart sink and I wondered, "Does *everyone* know how stupid I am?" I was feeling so hurt and frustrated that I couldn't express my feelings, nor explain what I was forced to put up with at home. However, I think it is fair to say that I had a lot on my plate during my school years, and this played a big part in how I did at school. At that time in my life, the belief that I couldn't succeed, and that I was unable to learn and better myself, was still very deeply engrained. But I didn't give up. I left school at the age of fourteen, and with the qualifications I had, I could have done good things or started a career. However, my mother's belief was that I didn't need an education, as I was going to get married and have children, and with my history at school I had no chance to get any further education anyway.

So, it was decided that I should do an apprenticeship, learning to make fur coats. I succeeded in my training, which was great, but I didn't want to stay in that kind of work. In fact, I wanted to become a nurse, but I was told that I needed more qualifications. So I tried attending classes at evening school, even though I was told from the beginning that I wouldn't make it, or that I couldn't do it. I tried anyway, but didn't get the support I needed to succeed so, eventually, I gave up.

Despite the negative comments that were made about me, I never stopped trying to learn and educate myself in the best way I knew, in my own way. I came across books like *Siddhartha* by the German author, Herman Hesse. *Siddhartha* is a novel that deals with the spiritual journey of self-discovery of a man during the time of the Gautama Buddha. I loved this book. It inspired me and, during this time, I started my transformational journey. I read many more books and some poetry of Herman Hesse and began to learn about spirituality. I found that this was a really good way of learning; it gave me food for thought and I connected with the ideas.

Having accepted that learning in a classroom was not the best way for me, I started to enjoy educating myself in my own way, although I wasn't conscious that this was what I was doing. I also read Carlos Castaneda, and that too made a deep impression on me and stimulated my way of thinking. I realised that I'm not stupid! I'm just different, and I learn in a different way. I was going to a 'better school': the 'School of Life'. All in all, I have to thank the woman in the job centre and my teachers for pushing my buttons and contributing to making me who I am today!

When I was seventeen, my family moved to a different town, so I moved into the first place of my own. It was great, but it was also lonely. Even though it was my choice to be there alone, I felt like nobody cared. I wasn't used to living on my own and I ended up spending a lot of time with myself and my thoughts: my negative beliefs continued to dictate my life.

Nearly two years later, a man came into my life, and once more that took me onto a different pathway to a very different way of life. He seemed to be really nice and he liked me: I thought he really cared. He was older than me, and it probably didn't take him long to realise that I was an easy target. He was the person who slowly manipulated me into becoming a prostitute. He would paint a picture of how much money we would have and what we could do with it. He persuaded me that it would be for our future and that it would prove my love for him if I would do this. I didn't know any different at the time. I didn't know that I had a choice: my self-worth and my belief in myself had been destroyed from the age of five.

It was these negative beliefs I had about myself that gave me the ability to do what I did. I believed, because I had no education and felt unworthy, that being an escort girl was the only thing I was good for. I believed that 'good girls' had a good education, and therefore had good careers, and that 'bad girls' didn't have an education, and so had demeaning or meaningless jobs. It was as if my dad had prepared me for this with his words and actions and it was in my belief system that this was what I deserved. I simply didn't know any different.

We moved to a city together and from my early twenties I started working as an escort girl. I used to go to some of the best restaurants and hotels when escorting businessmen who were visiting the city. I enjoyed fine food and wine, so it also taught me a lot. I met a variety of men: good, bad, interesting, educated, but also rude and ignorant men who treated me as if I was at their service, rather than appreciating me as a person. That part of my life was another form of education which I believe gave me the ability to read people and situations.

With time, I came to realise that if my partner really loved me he would have asked me to stop working as an escort girl. In fact, he never would have asked me in the first place. I know he had feelings for me in a way, but they were not the right feelings. He'd had his own experiences in life that made him the way he was.

Eventually, my feelings for him started to change and I wanted to leave him but didn't know how. So life went on, with me working as an escort and him continually upsetting and hurting me emotionally. In all those years, I couldn't tell his or my family, which also meant I couldn't ask for help to leave him and get away from escorting. I stayed in the relationship for nearly ten years, believing that as long as I was under his influence, I couldn't get out and do something better.

So how did things change? Well, I started to believe in myself more. I started to believe that there were different things I could do other than being an escort girl. I realised, once again, that I had choices.

Once I'd started making these decisions, however, this time I wasn't going to go back to my old thought patterns. I kept on thinking (just as

I had when I was a child), "This cannot be it, surely." My intention was to get out of the escort business and, after a while, my efforts paid off. I told a friend I was looking for a job and he helped me, putting me in touch with his friend who needed someone to work in customer service in the company he was working for. I couldn't believe my luck. Someone actually wanted to employ me! I was overcome by tremendous joy and fear at the same time, as escorts 'don't work in offices'. Not long after that, I started the job.

I had a new beginning, not only because of the job, but also, a couple of months later, I met my future husband there! After a few years together, we got married and a wish of mine came true: a new life, a new journey, and another new beginning for me. I'm sure this enormous change, to escape from life as an escort girl, was successful because I'd made the *choice*. I had put my heart and soul behind the thoughts and, feeling positive (and a little scared, too), I stepped out and took the action that supported what I wanted to achieve.

When we are pushed to step out of our comfort zones, we learn and have new experiences. It's about choosing to let go of those negative thoughts that lead to negative outcomes. Be aware of your thoughts and ask yourself if they are really serving you for the better, or if they are keeping you in old habits. Make the choice to create stronger, better, more positive thoughts to build an image of the best version of yourself.

In time and with practice, I learned to observe my thoughts, and when the negative chatter started I changed it to positive thoughts. It takes no effort at all to *not* be in control of your thoughts, whereas to be constantly aware takes supreme concentration; it takes time, it's a process. If you fall off the wagon, don't beat yourself up. Recognise your negative thoughts and change them to more positive, happier ones and you will start to feel better. When you feel sad, check what you are thinking about. What is your negative thinking pattern? How can you improve it? Don't let fear drive your mind; try telling yourself that it's not real, that it's just a thought creating a negative feeling, an emotion from the past that you have not managed to change yet.

We are not only affected by the words of others but also very much by the words we use when we speak about ourselves. Even small phrases like, "Oh silly me," or, "I could never do that," keep our self-doubt active and keep us stuck in negative beliefs. Choose not to get involved in negative conversations because even if it is not about you personally, it will still affect you. However, it's very important to remember that positive thinking alone is not enough to change your life. Your heart must be in it as well and you need to truly believe that you are worthy of the positive things you desire.

About fifteen years ago, I had a tarot card reading with a lady in Bath. I decided to see her as I wanted to have a glimpse of what might lie ahead on my path. When we met, I took a liking to her immediately and, during the reading, she gave me what she understood to be an important message. She told me that I had a natural aptitude for teaching and that she could see me facilitating workshops, and that I would be very good at it. I said to her, "No way! That is not something I can do!" Even so, there I was, being told that one day I would be facilitating workshops. There was no way, I felt, that this could be possible as it would involve writing. Plus, I didn't know *what* I would teach! I could see myself as a facilitator, but actually running the whole show, absolutely not!

But about seven years ago this all started to change when I was asked, "What is it that you are passionate about? What comes easily to you and takes no effort for you to do?" It was then I decided that I didn't want my challenging and 'colourful' life experiences to go to waste. I decided I wanted to work with people who were stuck, overwhelmed and feeling hopeless. I wanted to give people hope and inspiration and to demonstrate that, by sharing my story, anyone can change their life. No matter what we have or haven't done, no matter how low we might feel, each one of us is worthy of love.

So here I am, once the abused child, the dyslexic pupil, the escort girl, educated by the 'School of Life and Hard Knocks', having gone through the journey of ACCEPTING the challenges, changing my limiting BELIEFS about myself and making the CHOICE to do so, all of which has brought me to this very moment when I am writing these words. My experiences made me who I am. I love who I've become, and now I can only be true to myself.

My intention is not to impress you with what I have overcome, because everyone has a story and I just happen to be sharing mine with you. My reason for sharing my story is to give people hope that they too can change their lives, whatever the situation. We always have the choice to make some kind of change, and even consciously choosing not to make any changes for the time being is better than just letting things run their course. It's not necessarily about having traumatic experiences in order to find out what you're really made of. Sometimes, it's just a matter of realising that we may not be achieving what we would like because we're living according to other people's values. Einstein famously said, "If we keep doing the same thing over and over again, we will have the same outcome again and again." And, in my opinion, life is too short to just 'make do'.

So, what is your choice? Where do you want to be in your life? Will you let your limiting beliefs run the show and hold you back? In the workshop I have now created, I use my own principle called ABChange4life: simple, effective steps which can guide you to your path of change. The ABC steps become your building blocks from which you create the platform to change your life. The workshop is about exploring your self-belief and working through steps that can help to make those all-important changes.

This is the end of my chapter, but perhaps, for me, it's a new beginning! How about you? What will you choose? Will you let your past determine your future? What changes can you make today? As they say, sometimes your worst enemy lives between your ears.

I wish you the greatest happiness and the freedom to be you. We are all worthy of love.

Biography

Being strong and intelligent, Angelika realised that she could change her life: her past was not her destiny! Through a process of learning and self-development, she accepted her past and looked to the future, ultimately working in various fulfilling roles in the corporate world for many years.

Eventually, Angelika realised that her purpose and passion in life was to help others reach a place of acceptance and wellbeing. For the past seventeen years she has helped to transform many people's lives. At one stage she qualified and practiced as a Bowen therapist, but in recent years focuses on mentoring, workshops and speaking opportunities, enabling people to live a joyful, fulfilling life.

Helping you to move on from adversity and develop a positive mental attitude, Angelika's programme of workshops and one-to-one sessions highlights where your negative beliefs are, how they're holding you back, and helps you to achieve specific goals to recreate your life.

At the core of Angelika's work is her formula to living a life free from pain or shame, and to become full of joy:

Acceptance + Belief + Choice = Change

Change your story, change for life.

www.angelikabreukers.com

Gemma Freeman

As a naïve teenager, Gemma became trapped in an abusive and controlling relationship with an older man. It took many years to break free, and with her self-belief in tatters, other abusive relationships ensued. Once Gemma learned that love begins with self-love, she turned her life around and now works with a company which helps women who have been abused in childhood.

I WAS FIFTEEN AND LIFE WAS going fine. I had a happy home life with my parents and younger sister. I was doing well in school and always did my best to get good grades, and I had a small circle of friends. How on earth I got into the situation I did I have know idea. I remember being in the school music room one lunchtime with some friends, catching up with some coursework. My friend James's dad turned up to drop off some papers for our music teacher and got chatting to us all but he kept looking at me. I was not sure why. After relentless harassment I was somehow ended up in a 'trapped' relationship with this man.

I remember the first time I was alone with him; he took me down an alleyway and proceeded to put his hands all over me. I was too scared to tell my parents or anyone about this and about all the other encounters we had. I felt forced into meeting him as he found out where I lived and would sit in his car outside my bedroom window until I came down, as I was instructed to do via instant messenger. The only way to describe this is that, naive and vulnerable, I was brainwashed into thinking that I wanted this kind of relationship and that it was 'normal', although he insisted that our relationship was kept secret until after I turned sixteen. When my parents found out they were not happy and my sister was beside herself; we were very close and to her it felt like I was abandoning her.

Following my school exams he was determined that we should have our own place, and he left his wife to be with me. I didn't know any better and just went along with it; my mind was on starting sixth form and doing my 'A' levels. He found a studio flat next to the supermarket where I was working and so we moved in. Although my parents did not approve of this relationship or the fact that I was moving out at such a young age, they still supported me and helped with furniture for my new home.

The day came for me to start my 'A' levels. I was so excited: I was in a new school that none of my previous friends were going to, so it was an opportunity for me to make new friends, study the classes I wanted and to live the ideal sixth form lifestyle, embracing this exciting stage in my young adult life. Sadly this was not to be. John, the man I was with, drove me to sixth form every day and insisted in walking with me right up to the gate; this was embarrassing. People thought he was my dad. Only when the bell went did he return to the car and go to work. Over time the possessiveness grew and grew; I found that he would want to come with me to every social event and had a constant need to check up on me. I was doing 'A' level Information and Communication Technology and was the only girl in the class. This didn't faze me; I was just as bright as the lads and was doing well in the subject. I became friends with the lad I sat next to and we would often chat in the lesson and eventually exchanged emails. We got chatting on instant messenger, mostly about the course with a few conversations about what was going on the latest television show at the time. Nothing more came from it; it was just friendly conversation. John didn't like this and went out of his way to block my new friend so we couldn't speak to each other outside of college. He also took it upon himself to accompany me on a bowling night out with a few friends from the college; very awkward, these were my friends and I wanted to be with them on my own. I never went anywhere on my own, he had to be there. I found myself becoming isolated. It wasn't possible for me to have friends for myself. I started going to the library during my free periods and at lunchtime, using this time to do homework or just read. I became closed off from everyone. It was easier to do homework and coursework at college during these periods as when I was home in the evening almost five out of seven nights it was all about his 'needs'. He took great satisfaction watching me during the process and insisted that I looked at him as tears of pain rolled down my cheeks. I am ashamed to say that I lost my virginity to this man for whom, by this point, I felt no love at all; saying "love you" was more habit and had no real meaning, but having nothing to compare it with I knew no better.

During our time in the studio flat we had issues with damp which had an effect on my health, resulting in a few days off school. I still completed all assignments on time but it affected my attendance, which could impact my chances to go to university. I decided that I would leave sixth form having only made it through two-thirds of the year, a decision that was right at the time but looking back I wish I had at least completed the first year. I was now living in a tiny flat with a man for whom I had unexplained feelings and a part-time job at a supermarket. This still did not stop John from checking on me during the day. Whilst he was at work he would text me, phone me, and if I was working he would meet me from work and walk home with me – the supermarket was literally across the road. It was suffocating.

I still wanted to do my 'A' levels so I enrolled in several courses in the evening at the local college; by now I could drive so would drive myself to college and home again: such an exhilarating feeling having a car! This was for my eighteenth birthday from my parents, the best present I ever had. I remember the day I showed John my car that had been sitting on my parents drive waiting for me to pass my test; he didn't seem too impressed. I asked him what he thought and he just shrugged and said, "Once you have seen one car you've seen them all." A switch suddenly flicked inside me. How dare he just say that, it was my first car! It was new and exciting for me! If he really loved me like he so often proclaimed he should be happy for me and share my excitement. I was mad; I turned to him and said, "If you can't be happy for me and share my excitement about my car then you can just go back home." (I used other words here but I will keep it polite.) My sudden outburst shocked him and as he made his way to the front door I shouted "You can at least say 'bye to my mum and Nan," so he sheepishly said goodbye and left, leaving me alone with my family, something that rarely happened. I felt happy to be there. I felt safe. Of course I paid for this act of rebelliousness later that evening with his 'needs'. I never enjoyed this part of our relationship. I thought losing my virginity and having sex would be a wonderful experience but it wasn't. It involved watching pornographic films or performing certain acts for him which made me very uncomfortable, but how was I to know any different?

Now I could drive I sometimes drove to our regular night outs with friends – his friends, now mine – which often involved being home quite late. Whilst out I had to sit next to him and not go to the bar; he would order the drinks and I was not allowed to talk to any men. This possessiveness continued whilst I was at college. I enjoyed my classes there, I was making friends with my peers and we would often meet half-an-hour before class to grab a coffee and discuss the course. John started meeting me after the course had finished in the evening: he drove seven minutes up the road to meet me outside then follow me back in my car to make sure I got home. The suffocation of this relationship was starting to take its toll.

Then I met Elizabeth, who had been a year below me in school. We soon became friends and she started joining us on our nights out. One night there was a band playing and Elizabeth wanted to invite her two friends, both men in their late twenties. Reluctantly John agreed and we all went in his car. It was a good evening, the band were playing a mix of music. Elizabeth, her friends and I were chatting. John came to sit next to me and insisted I sit on his lap; his way of stating his claim on me, that I was off limits to anyone else. I was quite happy sitting on a chair having a pleasant conversation with Elizabeth and her friends, so I said "No." I could see in John's eyes he was not happy but being amongst friends, he didn't make a scene. That night was the night I decided to call the shots on what *I* wanted to do; no more being told, being supervised, being chaperoned or prompted with what to say. The night continued and for the first time in the two years we had been together I was actually having some fun. I danced with Elizabeth and her friends. As the night came to a close John helped the band pack their things away and load their van; whilst he was doing this I was stood outside talking to one of Elizabeth's friends, Anthony, just chatting about what music we like, just usual mundane things. Every time John walked past he would give me a disapproving look. Then I did the unthinkable; I exchanged numbers with Anthony and thought nothing of it. The following morning John came into the bathroom and held my phone up to my ear. I heard a voice message from Anthony saying he had enjoyed last night and could he and his friend Eric come to the next one and that we should all go for drinks sometime. The message was innocent, but John had taken it upon himself to listen to a message that was intended for me. I flipped. This was it; no longer was I going to be kept in this suffocating state. I was already angry that I had lost all my school friends, college friends and had even distanced myself from my family. I had lost the closeness my sister I once enjoyed, all because of this man. I had been held back, been told what I could and could not do, to whom I could speak, and was bound so tight in his invisible rope that I couldn't grow and develop my individuality. But I was now fighting back!

I told him that we would discuss it later. He insisted on talking now and grabbed my wrist. I broke free and said again that now was not a good time and that we would talk this evening. I grabbed my phone from his hand, walked past him, picked up my handbag and made my way out of the door, only to be followed by him. His car was parked behind me and I needed him to move it before I could leave. He refused. I was going to be late for work, so I started my car and reversed, my bumper just touching his but I was able to drive my car forward and make my escape.

The day at work passed like any other and eventually it was time to go home. I made my way to my car which was kept behind security barriers – to find John standing next to it. I was mortified; he couldn't come in here without a pass so he somehow got through security to find my car. I told him that they needed to check employee's passes before leaving the car park so he had best go out the way he got in and meet me on the corner of the road. I am so grateful he actually did as I asked. I drove up to the barrier and showed my pass. The barrier started to go up and I could see John on the corner waiting to get in the car. It was in this moment I made the decision that enough was enough and I was leaving him. I locked the car, edged my way through the barrier and when I was sure I was clear I sped off round the corner down the road and straight back to our flat, leaving a very shocked and angry John behind. Once home I grabbed clothes and personal belongings and threw them into the boot of my car. I drove to my mum's and told her I had left him and that I could not go back. John appeared at my mum's and insisted I go back with him. I said no. He pestered me to go back to him. To get him off my case I told him I needed space to think and that in a month I would make a decision; this seemed to appease him. One afternoon I was in the pub with my friends when suddenly I was pulled out of my seat. It was John; he practically dragged me outside and accused me of being deceitful. Eric saw what was going on and called the police. I gave a statement and John was given a warning. Later that day Anthony and Eric helped me collect my last few things from the flat.

This was the start of a new life for me, but so much damage had already been done; my family relationship had to be rebuilt, my perception of love and relationships was broken and confused, my confidence was weak and my own self-belief was in tatters. What followed would still be a very hard few years. Anthony and I started dating and eventually moved in together, but this was also a very negative relationship. Sex was not an issue as after I told him I had such a bad experience before Anthony took things slowly. I began to enjoy that part, but soon the relationship would turn a dark corner.

Anthony suffered with severe depression, mainly because his previous partner refused to let him see his son. Quite often he would turn to drink and become physically abusive. John was lurking in the background and would often feed Anthony's depression and anger with remarks and text messages. One night the physical abuse was terrible. Anthony had a great deal to drink and was on his phone a lot. I had a sixth sense that something was going to happen so got dressed. I felt the back of my hair being pulled and I was punched multiple times until I crumpled to the floor, being kicked in the head and ribs. I managed to stand up but he was blocking my way out. He locked the door, took out the key and put it in his pocket. We were in a flat on the third floor…there was no other way out. He marched past me and went onto the balcony and back on his phone. I found some shoes and grabbed my phone and keys. I would find a way out. Luckily the fan light window was open. It was a tiny gap but I didn't care, I just wanted to get out. I climbed onto the worktop and managed to squeeze through the gap and ran and ran until I could run no more. Surprise surprise, John was there; he was always there! I can't remember exactly where we went but soon the police arrived and took a statement. Anthony was taken into custody for the night.

I spent a few nights at my mum's. I think it took for me to be beaten black and blue for John to finally realise that I was not going back to him. I foolishly did go back to Anthony but it was not long until I saw the abusive traits starting to manifest themselves again, so I asked my dad to help me and I moved back to my parents.

I went through another three bad relationships. The first two had such a detrimental effect on my confidence and self-worth. During the third relationship I took out loans to help buy my partner buy a new car and to put money towards the flat we were renting. When he left me I was in about thirteen thousand pounds worth of debt. Quite a lot for a twenty-one year old! I worked at several jobs to pay off the debt, having only one Sunday off a month. After my relationship with Anthony, I did something which you would probably think is crazy given my previous history with relationships, but I signed up to a dating website, not necessarily to meet anyone, but to make friends. I made one and his name was Graham. We met online in 2004 and continued to bounce emails back and forth every couple of weeks and send Christmas cards – but we never met. It was after my last relationship and in the process of moving back in with my parents yet again that we decided to meet: we met at the cinema and had a few drinks afterwards. It was not love at first sight but we had a really good time in each other's company. I had already shared with him in brief my past relationships so he was aware that I came with a history and that I was working crazy hours to pay off a debt. This did not faze him.

I continued to meet with Graham for drinks, a walk, a meal, but we were not actually dating. A job came up as a receptionist for the education department in the National Health Service which would pay more than the three care home jobs I was doing. I was lucky enough to get the job so was able to work Monday to Friday and three evenings with the other job: I now had weekends back where I could meet up with Graham and other friends. Eventually Graham asked me out properly. I felt I already knew the man to whom I had been chatting for years and meeting on a regular basis, so in 2007 we became a couple. In time I was able to clear my debt, give up the evening job and gradually work my way up the career ladder. After three years of dating, I eventually moved in with Graham. Three years later we were married. Life had finally turned a corner. At this time I was asked by the police to write an official statement regarding John. He had been caught grooming teenage girls online and was sentenced to a considerable time in prison, where as far as I'm aware he remains. To my horror I started to receive letters from John whilst he was in prison; not just letters, they were six A4 pages front and back, all of them declaring how innocent he was and how much he still wanted to be with me: one letter was extremely graphic to the point where I could not read it. Another which caused great concern detailed what I was doing with my life and where I was working: I hadn't seen John for a few years nor had contact with him so how he got hold of this information I will never know. The prison governor was very understanding and shocked at what I was receiving, and asked me to photocopy the letters and write a covering note explaining I wanted no further contact with John. I still have his letters locked away for legal reasons should I ever need them. I received no more letters, but it still concerned me how he knew so much about my life from inside prison.

I now have the reassurance that the nightmare, which began my series of destructive relationships, is finally over. Graham's presence and understanding has shown me that relationships can be filled with love, respect, understanding and trust, and for that I will always be grateful.

Graham has helped my confidence grow and has encouraged me to discover my self-worth. I now have a wonderful circle of friends with whom I enjoy spending time. I do not have to justify myself to anyone or explain my decisions. I never had counselling following any of my relationships. I have always been a firm believer that something good always comes from the bad and that if you remain positive and keep going you will be rewarded: I certainly have been rewarded now.

Despite all the positives that were now filling my life I still felt cheated out of what should have been an exciting part of my young life: I missed out on the whole college experience and going to university; all the things a young adolescent normally experiences. It's usually during those years we discover who we really are as individuals and where we want to be. I was now in my early thirties and still had no idea who I was as an individual. Something was missing.

While I was on maternity leave with our second child one of my friends (who knew nothing about my past) introduced me to the world of 'Younique'. I was working eight am to four pm Monday to Friday, leaving my children for a job which was not fulfilling me. 'Younique' she explained was a company which sold makeup and skincare to help raise money for the 'Younique Foundation' helping to build and run retreats for women who had been sexually abused in childhood. That spoke to me in huge volumes. I have always been passionate about helping people and 'Younique's' cause spoke to me on such a personal level as I could relate to what these women had gone through. I had no clue about makeup or about network marketing, but I felt that this opportunity had been presented to me for a reason and as I was on maternity leave it felt like a good time to try. I took a leap of faith and joined the huge 'Younique' family which has to be the best decision I have ever made. It's not just about makeup and skincare, it's all about developing confidence and self-worth and helping other women do the same. This business has been a rollercoaster journey but I have loved every moment of it and met so many women who are now overcoming their fears. This is and will continue to be the therapy I need and the personal growth I have craved for so long. In July 2018 I went self-employed building my 'Younique' business so I can help more women in the 'Younique Foundation' to change their lives. On reflection

I feel I needed to have experienced all these toxic relationships to really understand who I am and what I want to do with my life. Whilst at the time of the relationships I felt so low, I never let them get me so far down that I could not get up again, although there were times when it came very close. I made a friend when I worked at the care home called Louise who has become my best friend and we always talk to each other, putting the world to rights. If it was not for her and her support and friendship I may not have survived through the worst relationships.

My advice to anyone going through an abusive relationship, whether it is physical or mental, is to *get out of it as early as you can*. You are worth so much more and you deserve more. It is *your* life and you need to enjoy it and be happy and love yourself first – love starts with *you* before anyone else. Once you can love yourself, finding other people to love you for who you are and finding that one person with whom you want to spend the rest of your life will come so much more easily.

www.youniqueproducts.com/gemmafreeman

www.childline.org.uk/info-advice/bullying-abuse-safety/online-mobile-safety/online-grooming

www.childnet.com/parents-and-carers/hot-topics/online-grooming

Minnie von Mallinckrodt-Grant

To say that Minnie had a dysfunctional childhood would be an understatement. It is a wonder that she has, with great emotional intelligence and determination to thrive, forged a way forward which is healthy and functioning – both as a daughter and as a mother. Her courage in speaking out and creating strong boundaries is an example to us all.

What being kidnapped by my father taught me about love and parenting

When I was three years old I was kidnapped by my dad. He picked me up from nursery one day and took me without my mum knowing. My parents were splitting up and when mum arrived at nursery they said I had already gone with my dad. I can only imagine the feeling of her blood running cold and sheer panic coursing through her body, mind racing and heart palpitations, wondering where her child had gone.

Not knowing where he was, she enrolled her brothers to help her find my father. My great aunt knew where he was so told mum: dad had gone back to Germany. Mum found him, and persuaded him that they should get back together and return to the United Kingdom to sort everything out. However, mum flew home to the UK with me but without dad. On her return home she took out an injunction against him, which meant he would not be able to see me or come near me; she had no intention of being with him after this incident. I can understand her stance. But what a blow and complete life changing moment that was for my dad: in a moment of madness, his whole life and mine were changed forever.

This whole tale unfolds because my parents had the most bizarre and frankly outrageous meeting and marriage. In 1975 mum left Suriname, a Dutch colony, to go to the Netherlands because a military coup had left the country unstable. All those who could leave, did so. Mum had a large family, so family members departed in stages. Her brothers, whom she had called upon to help find me, had gone to the Netherlands before her. They had met and befriended dad before mum arrived and decided that she would be a good wife for him. Somehow, and I can't get the truth from anyone as to what exactly happened, they arranged for my parents to marry in England.

Aged only seventeen, mum went first to the Netherlands then to England where she met dad, a total stranger. They were married and she was left with dad and his mother for a week to 'enjoy their honeymoon'. After that she was left alone in a foreign country married to a stranger to start her life in England. This seems mind blowing; it was in the 1970s, yet it still goes on today.

It must have been scary and confusing for mum. She was bright and doing well in her studies and had she stayed in Suriname she was destined to attend university. Instead, because of a military coup and three brothers who decided her fate, she was now on the other side of the world, away from her family, unable to speak English and married to some German guy.

She told me that when she came to England she was excited because she thought it would be as she learned at school; everyone still living in a Victorian England. Instead she found people wearing flares and men with long hair; quite a culture shock. Obviously her brothers must have convinced her the move was a good idea.

According to mum, dad was overbearing and violent. I remember finding her trapped behind upturned beds and shut in cupboards. I thought she was playing hide and seek. Mum said when I was born at one point we were homeless, sleeping on friends' sofas. Later, when dad's violence became unbearable, we escaped to a women's refuge. I don't remember much about this time apart from meeting an older, nice girl called Sarah whom I liked.

I also don't remember much about being taken by dad, apart from going to a doctor's surgery then being in an apartment. Following the kidnap I was very sad because things changed. I didn't miss dad particularly, but I did miss our two dogs which were given away because mum had to work all the time to pay the bills. I was left with various child-minders and learned to play alone and entertain myself. I took the entire situation to mean that I was an inconvenience. I went from one child-minder to another. I can't even remember their names and I certainly didn't speak up.

Over the years mum told me stories about dad, all very poisonous. This was her version of events, I'm sure the stories are all valid, but they are one side of the story. Dad used to call me from time to time when I was very little and cry on the phone, say my mum was a witch and that one day we would be reunited. It was like talking to a crazy person whom I didn't know or have any real connection with. It was surreal, quite disturbing listening to his sobbing, and to be honest I felt freaked out and scared by him – especially given all the stories I had heard. He seemed like a monster to me. I was living with my mum and still very young so I didn't want to upset her by showing her that I had any alliance with my dad.

When I was thirty I returned from spending a year travelling. An uncle rang to tell me that dad had terminal cancer and wanted to have a relationship with me. My mum was fine about this; I will never know what happened, but she said she had forgiven him.

I was apprehensive about having my father in my life; after all he was a stranger. I saw him the year before he died and it was very hard for me to get to the truth of what had happened between my parents. I realised that here was a man who had made a decision based on fear, and he had paid the ultimate price of never seeing the one thing he loved most of all: me. To be separated from your child and never be a part of their lives must be utterly gutting, particularly when you made such an impulsive decision based on anger and fear, so really you have no one else to blame but yourself.

What happened with my dad did impact my relationship with mum. She was a child herself, raising a child, without any support from family. I do think family can give you a whole different dimension of bullshit you have to deal with on top of everything else if the dynamics are not there to be supportive. Mum firmly believed she was doing all of this alone, that she was better off on her own and I think it was right for her. But all the stresses and strains of what she went through were taken out on me, because I guess you do that – you take out your frustrations on those you love the most.

Growing up, I never felt enough. I never felt that anything I did was right, or good enough. No matter how hard I worked at school, or with hobbies, it was never good enough for her. "You can do better," was the mantra. Now I'm older I realise she was trying to push me to reach my full potential, but as a straight 'A' student who really did everything she could to do well and do right, my mother's words just felt like a constant put down. Often I gave it my best yet I learned my best wasn't good enough for her. All I wanted to hear sometimes was, "Well done, you did good." We all seek validation and I just never got it from my mother, so I realised after some time to learn to disconnect from her. I was without a father and now I often felt without a mother, because she was just not able to be present for me.

Part of the challenge of dealing with mum was her perfectionism – although she is less rigid nowadays, or perhaps she has learned to keep her opinions to herself. She was always obsessed with the house, which I see now was a form of having control over her own situation; at least the house was perfect! She really didn't have time for me as she had too many jobs to do, jobs that never ended, yet my childhood would end and did end, quite abruptly in mum's mind.

She confided in me recently that when I went to university she thought it was just a phase and that afterwards I would come home. It never occurred to her that I was grown up and gone. I didn't return home. That was a big shock, yet I can't understand how because she seemed to be in love with the *idea* of who I was. She had been blind to *me*; totally focused on her own problems and not paying attention to me, rather she was focused on what she wanted to achieve. Some of what she wanted to achieve was clearly important – and certainly it wasn't all bad. She had a strong work ethic and was a real achiever. She took risks, started her own business and was a great role model for me in that sense. As I was left to my own devices from a young age, I was very independent and capable of looking after myself. I was street wise and unafraid of leaving home and starting my own life. But, oh the years wasted on stuff that didn't really matter in the big scheme of life.

However, roses grow stronger and more beautiful when they are steeped in shit. I wanted to understand what beauty could come from this situation that was my life up to this point.

After many years – decades – of feeling angry with mum, not understanding why she was always so critical, not understanding why she was so abusive to me, not understanding what I did wrong to make her so negative and depressed, I sought some help around this. I was sick of asking myself "why?" and wanted to know what to do, because I was holding on to a lot of anger, resentment and pain and this wasn't serving me.

I think that emotional neglect as a parent is one of the harshest things you can do to a child. It pushed me to my absolute limit. The best lesson came from that place of sheer hell and desperation: that I was capable of hitting rock bottom, and no one was going to care, help or save me. Not my mother, no one. But I was alive and I survived. I made a clear decision that day that I would never let anyone control me or make me feel bad about myself. They would have *no* control over me.

I didn't ask for this situation, as far as I am consciously aware.

What I did know was that I was good enough; I was and am worthy of love. I had to learn to love and respect myself and that meant I had to break free and live my life on my terms. I had to become the mother I didn't have, the mother my mum couldn't live up to, after all she too is only human: she tried her best.

After years of the same old repeated patterns and anger it all came to a head. I had a massive row with her in front of my young daughter, who was scared by how angry and enraged I was with mum's undermining and 'gaslighting' behaviour. That was the day I decided something different had to happen because what I had been doing wasn't working. My daughter was scared and crying because I finally lost it and gave mum a mouthful about her constant undermining comments and behaviour. I couldn't change mum, but I could change myself, my responses, and what I'm willing to put up with. I could take back my power and not allow mum to continue to treat me like a child with her negative comments, limited thinking, fearfulness and trying to control the narrative.

No more. It was over. And if I never saw her again, so be it. I'd had enough! I believed I could still have a relationship with my mum through setting healthy boundaries and standing my ground if these were violated. But if she didn't agree to the rules, it was over.

I hired a mentor to help me reinvent my relationship with my mum, which was the best thing I ever did because I just couldn't find a resolve for this on my own. My mentor explained to me that in order to move forward I needed to understand what *I* wanted and to let go and leave behind anyone who didn't like it and agree with it. In order to become the person able to do this I needed to forgive my mother and all the past so that I could move on.

I called mum and we spoke about what upset me all these years – and ending up rowing again. We were accidentally cut off which was a good thing as I was able to calm down, breath and call her back. I knew exactly what I wanted to do and say. I told her, "I forgive you and I absolve you for all that has happened in the past." I nearly choked on those words, but actually felt so much better afterwards!

You see 'forgiveness' in my mind was letting someone off the hook for past deeds they committed. In fact forgiveness is about letting go of the anger and resentment you feel towards that person so you can be free of negative emotions – and so move on. It's not about righting wrongs, or letting someone walk all over you again. Forgiving allows you to move on and stop dwelling in the past. You forgive to set yourself free and find peace.

I also decided how I wanted it to be moving forwards in order not to keep repeating the same old patterns. That was all about setting the rules and healthy boundaries I wanted in my life and asking my mother to agree to this for the common good. I also asked her what she wanted me to stop doing; I'm not perfect and this must be a two way street. However, when either one of us starts to break the rules and overstep boundaries then we are to inform each other and gently yet firmly reinforce the boundaries. Mum took this really well. In fact it is probably the first real grown up conversation we have ever had where she stopped treating me with contempt and instead listened to what I had to say. She was always very dismissive, disrespectful and often laughed at me when I told her how upset I felt. I think fundamentally she knew that this was the final straw and that I could, and would, walk away from her. Putting my cards on the table really helped to transform our relationship. It's not perfect, but it's now the best it's ever been. It may never be perfect and we still have ups and downs, but we try not to argue in front of my daughter, which is what I wanted.

My journey isn't over, because I am now a mother. What my parent's dysfunctional relationship and the traumas I experienced and witnessed taught me is that love is simple, but humans make it very complex. Parenting is about listening to your children and guiding and supporting them so they feel empowered to make their own decisions and to see they have choices in every situation.

The more you push the more you push them away. My mission is to remain open with my daughter and try not to repeat what happened between my parents and me, which can be hard as it's all I've ever known, but it's my mission to create a happy family.

If you are reading this and you feel lost and lonely and that no one understands you because you have similar issues in your life, I want you to know that you are worthy and you are loveable. I want you to know that it's not your fault, but you do have a choice to allow this to take over your your life or to move on and do what you want, how you want it, when you want to. Other people cannot control you unless you allow them to. I invite you to forgive yourself first for feeling any emotions you have felt and I also invite you to list the people who have upset you and forgive them, not for them but for yourself so you can let those negative feelings go. You do not have to be friends with that person anymore, but once you forgive you can use that energy towards something much more positive. I wish you the best for your future.

Biography

Minnie is a TEDx Coach who helps her clients nail their high stakes talks first time so they can command any room and make more money. She works with public speakers, TEDx speakers, professionals, executives and business owners who want to master speaking to grow their business and career success.

Gina DeVee was Minnie's mentor to help her learn life-coaching skills and help her learn to forgive.

Minnie recommends:

The Four Agreements – Don Miguel
Dark Side of the Light Chasers – Debbie Ford
The Big Leap – Gay Hendricks
The Divine Matrix – Gregg Braden
Sally Dibden – life and health coach, personal mentoring

Whilst many books have been helpful the Debbie Ford one was the most transformative, and personal mentoring was the real catalyst for change. Mentoring was not cheap but what Minnie wanted was a life changing transformation and that was what she got.

www.minnievon.com

Tracey Jayne Inglis

Abuse, rejection and loss have been a major part of Tracey's life. That she has turned her life around while coping with yet more serious challenges is admirable; that she has turned her life into a positive one where she now helps others in the health and medical field is truly inspiring.

IT IS DIFFICULT FOR ME TO know where to begin. For years I have kept my story hidden for fear of the anxiety or not being believed.

As a solution focused hypnotherapist it is within me and our mantra to be solution focused, not problem focused. However we have all faced problems and adversity within our lives and if I sat here to only describe the good, my story and my healing would never begin. Life is never perfect for anyone.

I have memories of a happy childhood up to the age of about eight. For years I looked up to my dad, the man who I thought would always protect me. On school journeys, accompanying him to his place of work, colouring in the quiet corner at the weekend if I did not go to Saturday matinee with my brother. I had a childhood where my mother seemed disinterested in her children yet was besotted with infidelity. Of course at such a young age I was oblivious to all of this.

My dad became my safe haven: he was my protector and my guardian. I don't remember my mother being at any parents' evenings or sports days, to watch me as a sunflower in the summer fayre, or to hear me sing. I don't remember my mother giving me advice on school, on my fear of swimming, or her brushing my hair or playing along with my dolls. However I do remember my stepmother attending school functions, offering relationship advice, support with school and most poignantly supporting me over every day life issues.

My mother was at home but was never really there as her mind was always elsewhere. My older brother, sister and I were never her priority. Would this be the initiation of the insecurities I grew up with, the feelings of doubt about myself and my ability to do well? Looking back this was never an issue at the time; only with maturity and life experience, when you compare yourself to others, do you realise things were just not right.

At the age of nine my parents split up, which was probably for the best. I lived with my dad and then my step-mum whom I now consider my mum, the woman who was there to rub my knee when I fell off my bike and the one I would call when I needed a recipe idea when I had my own home yet still needed some cooking advice! To this day we remain very close.

We moved around a lot due to dad's job, and the family finally settled in Wales. Here I met a man who took over my world and whisked me away to a new world which I found later to be full of false promises: he would provide financial stability, nobody would ever love me as much as he, and he promised the security of a mortgage and a home to start a family. Things went awry almost immediately, the honeymoon included. It was all too soon for me at nineteen. There were Universal messages I was not quite taking notice of and I thought it would all be fine. Perhaps retrospectively I wonder if I was holding onto something, filling a void from my mother's rejection and holding onto the first person who showed me affection other than family – but in the wrong way. I was put down and my self-esteem was minimal; I felt emotionally ready to crumble.

At the time of our wedding I was pregnant with my daughter. The abuse became worse to the point of being followed, being lied to, being pushed, shoved, and being threatened. Hospital visits for injuries occurred, and an attempt to push me out of a moving vehicle. I had to deal with a punch to the stomach whilst pregnant, and being told I wouldn't be believed if I reported it made me too frightened to speak out. I became scared for my life. I realised there was so much control on his part entwined with manipulation where I had absolutely no control. Who would believe me, why did I not report it sooner? Had I been the problem? It must have been my fault: my apologies, thinking I was the instigator, became as frequent as the abuse.

After three years of abuse; emotionally, physically, financially, experiencing assault and neglect, being locked out of my home late at night while pregnant, having my bank account emptied, being forced to ignore my family, suffering neglect and being followed and feeling totally unsafe, uncared for and generally unworthy of someone's love, I could take no more. The belittling became unbearable. There were moments where I would wake up and find him sitting on the bed watching me, moments when I was forced to the ground and attempts were made to force me to have intercourse without my consent. At this point even my colleagues were worried for me as he came to work falsely accusing me of having an affair with a male colleague.

It was time to go.

On our third anniversary I decided to seek a solicitor's advice for divorce proceedings. He laughed at me, saying I was not brave enough and he would make my life hell, suggesting he would rape me and get me pregnant so he could also take this other child from me. That was it. I left at night when he was out, with one bag of clothes and my daughter: our escape had to be carefully organised so I knew we would be safe. We had no money yet I felt freer that I had ever been. I felt the richest I had ever felt because I was lucky to get out alive with my precious gift: my baby. I moved to the north west of England with my sister. She was immensely supportive during that time, however it was later that I was to learn her support would dwindle along with my mental health.

For almost eleven years I was the one who had to fight for custody of my daughter, battling eleven court cases to prove I was a fit mother. I fought for my sanity and to convince the courts that I was not abusing my daughter, that I was not a prostitute, that I was not hitting my child and hiding the bruises, that I was actually feeding my daughter. I learned that he had a criminal record and that he was known for violence. Why did it not see it before? Surely I should have been aware of the signs?

The most humiliating time of my life was about to occur. I had to fight the judicial system when video footage of which I was totally unaware was sent to family and work colleagues. I discovered that years before I had been violated during intimate moments and this had been recorded. He was laughing whilst he was recording me, a premeditated act to hold against me, to humiliate me, to ruin the core of my confidence, and to make me feel disgusting about myself.

The stalking laws then were very lapse and lacking in support for people like me. I had to protect my daughter yet there was nobody to protect me. Where was my dad? The humiliation of failure in my marriage was too much to bear so I kept a lot of this hidden. My dad was my hero, an ex-army drill sergeant, very well respected. I could not let him down. He finally found out the bare minimum and I felt ashamed as if I had played a willing part in it. We went to court but the judicial system failed me. My husband was clever. Manipulative. He won.

If I had told my dad he may have felt helpless that he could not protect me. Legal advice suggested I move with my daughter to the north west of England to safety. Yet he found me. I was stalked, letters were threatening. I was afraid again. Finally I found the strength to divorce the man who had made my life unbearable, and two years later married the man who saved me from this terrible past.

A while later I joined the police force, yet this also caused issues as my past came back to haunt me when my daughter's father decided he wanted to ruin my chances, causing me inconvenience, anxiety and fear. He was finally cautioned for wasting police time and I was able to commence my career in the police force.

After four years we had a son who has special needs. I left the police life; I miss it, however with all the tests, paediatrician appointments, consultant visits and occupational therapy life seemed to be a field of negativity and schooling was a challenge. I decided to embrace our son's needs and issues and just got on with it. The life of a special needs family was very lonely and isolating, particularly as my husband was a workaholic and thrived on moneymaking. I still believe to this day my son's father, who is a caring man, is in total denial about his son's learning difficulties. The issues he faces in life won't improve, they will just be different as he matures.

I decided to enter into the field of midwifery and worked hard to look after my son, my daughter, who was now being emotionally manipulated by her father, our home and also to study. My husband was away much of the time either with promotional work or sales that took him abroad. I felt like a single parent, yet we were mostly happy. Then my world fell apart.

In 2011 my dad, my hero, passed away. I was in the third year of my midwifery degree. My world had ended: that's what it felt like. I needed to support my step-mum. My marriage ended and I felt so alone. I did not receive the support I thought I would. The hugs at night were invisible and I found myself crying silently, feeling like my world had disappeared – I was the closest to my dad of all siblings. Family members had become distant since we found out my son had learning difficulties, so that just became worse.

Life was tough; more court cases ensued with my daughter's father who wanted custody of her. When she was thirteen, he eventually succeeded; she remains with him to this day. She is now a beautiful twenty-four year old, intelligent, vibrant, yet often feisty towards me as I am not believed, which I feel is due to her father's manipulation. Little does she know he tried to ruin my life, even having threatened to end my life. One day she will come back to me. One day she will need me and I will be here for her. For now I know the truth and that is my strength.

The court cases were in fact empowering: I stood up for myself, I was my own barrister and I questioned him, I made him feel uncomfortable. It felt incredibly powerful to put him on the spot and to make him feel inferior for a change. Recalling moments when I was threatened with electrocution; moments of being punched, both behind closed doors and in front of others; the moments of intimidation and countless incidents with the police where I had to stand by him and deny I knew anything about the stealing, violence, assaults, or drugs he was involved with. I was empowered and then I put an end to it. Standing as my own barrister, he knew I would take no more abuse, even from a distance.

I decided I could either curl up and surrender to the past and allow it to define me or I could fight. So I continued my degree in midwifery and completed with Honours. Yet my marriage was over; I felt a failure although I had gained a degree and academically I was a success, in my marriage I felt I had failed. The court cases, my dad's passing, my studying with night shifts and long days; it was hard to maintain the happy positive life we once had. I was haunted for years by the past rejections, the neglect and abuse. Was I to allow the abuse from when I was younger, my mother rejecting me as a child, and choosing a man who had a history of prison life to define my future? I always felt looking back that perhaps as a child I had done something wrong for my mother to leave.

What did I do to sort myself out? I entered into abusive relationships which failed and again where I had no control. I decided to have a couple of years to find myself, yet along the journey of self-discovery I fell into depression, feeling guilty for putting my son through a move away from his dad, although he is now settled in his special school and thriving. I felt it was my time to look after myself, besides if I cannot look after myself how can I be a good parent? Everyone I loved had either passed away or hurt me and let me down. The relationship with my sister, brother and biological mother had all dwindled to nothing significant. After years of trying to build relationships yet to fail again, it was all too much.

Searching on the internet for how to self-improve, I came across hypnobirthing. Having studied holistic therapies a few years previously and enjoying working with clients with mental health issues, I decided that merging the midwifery experience towards the preparation for labour in another natural way would be ideal. I trained in hypnobirthing and then discovered clinical hypnotherapy. I enjoyed this so much I felt like my path to success was finally calling me.

Believing in myself and my abilities, instead of what I've gone through and what I am unable to do, now seems more relevant. I see how far I have come through adversity and realise I am stronger that I ever thought. Now I am aiming to go into the fertility field and become a fertility coach, to allow my hypnobirthing, hypnotherapy and holistic therapies to all merge into a one-stop shop for mental health and wellbeing.

I'm now in a very happy relationship with a man who respects my ideas, views, choices, decisions and crazy ideas and yet he is my rock, my guidance and someone without whom I cannot imagine my life. This man is truly the one who brings out the best in me: I can be myself. He is a fantastic role model for my son and his own children. One day we will be a family, the family I have always dreamed of having.

I live believing that one day my daughter will realise I did nothing wrong but to save her from a life of cruelty and abuse – only for her to choose to love the man who caused it all. I will always keep the lines of communication open. With open arms I will always love her with my whole being.

My son has taught me to live again and to enjoy each day; he has been my inspiration all these years, to live and learn through adversity, to turn a challenge into a positive and to allow life to unfold naturally, organically. I choose now to not waste energy on the past, or it will be all consuming. I choose to encourage my clients and to nourish myself with healthy foods, to enrich my life with good people around me, to offer as much help as I can to those who also suffered domestic violence in relationships to live their lives as freely as they can, with no detriment to themselves or others. To say to people "It's ok to not be ok all of the time, to allow yourself to just 'be' without having to explain yourself. To learn to say 'no' when you feel the need. To be a role model to others and to learn from others in a positive way." I love to teach, to reduce anxiety and fears in my clients and to watch them blossom into incredible human beings.

I feel a strong urge to help others so that they can avoid as much as possible the depression and anxiety I felt, constantly looking over my shoulder through absolute fear of failure, fear of being hurt, fear of not living. Failure is just not an option in my mind: it is with sheer bloody-mindedness that I thrive to be independent, to support my son as best as I can with his severe learning difficulties, to support my daughter whenever that may be, and to support my partner of two wonderful years as he has supported me more than he will ever know. There is such kindness in the world and I am forever grateful to those around me who have believed in me, in my truth and in my integrity.

Kindness is something I did not experience from my mother, from my first husband, from other family members. However my son, partner and my step-mum have all seen my hurt, and they stand by me, knowing my truth. My step-mum firmly believes I am a fantastic mother although sometimes I still doubt myself. Don't we all? I choose to eliminate the toxicity of those negative people in my life and to engage in the positive. Life gives you choices and there is the path I believe we must go down to find our own strengths. There will many things I will never speak about; too daunting for others to read, to despairing to re-live. I have overcome the haunting of my past, and it is enlightening, invigorating, knowing that I am no longer terrified of anyone or of my own feelings, neither am I scared to speak out. I have learned to heal myself through hypnotherapy and kindness.

There have been times where I have not wanted to walk these paths and wanted to end my life. A doctor once saved me, emotionally, my son once saved me, emotionally without really realising it, and I have now saved myself: I am stronger than I have ever been. Often my partner calls me at just at the right moment when I am in need of comfort; we are in sync. I've never experienced this before; it's as though he is my guardian angel who also saved me. They say people walk into our lives for a reason. He is not my reason. He is my How and my Why.

I have only a handful of people I trust; I guess the feeling of being a little lost may never ever leave me, so I am still finding my way, yet I'm getting there and I will succeed. I've learned to never allow anyone to treat me, or anyone I care about, in the way I have been treated. My story is by no means isolated: there are many men and women who have experienced such atrocities. One point two million crimes were committed against women in 2017, and seven hundred thousand against men (Office of National Statistics).

With hindsight, domestic violence, bullying, lack of nurturing from my biological mother, rejection from my sister whom I once adored, accepting a wonderful child with special needs and the passing of my dad were enough to deal with in isolation, yet when you deal with them in their entirety in one lifetime it is often too much to bear. In November 2017 my brother, a strong man, ex-army, passed away in his early fifties. Although he fought for a few years and worked during this time, cancer took him, too soon. He was my big brother. When I was nine and he was on leave from the army I used to sit by the window waiting for him, looking out for him walking in the rain towards the house wearing his beret, looking so smart! A second bereavement in seven years: two of the strongest male role models in my life. Life can be cruel yet it is also truly wonderful when you stop for a moment in time, breathe and embrace it.

I've recently been diagnosed with Coeliac Disease, an autoimmune disease which destroys the villi and gut flora. Often people mistakenly view it as an allergy or intolerance. Coeliac Disease is a challenge on a daily basis with chronic fatigue not being kind to me at the moment, yet I cope because I have no choice. Foods I used to love are now in my past, so I choose to nourish my body with fresh ideas and recipes. I look at it as a positive aspect in my life to encourage more nurturing. Through hypnotherapy I have learned how to cope; my journey of self-discovery continues.

I've had a successful interview to attend the NHS to return to my passion for midwifery. It is called a 'return to practice' so I can do a short refresher course to return to what I spent three years at university studying hard for: being a midwife!

I am grateful for the opportunity to do what I do best: to care, love and nurture.

My heart still aches for those loved ones who have chosen to leave my life, in particular my adult daughter and my sister. I am left heartbroken over wondering how family can turn their back on someone when they are needed for support. Reaching out for help is nothing to be ashamed of. Mental health is nothing to shy away from. Isn't there supposed to be a bond between sisters, and mums and daughters?

I choose wisely with whom I spend my time. This is not the end of the story, but the start of something incredibly wonderful. As I prepare for my own future and that of my son's, with my recent engagement this is just the beginning…

The incidents above are moments, just moments, yet I cannot get the time back. If I could change all of the above would I if I had the chance?

No, probably not as these experiences have made me who I am.

I often wonder how we cope with all that is put in our way. We just get on with it don't we, because indeed, failure is not an option.

Biography

With domestic abuse, rejection from those she loved and bereavement from her father's passing, Tracey struggled to come to terms with everything that was crossing her path. Having a child with special needs and coming to terms with depression, Tracey has now turned her life into a positive one by helping others who have been through similar challenges. She now works in the health and medical field; mental health is her passion and she strives to continue a positive life, gaining learning and strength in everyday situations.

As well as her degree in midwifery and diplomas in hypnotherapy and hypnobirthing, Tracey holds numerous wellbeing qualifications, including maternity reflexology and an infant massage instructor certificate.

www.cotswoldhypnotherapyrooms.co.uk
www.nationaldomesticviolencehelpline.org.uk
www.cruse.org.uk
www.specialneedsuk.org
www.facebook.com/cotswoldfertilitycoaching
www.facebook.com/cotswoldhypnobirthing
www.facebook.com/cotswoldhypnotherapyrooms

Two

Failure is Not an Option

The best day of your life is the one on which you decide your life is your own. No apologies or excuses. No one to lean on, rely on, or blame. The gift is yours – it is an amazing journey – and you alone are responsible for the quality of it. This is the day your life really begins.

Bob Moawad

Carie Lyndene

In her early twenties, everything in Carie's life seemed perfect. With the love of her life also her working partner and mentor, she felt she needed nothing more. When tragedy struck it was impossible for Carie to see how to move forward. That she went on to create a life full of purpose, while she helps others change their lives and live to their full potential, is testimony to her strength of character and warm heart.

Selling: A Love Story

The beginning.

On the nineteenth of July 2013, when one of my workshop delegates told me she was going to write a book about women who have overcome major issues in their life and go on to create success, I really didn't give it much thought and certainly wasn't imagining myself five years on, writing a chapter to contribute.

When this woman told me of her intention, I was in the middle of delivering my first paid workshop in my new business 'The Success Coach' and really my focus was to blow my delegates away with my in-depth knowledge, profound insights and astounding expertise!

I had called the business The Success Coach (primarily as a little in joke for me) but really to reinforce my belief and ethos that we *all* start from a place of success. I had just come through another testing period in my life and my intention was to share that, whatever curve ball life throws at you, there is always a way forward.

It has always fascinated me that we are the one in three hundred million spermatozoa which is released at the point of ejaculation and made it through to fertilise that one egg in our mother's womb: I think that classes us ALL successful from the get go, wouldn't you say?

The workshop was going well with a mixed group of eighteen, all of whom seemed engaged with the content material. Truth be told, I had no idea what the problem I was going to solve for my clients, so this workshop was a complete stab in the dark to gauge the reception of what I had to offer. One of the delegates who seemed to get the most from what I was sharing was Susie Mackie. She of course is the creator, organiser and facilitator of the *Women of Spirit* books (nay, movement), who went on to become a business consultancy client and one of the strongest advocates for my work for many years.

This part of my story goes back to January 1982. I was twenty-one and had just come back to work from a fabulous New Year celebration in Glasgow – New Year lasts about a week there!

I loved my job. I worked as a design assistant to a successful interior designer in Edinburgh. I adored her. Not only did I aspire to be like her one day, but she was also the funniest person I had ever met and although there was an age gap of around fifteen years between us, I thought of her as a friend as well as my boss. She laughed as I told her all my tales of the people I had met and parties I had attended over New Year and regaled me with a few of her own in her younger years.

It was only a couple of days after this that I found her crying in her kitchen when I arrived for work. She was upset because her brother's wife had walked out on them, taking their baby. She said he was devastated and asked me to drive her to her cottage where she had arranged to meet him and her mother. We packed everything we needed, jumped into her jeep and set off to her cottage. Her brother Bob and their mum were there when we arrived. In spite of my young years, I saw something wrong with the picture when I met Bob for the first time; he was twenty-two, towered over me at six feet tall, had piercing dark eyes and was wearing the most awful (what looked like army issue) sheepskin coat. He didn't strike me at all like most twenty-two year olds I knew. Being on the outside looking in, the main thing I was sensing from him was that he wasn't devastated at the loss of his wife or baby. He was certainly saying the words to his mum and his sister, but it was clear to me that wasn't what he was feeling at all. This made me very suspect of him and I decided I didn't like him very much so kept my distance from them, making myself busy with other tasks. For a few days after this, there was something niggling at the back of my mind about my boss's brother. He was on my mind and I didn't know why.

Later that week, my boss sat me down and said she had a favour to ask me; because she saw me as this young free and single party girl, she wanted me to take her brother out for a drink to 'cheer him up'. My first reaction was one of resistance. I really didn't want to get involved, I hadn't even liked the guy. It bothered me about the disconnect I felt from the words he was saying to the energy I was sensing from him. It felt like a major imposition but as I thought of her as a friend and she was genuinely upset about the situation, I said yes, I would meet him for a drink.

Within the hour Bob called me at the office and we arranged to meet at a little pub around the corner from where I was living in my tiny flat in Dundas Street in the centre of Edinburgh. The pub was The Laughing Duck, Edinburgh's one and only gay pub at the time. It was somewhere I had frequented with my best friend Gavin, who was gay, and it felt like a safe environment to meet this all but total stranger. I really hoped he wouldn't turn up in that awful sheepskin coat; bad enough I was going to have to make conversation with him, but it would be the tin lid on it if I was embarrassed to be seen with him too.

As arranged he arrived at 8 pm. I watched him drive up in his car and went out to meet him. I was in for a shock: bouncing out the car was not the guy I had met the week before. This guy was beautifully turned out, shiny dark hair, smart suit, shirt and tie and with a grin that went from ear to ear showing off the most beautiful smile. His eyes were still piercingly dark but now looked alive and warm in their chocolate brown-ness. Was this the same guy?

We decided to walk to the pub and by the time we got there, I knew this wasn't going to be a normal night. We seated ourselves at the bar. Bob didn't drink as he would be driving later but I had some wine. I don't know why or how I had the courage, at that young age I wasn't great at articulating myself or my feelings at all well — maybe it was the wine or the strange circumstances, but probably for the first time in my relatively young life, I was one hundred percent honest. I told Bob how I felt about what I had sensed from him on our first meeting — that he wasn't upset about his wife leaving and taking the little boy with her. While I challenged him about this he kept his dark eyes looking down to the floor and his head tilted as if to be listening intently. He was silent for what seemed a long time after I finished speaking.

When he looked up his eyes were full of tears and he said in a voice choked with emotion, "You are right." He told me how at nineteen, he had been going out with a girl (not exclusively it seemed) and suddenly she announced she was pregnant. Bob literally had no idea if the baby was his or not but by that time it was too late to do anything other than get married. He told me his mum and sister (my boss) were insistent and between the two families a wedding was quickly arranged. Before he knew it he was married to someone he was not in love with and with a baby on the way – which may or may not been his. No one asked him what he wanted, no one asked him if he was happy, no one asked him full stop. It was decided and that was that.

After a very unhappy eighteen months of marriage and all the ups and downs of looking after a young baby, the truth was that for Bob, it was relief when his wife left. He said she was a lovely girl, but they should never have got married.

Bob and I went back to my flat that night and we talked until four in the morning. He drove home and promised me he would be back at eight-thirty the next day to take me to work. He was, and from that point we never spent a day apart for the next two years. We lived together, ended up working together and played together; we were partners, best friends, boyfriend and girlfriend. We adored each other and almost from that first night, we were planning our future together.

Bob was a direct salesman in home improvements whose business took him out in the evenings to meet potential customers. Because we couldn't bear to be apart, I would go on Bob's appointments with him; this was the beginning of a whole new world to me. I was used to earning fifty to a hundred pounds a week for around forty hours' work. However, here was Bob who could do a few hours' work and be paid anywhere between two hundred and three hundred and fifty pounds per session. You see Bob was a salesman: not just any salesman but someone who had mastered his art.

I watched and learned, listening to everything he said and watching how he conducted himself in these appointments. What was amazing to me was that I never saw Bob actually SELLING anything, it was so much more than that: it was the ability to connect with his prospect at such a deep level that literally no 'selling' was required.

Before long, I was able to do appointments on my own, but the truth was we missed each other too much to work separately and decided that we were earning more than enough as a couple, selling to other couples.

Soon we became top of our company. The manufacturers created a range named after us and we won several industry awards. We were a 'Golden Couple with The Midas Touch'. We began to treat ourselves to the trappings of success such as our smart sports cars and had purchased our first home together: life was good. We loved each other more each day and nothing could blight our future together.

All good things…

One dreary winter's day I dropped Bob off at our office while I went to get my hair done at my sister's hairdresser. I was quite late picking him up for two reasons: my sister and I had been catching up and there was a bus strike in Edinburgh. It was Monday the ninth of January 1984.

Bob was standing waiting outside the office and because we were so late for our appointment he jumped in the passenger seat and, very unusually, I drove. We were barely in the car for twenty minutes when suddenly, coming around the corner on the wrong side of the road, was another car. Bob shouted "Where is he going?" and the only thought in my head as the car hurtled towards us was "We are going to become a statistic, we are about to die."

Because of the bus strike, the traffic was heavy on both sides of the road and there was literally nowhere for our car to go but into a head on collision with the other car. The two vehicles impacted, and the velocity lifted and catapulted our car into the fifteen-foot wall on the near side of the road. I never for one second thought I was going to survive this crash. But survive I did. However, Bob did not. The loss was devastating: for me, his family, my family and everyone with whom he had contact. Bob was a one off and the world was a lesser place without him.

How do you come back from something like that aged just twenty-four? Although of course I was massively supported by my family, not only did I have no idea how to deal with bereavement, I also didn't realise I was suffering from Post Traumatic Stress Disorder.

This took the form of agoraphobia and is something I still have to manage to this day. I am writing this in San Diego Airport (I live in Gloucestershire in the UK) and I have to dig very deep to be able to travel, in fact to leave my house for any length of time at all, so it's always a massive stretch for me to make a journey of this type.

The middle

When I was age thirty a very good friend of mine who lived in London called me up and asked me "Do you trust me?" "Yes of course I do." I replied. "Then get on a plane and meet me here on Friday." he said. So, I did!

Bill picked me up from Heathrow and we drove straight to a lavish house in Earl's Court. I must have really trusted him as I had no idea what was going on. We joined the group that had gathered there and when the meeting began, I sat in silence, and more than a little bemusement, as others began to share emotional aspects of their life. I had never heard anything like it. Over the course of the weekend, the workshop facilitator, a wonderful man called Mike Portelly, worked with the participants using a healing model that I was to learn was called 'The Psychology of Vision', a model of psychology originally created by Dr Chuck Spezzano and his wife Lency.

I was very moved by the participants and their stories but I couldn't see how it all related to me. The whole emphasis of this healing model was about taking one hundred percent responsibility for everything in your life – good *and* bad. It suggested not only were we responsible, we had actually created all these situations with the power of our unconscious and subconscious mind.

All weekend, I was in turmoil

My mind was completely rejecting this theory and it was just making me angrier and angrier. By the end of the Sunday, I could hold it in no longer. I challenged Mike by saying "If what you are saying is true, that means I am responsible for my car accident and my partner's death!" Mike looked at me with the most compassion I think I have ever seen in anyone's eyes and said "Don't worry about that for now, first let's deal with the grief."

He continued to look into my eyes and very lightly laid the palm of his hand flat on my heart chakra. Something happened in the room. All I could see was everyone looking at me with the same look of compassion that I saw in Mike's eyes but in the distance, I could hear a strange sound. It sounded like a wild animal howling and it took several seconds to realise that the noise was coming from me. It's hard to say long it went on for or how it ended but what I do know was in that moment, I let my grief go. After the process, for the first time since Bob had died, I felt like I had re-joined the land of the living.

I didn't sleep much that night. I was processing everything that had been said over the weekend, especially the part about being one hundred percent responsible for everything that happens in your life. Eventually, when I woke up the next day, I got it. I understood the whole thing: how we write our life scripts, how we collude in each other's script, how our higher mind guides us and how everything is happening for a reason – and how to trust the process.

Moving from being the victim of your life, to the architect of it, is huge

I knew this was not to be learned in just one workshop. From that day to this, I have studied The Psychology of Vision – it has taken me all around the world – and lived and taught the principles of Chuck and Lency's work. I believe The Psychology of Vision model saved and transformed my life and I am forever grateful to my beloved friend Bill Johnson and to Mike Portelly for facilitating that turning point in my life.

The end?

Now, at the age of fifty-eight, one marriage/divorce and two grown up children later, there is never a day goes by when I don't think about Bob and bless him for the legacy he left me. He taught me so much about life and relationships, but from a business sense he bestowed upon me my love of selling which has guaranteed me an income for life. It's been the gift that keeps on giving too, as I have been responsible for tens of millions of pounds of products and services moving into the market place, not just through my business but through my coaching and training of thousands of others in business who benefit from Bob's gift to me.

Every day I bless too The Psychology of Vision for creating the healing structure by which I live and for giving me a profound understanding human nature, of the mind and how it works.

So, indeed this is not the end, this is still the beginning for me

In my latest project, I have partnered with a Master Coach in The Psychology of Vision model, Alex Patchett-Joyce. I believe that the combination of what we teach for those in business is a marriage made in heaven and also will allow them to make their success inevitable.

In our 'Success Accelerator Intensives', we teach Mindset and Marketing Mastery to result-driven professionals to launch or scale their business online, so they can live life on their terms without wasting any more precious time or fear failure.

It's so rewarding seeing others break free of the blocks that hold them back from the success they deserve in their lives. The combination of working on their inner game and putting in place all they need in their outer game makes what we do unique and highly sought after.

So, in conclusion, thank you for reading this chapter, and thank you Susie Mackie for asking me to write it. Putting down onto paper these two defining experiences in my life is something I may never have done without you.

I will end now with the phrase that stays with me from that very first Psychology of Vision weekend to this day — and that most people I know now associate with me:

Trust the Process, it will NEVER let you down.

Biography

Carie Lyndene has been helping businesses with their marketing and sales strategies for over thirty-five years.

She has sold over ten million pounds' worth of her own products and consultancy services but is most proud of the tens of millions of pounds of goods and services that her clients have sold as a result of her Success Accelerator Training Intensives.

Carie focuses on helping coaches, agency owners and consultants, both nationally and internationally, to shift their business model and successfully launch and scale their business online.

This allows them to break free of the geographic and income limitations of working locally and to truly live life on their terms by creating the 'Six Figure Plus' laptop lifestyle.

Using a certified time tested and rapid results method, her clients can launch their business without technical frustrations, information overload or without the fear of failure in just twelve weeks. Please contact Carie if you would like to get clear on the one thing you need to focus on right now to launch or scale your business.

Carie lives in Gloucestershire with her acting student son Rory and dog Jack.

www.carie-lyndene.co.uk

www.thewisdomworks.com

Tereza Matysova

Leaving her dream job as a Czech television presenter to begin a new life in London has presented many diverse challenges for Tereza, who has faced these with a stunning smile and a wonderful sense of humour. Never one to simply give up, she has no regrets, loves her life as a Londoner, and has finally become her true, authentic self.

Coming back home

Turning thirty wasn't exactly what I expected: I got divorced. Years before I promised myself that this will never happen to me – my father did it four times. Yes, FOUR times. Therefore, that clearly wasn't an option for me; all that heartache and trauma. Until it happened.

And it was actually my own decision.

After eight years of my soon-to-be husband being unfaithful in our relationship and a short six-month marriage to try and fix everything (because he was always going to change his behaviour after that, right?) and yet another telephone call about what he'd been up to from a concerned husband or boyfriend, I'd had enough. The divorce was costly: I had earned more in the relationship, he was angry at my 'irrational decision', supposedly still loved me, yet now he wanted everything and I lost a great deal.

After the third day of sobbing on the bathroom floor wondering who would ever love me again, I used my only spare money to vaccinate the cat. I know it sounds irrational now but I love that cat and he was my rock. Prickly, difficult, thrown out by his previous owners as a kitten and not a big fan of people, physical contact or other cats, Meowglish had never betrayed me and it was the least I could do for him.

I felt guilty of course. I always knew that divorce was a 'couple thing' and each person contributes in their own way to a relationship ending. I kept asking myself if I'd been somehow better would he have been faithful? Could I have done more? But in the end I realised that the only things I've ever really wanted were trust, friendship and loyalty in a relationship and anyone who truly loved me would understand and nurture that.

It took me a while to get back to myself; or more accurately, to reshape and grow into myself. I started thinking about when I'd been truly happy and what happiness actually meant for me. It was hard to articulate. I started thinking about different times in my life and trying to remember how I'd actually felt; again, not easy, as I looked back on my life through broken glasses.

I was born in Prague and was a child of Communism and food queues. But when I was three and a half, my parents and I moved to Hampstead in London for five years. Was I happy in London? It was again hard to say as I was currently unhappy and that maybe influenced how I saw the past. But I thought harder. Lots of people have had far worse than me. And there *had* been happiness in London. There were trips to the country, smiling people, warm summers, lights at Christmas and a lovely upbeat, positive feel about the city, where we were a complete family. We did things I could never have dreamed of in Prague. There were friends too (and security men following us to make sure we didn't defect), and I remember how the people always seemed to be busy planning and looking forward to something. Maybe it's just a British thing, but I liked it; I wanted something to plan and look forward to something too.

On our return to Prague I worked hard at school. Indeed as a young adult, work was my savour on so many levels. I applied for a posting to return to London and threw myself into my career in Prague to hope, wait and temporarily forget – and thanks to my beloved work, my request happened rather sooner than I expected. At the time I was a television news reporter and presenter and a radio newsreader and I was pretty busy. But that particular year maybe the Universe knew I needed some help. Work grew and grew and I found myself almost everywhere on the TV and radio; every opportunity seemed to create three more. People sought me out, valued my opinion and asked me to share it with millions of others. I found myself on a government jet accompanying the Czech Prime Minister to the White House and asking Barack Obama questions for my TV news channel (while the secret service kept a close eye on me after I started nosing around the Oval Office – well, who wouldn't?!). I really didn't have time to reflect on the black hole of my personal life.

Life is often about people helping each other and my boss really helped me: she gave me a glowing recommendation and suddenly my posting to

Britain was 'go, go, go!' Something good often comes from dark places; when I was broken and on my own again, I had time to think about me. Not about rumours or accusations or others, but just about who I actually was and what I actually wanted to do with my life. I have always been a strong believer in dreams and making them happen. Maybe it's my inner London child. But like many dreams, there were obstacles and barriers and others telling me to let them go. Why do people do that? Is it not easier to believe in others? Nothing happened for a year and I was starting to forget. There were men, coffees, advice about the latest catch, a few blind alleys and my saviour of work was starting to become my distraction. And then, when I was at the very top professionally, intellectually fulfilled, able to afford two whole meals a day and with a slightly fatter cat, the offer came.

It was just one sentence: "We want you in London in three weeks' time."

Back then, just my boss and my best friend knew what I was up to. I didn't want other people blocking me or advising me against 'throwing it all away'. All of what? I was lonely. I can tell you now, if the time had been longer between the offer and the actual move, I might have never done it. When I broke the news, dad and his parents were happy, at least that's how they looked. They were always anglophiles.

But my mum and gran? They took it really badly. "Who will help with shopping now?" my mum cried, as she got into her car. "I'll be dead by Christmas!" said gran, as she says every year. "Won't we all." I thought.

I flew to London, and in one day saw twelve flats: they were really expensive! But I managed to find one that seemed to have hardly any mice, so I put a deposit on that one and paid the twelve-months rent in advance. Within three weeks, I had finished my dream job in Prague. My boss was amazing and smoothed everything over for me. My two best friends offered to drive me to London, so we packed up my life, eventually caught the cat and stuffed the whole lot into an old Skoda. Meowglish was especially prickly but he settled down after only eighteen hours of hissing and squawking and the last few miles of the journey were reasonably quiet. I later realised he'd had his arse up against my cactus and had crapped in my shoes so I guess he had a cat-based point. I'd promised myself a fresh start and a new, happier life and that's exactly what I intended to have in London. That, and some new shoes.

But as you can imagine, it was much harder than I thought. Starting with getting a mobile phone SIM card and coping with the language barrier (I thought I spoke English, but, judging by the startled looks, clearly not) and continuing towards finding new friends. An odd personal discovery was that over the previous year, and unbeknown to me, my core values must have changed and now I didn't want to give my friendship to just anyone. I was much more selective and I realised that new people must fit into my 'box'; they need to be *my* type of people rather than just someone with whom to spend time.

Another struggle was coping with my new 'position' in the world. One day I was a top television and radio presenter whom everyone knew; running a camera crew, framing theories and producing news stories for millions, and the next I was an office mouse in whom no one was interested. And I wasn't ready for that!

I had made a classic mistake: I walked into my new life thinking I had been there and done it all. It had taken me thirteen years to get to the top in my chosen field and like many, many people who have moved countries before me, I learned the hard lesson that often no one cared about your previous life or expertise or qualifications. This is Britain: Britain has its own way of doing things and it is all about the work you are being paid for here and now. I really didn't want to do another thirteen years' of work just to get back to where I was before, and in all honesty I didn't believe I could do it; I'd had great people around me before and had the luck you often need to succeed. But now? In a city where I had no friends or family and where I would be competing against the best in the world? But there were bonuses too. My new job was really easy, I was home by six o'clock every day, and I had every weekend off. I had lots of time to think, read, explore London and get myself fit. I also had a two hundred pound monthly budget after everything else was paid and I was living on soup. Yes, I was definitely getting thinner.

But I was never homesick, quite the opposite. No matter how many obstacles I've had to fight, Britain has never put me off. It really is happy, upbeat and plans for the future and it's always been good to me. My first year in London flew by and I decided to stay longer. Again something my mum and gran didn't take lightly. But I have been persuaded that I now simply have to live *my* life, so I stuck to my new dream. After deciding to put down roots, I rented out my little flat in Prague and bought (well, hugely mortgaged) a 'Bridget Jones flat' in Zone Three, with the stairs right in front of you when you walk in and close to the tube station. It was a complete mess of course at the price I had paid, but I had done it: a new nest and a new home.

It sounds like a bed of roses, but it wasn't, obviously. My tenancy was running out, they wanted another year of rent and my first property fell through. I did my usual dozen houses in a weekend thing, put an offer in on one (the agent wouldn't let me offer without seeing it even though I just 'knew' it was the one from the pictures), lost the mortgage, found a new one and badgered the poor sellers and agents so I could have everything signed within my seven weeks till homeless deadline. Meowglish mostly slept through this challenging period.

And then John came into my life. In fact, we met on a dating site, as most people do in London, where everyone just works hard. After a few emails he called, and the first phone call was just like a date; we didn't put our phones down for eight hours. And off we went. On the second date we went on a driving tour of the Cotswolds. John obviously had a convertible. It was January, minus five and alternating between sleet and snow. Eventually he put the roof back up. The Cotswolds was flooded after extensive rain and our umbrella broke. We were smiling and happy and found a pub with a fire and no vegetarian options. John had chips. The pub was almost empty (it may have been 'off season') so we cuddled up. The only three people in the pub, all women, eventually came up to us, smiled and said they wanted the love we had and asked how long we'd been together. John happily explained: "Nine hours." And we knew we were going to get married, and that we were each other's person. On a side note, I'm sure it was actually nearer to thirteen hours by this time all things considered, but hey…

Eventually I left my beloved 'Bridget Jones' home and moved into John's flat – first to try it for a week with the cat, and when John came knocking on my door at eleven pm the day after we moved out after the 'trial period', we simply moved back in again to try a longer trial period and we never moved out. Meowglish crapped everywhere of course, but he soon settled down. It's understandable – he was only four and John had a lot of cacti.

Have I mentioned that Meowglish is asthmatic? As a special gift to John, a week after moving in he had a huge attack and had to be rushed to the vet and stuck in an oxygen tent with lots of tubes sticking out of him. We were told he was the angriest cat the vet Mark had ever met, and that he was about to leave us. Naturally, my soup-based diet had not stretched to cat insurance. Mark was amazing and he saved Meowglish's life. John spent the price of a small car to fix him. Meowglish is now 'not allowed to die, ever' because of John's ideas around 'value for money'.

John's business was doing really well which meant that he spent night after night working past midnight for two years to keep the quality and standards high. I hardly saw him.

Naturally, we had so much spare time on our hands (!) that we then decided to look at over one hundred and fifty houses (have I mentioned that I'd have been happy after seeing three, but John is, and how can I put this, a little bit fussy?) and put an offer on one that was beautiful but run down, so needed a lot of work. Was this our best idea?

John had also not learned his other lessons and had been feeding a badly injured and starving cat on the street for a few months; it looked like the cat had been attacked by a large dog or fox. A few days before we moved out (November and about minus ten this time) John decided the cat might die if we left him. He managed to catch him, take him to Mark and spent another few months' food money on getting him cleaned and hoovered. 'Johnson' had issues – and he was about to join our family. Have I mentioned that Meowglish is tiny? And that he hates other cats? And that Johnson was a huge, balloon cheeked, badly scarred and often quite scary battle cat, now newly neutered? We were all a bit tense about this new arrangement...but we outvoted Meowglish and bought another litter tray.

Of course, house sales in London are often tricky, so everything went wrong and we spent four months renting an 'Air Bed and Breakfast' until our saggy old house was ready. John chose one rental based on arty website pictures and we spent a couple of months in some sort of soggy, gothic funeral brothel in the middle of winter and to be honest, we didn't feel too romantic there. The cats were fighting every night and there was a fox dating site going on outside. Incessantly. We didn't sleep much.

Eventually however, we had our dream home: a broken down Victorian property in Islington, with huge windows, beautiful views and a jungle for a garden. Like the cats, it needed love to help it bloom. After a year and a half, we still don't have a decent kitchen and bathroom but hey, we're lucky to have our own home and we are getting there. Just this week our first mouse moved in too… I'm sure that will work out well for it…

I was made redundant (twice) and was feeling rejected and lost again. John was also worried that I saw my 'best days' as being behind me in Prague. So he had the idea of me setting up my own business and although I was terrified, something about it sounded just right: the idea fitted me. I made a vision board, and I wanted all the usual things…you know, happy cats (they are now best buddies, collaborate and are in food-based league against us), a healthy child, to become a children's writer, maybe a professional business coach, to be a journalist again, maybe a media trainer and to be at the heart of world politics again…world domination… usual stuff…start small I thought…!

And so I began. Through tears, self-doubt, rejections, knock backs, training courses promised and lost, more rejections, good advice, bad advice, blocking advice…the same journey so many business owners and authors know so well. But I made it happen.

The only thing John forgot to tell me (and which I 'knew' but didn't really 'get') was how hard it would be at the very beginning. It's so hard you always want to stop. Find an easier option, an easier way of life. People often say how lucky John is to have a successful business. Maybe people think and say the same things about people who have a happy family, successful relationships and good health. But for most of us, all these things take hard work, determination, risks and sacrifice.

I also insisted that I did it myself, I did not want John's help. I needed my personal part of this world that was exclusively made by and for me, and he thinks differently to me; what works for him is not my way and I've learned to trust myself. I was left to learn every day. It was not as easy as I initially thought (obviously!) but I kept on going and learned from my mistakes and successes. And things happened unexpectedly: one Sunday morning while lying in bed, laughing, chatting and reading the papers I remembered the old stories I used to tell myself when watching wildlife by a stream. All the old characters came back to life and I started writing that very day: my stories have now been endorsed by Members of Parliament, head teachers, children, parents and psychologists. My agent is working hard to help me publish them and enable my childhood dreams to become a reality.

My business has grown too. I've trained and coached legal departments, politicians and teachers. I do regular television and media reports again and of course Britain's events have helped with royal weddings, babies, elections, Brexit and the whole day-to-day rollercoaster on which we find ourselves.

Do you remember Nelson Mandela's sentence: "It always seems impossible until it's done"? Yep, that's exactly my life story. My last six years have been just like that; things I thought I could never do or achieve all by myself have now become my bread and butter. My mum says I am different, more distant, but I believe it is not the distance that causes the sudden gap of misunderstanding; I've just become someone else, who may be different to others but more familiar to *me*. I am no longer a stranger to myself: at thirty-seven years of age, I have finally become Tereza.

I came to Britain to try a new way of living and I feel I have been given 'the full English'. I look at the world differently now, most of the time more positively. In this wonderful cosmopolitan city that is London, which gives you space to breathe and reinvent yourself every day, I have also become a Londoner with all that this means. I love the buzz of the city and the tastes and accents from all around the world. It's a city that demands and values hard work and personal success rather than envying it.

I have also learnt that everything has it's own time, although being the most impatient person in the whole Universe means I am still getting used to this. Things usually happen for a reason, as much as it hurts sometimes. Sooner or later we work out why we had to walk through so much mud.

I learned to think "when" and not "if", because you simply get out what you put in. I have always been grateful and said, "thank you Universe" but now I understand that I'm an equal partner in how the world turns. I'm now responsible for my life, and I know that if I need to climb a mountain no one will do it for me, but I can still climb alongside the people I love.

I now know there are no failures, only opportunities and we can never know how everything will pan out. When Johnson was abandoned and then savaged by a dog, every day must have been a cold, painful, hungry, lonely torture for him. How did he make sense of this world? If he had not been injured, would John have fed him and taken him in? If Meowglish had not been thrown into the trash as a kitten, would he ever have found his way to London and been saved by Mark? Who knows.

When I look back, I genuinely think: "How have I done it all?" but I now see myself as a fighter, and when I decide to make things work, I get things done. So six years, four house moves, one fiancé, two jobs, and setting up myself as an entrepreneur later, I can honestly say: "It was all worth it!"

I don't regret a single minute, because if I had changed one tiny little detail in my story, would I have been here writing about it today? I now love my life and the challenges it brings and I can't wait to see how the next chapters unfold in my journey: onwards and upwards with John and our two rather troubled cats by my side. And did I mention my new friends, our fish, roses and some sort of bee hotel/'Trump Tower' thing John is building in the garden…? Ahhh…that's another story.

Biography

Tereza, a former television news reporter, television presenter and radio broadcaster, is now a public relations professional with over eighteen years of experience as a media expert.

During her thirteen years with Prima TV, Tereza worked closely with and interviewed Czech and world politicians on a daily basis. She accompanied the Czech Prime Minister to the White House to cover his Presidential meetings, and asked President Barack Obama questions for her news channel both in the Oval Office and during his state visits to the Czech Republic. In her role with Czech Prima TV, Tereza created independent reports for daytime television programmes, completed regular voiceover work and has written political and women's columns for magazines and political interest websites. Tereza is currently an official British contributor to Czech Radio and Prima TV and examples of her recent work can be found on her website.

Tereza is a qualified coach, and specialises in transformational coaching and finding positive, achievable outcomes based on the client's own particular needs. She is a board member of the British Association of Women Entrepreneurs. She is also a fellow at the Royal Society for the encouragement of Arts (RSA), Manufacturers and Commerce and a member of the Executive Committee at the Czech British Chamber of Commerce; you can read a recent interview with Tereza at the website link below.

Tereza is currently working on a series of children's books which are fun and which educate children about friendship, loyalty and environmental issues. She lives in Canonbury, Islington with her fiancé John, and somewhat troubled cats Meowglish and Johnson.

www.mpaoflondon.com
www.cbcc.org.uk/News?News=154
http://bawe.org.uk

Ruth Mary Chipperfield

Sometimes, something which appears to be fragile, is inherently strong; this is the case with both Ruth and the jewellery she creates. Not one to allow chronic, debilitating illness interfere with her life, Ruth has a bright and beautiful future ahead of her. She truly deserves the awards she has won – so far!

Growing up, I heard too many stories of people who pursued their 'creative side', only to find it unfulfilling in the end, or that they fell short of their dreams. To me, science seemed like a sensible option and as I pursued academia, I became fascinated by the way molecules move in three dimensions. I started my chemistry degree at Warwick University in 2009, the same year I married Paul. I was ambitious and planned to have a career in research. Drug discovery and cosmetics were two areas that particularly fascinated me, but as my health deteriorated I found the course incredibly challenging. In 2010, my second year at university, I was finally diagnosed with narcolepsy, and by the time I had medication that gave me the ability to function sufficiently, I had missed almost half the year. I was advised to go back to first year, but I fought back and taught myself what I had missed: I didn't like the idea of giving up.

The following year my health worsened. Narcolepsy is a sleep condition whereby the person doesn't get the deep restorative sleep like that of a healthy person. A healthy person sleeps deeply at night, meaning they are fully awake during the day. However, a person with narcolepsy doesn't sleep deeply and so is incredibly sleep-deprived as a result. Sufferers therefore spend their entire time falling asleep, without getting the rest they need.

As if this wasn't enough, I also began having frequent cataplexy attacks. This is when the body loses muscle tone in a similar way to someone who is sleeping, except with cataplexy, the sufferer is awake. This happened multiple times per day, with many collapses in crowded public places. During an attack, I would be able to hear everything going on, but be unable to move until it passed.

One of the more bitterly amusing stories was when paramedics were called and weren't aware that I could hear everything. They had never encountered anybody with narcolepsy before, so I had a two-hour trip to Accident and Emergency while they looked up narcolepsy on Wikipedia! By Christmas 2011, I had dropped out of my course. I was sleeping around eighteen hours a day and could no longer leave the house alone because of the cataplexy attacks. My husband Paul became my full-time carer and we set out on the long road of bureaucratic applications for National Health Service funding to receive the only drug available that would alleviate the symptoms. Incidentally I could have made the drug in the lab very cheaply – illegally, but very cheaply. We had applied for the medication, only to have the application rejected. We put in an appeal, which was also unsuccessful, but this medication was the only way I would be able to lead a normal life. Again, failing was not an option. In 2012 and eighteen months after the first application, on the third appeal the funding was granted. Hurrah!

Up until this point, I didn't have many functioning hours in the day to do anything, but the few hours I did have were spent making pieces of jewellery. As these became popular, and with people around me buying my pieces, I realised this was a business opportunity. Creativity was always the driving force and so I experimented with inexpensive pieces of vintage jewellery sourced from antique fairs. These became a great source of inspiration.

Having received funding for my medication, I had a simple plan. Namely, launch a business, grow it quickly, let someone else take it over while I finish my chemistry degree, come back to it and grow it into a successful enterprise.

Unfortunately, things weren't that simple. My new medication was designed to make me sleep deeply at night to enable my body to have the rest it needed to be awake during the day. What I didn't know was that this medication would prevent me from experiencing another type of sleep, called 'REM' sleep. A person experiences 'REM' sleep (or rapid eye movement sleep) while they dream, and it's this phase in which the mind is recharged. Pre-medication, I experienced mostly 'REM' sleep, but suddenly this stopped and I experienced mostly deep sleep. I had never felt so healthy before in my life and I couldn't imagine anything stopping me from charging ahead with my business.

Then came a day when I suddenly experienced overwhelming and irrational fear. It was as if a baby had suddenly been put in an adult's body and was expected to function normally. I could no longer cope with my new responsibility, having been so reliant on Paul. My brain became over-stimulated and I had no 'REM' sleep to help process new experiences. My mental health took a really big hit: I experienced severe anxiety, depression, several psychotic episodes, and in the process, my body weight dropped by almost a third in four months. All this was simply explained away as side effects of my new medication.

As time went on, there seemed to be no other option but for Paul and me to keep developing our own business – there was no 'get-out clause' by this point. I needed his support at home, so we had to find a way to earn a living in the situation in which we found ourselves.

Inspired by lace making

Shortly before this crazy episode in our lives began, I had visited my favourite antique fair in Malvern. My mum took me on this occasion, as I was still unable to go anywhere safely on my own. Mum knew a lot about lace making and had been a keen lace maker herself before I was born. She pointed to a curious looking object called a 'tatting shuttle'. It was a piece of plastic with a crochet hook attached and she suggested I buy it. The plastic part acts as a shuttle, around which thread is wound to make 'tatting lace', whilst the hook is used to pull the thread through the occasional loop. I discovered a tutorial online and picked it up pretty quickly. I have never liked playing by someone else's rules, so I developed my own designs and patterns.

At the same time, I had decided it was time to move on to using precious metals. From a business perspective the choice was simple; either use low cost materials to create vast quantities of identical jewellery at low prices, or use precious metals to create luxury pieces. I had no desire to contribute further to the amount of costume jewellery in landfill, so it was time to teach myself silversmithing.

My approach to creating jewellery became much more design-led when, in 2013, I discovered the possibilities of mould making. By creating a mould around a small object, a precious metal version can be created. I decided to try this process with delicate pieces of lace, which I had hand stitched using my new tatting shuttle.

I progressed my idea a few months after receiving the new medication. At this point, I was awake for more than six hours a day, but the turmoil my mind was in had an even bigger impact than being restricted to six waking hours. Nevertheless, because I don't do things by halves in life, I invested in having several moulds made around my unique lace motifs and cast them in solid silver. I just wasn't in the frame of mind to consider the implications – the numerous techniques I would need to learn to get from the silver lace to finished pieces of luxury jewellery.

Instead I learnt the techniques of silversmithing, one step at a time, purchasing the necessary equipment as I went along. It was a bizarre domestic scene: I placed my soldering equipment on the gas hob in the kitchen and destroyed our slow cooker by using it as an acid bath to pickle the silver (post-soldering). Incidentally, I later discovered that a chocolate fondue kit makes a much better acid bath! The tea light candle doesn't last long, so it's a bit like having a built-in timer.

One of my big practical challenges at this point was maintaining a sufficiently steady hand to work. Because of all the drugs I was taking, around thirty-seven tablets a day, my hands were shaking all the time. I somehow used this to my advantage by positioning my hand so that the shaking nudged the solder into position.

Back to university

Despite the creative breakthroughs, the medication continued to have a serious effect on how my mind worked. I went from being someone who had been confident, to someone who was afraid of everyone and everything. I had already taken two years away from university at this point and I was about to take a third year out, the maximum amount possible without starting my degree from scratch. I really wanted to see this degree through. My brain was in constant survival mode, which made it impossible to plan ahead – an essential part of building a business. Again, failure just couldn't be an option, as I had no alternative to self-employment, regardless of whether or not I completed my studies. I still relied heavily on my husband and couldn't imagine not having him around during the day. The jewellery business wasn't at the stage where we could earn a living from it, and as winter came and went and spring drew closer, the summer of 2014 became my last chance to return to my chemistry degree. We decided it was time to put the jewellery business to one side to free Paul up to pick up his career as a graphic designer – something which had itself been in limbo.

I had fought pretty hard to get back to university, and now back there I found the course far from easy. When it came to laboratory work, it was decided that I was unsafe to use the facility in case I had a cataplexy attack. Personally I found cataplexy attacks, which were thankfully rare by this point, more of an inconvenience than a threat, but then I was used to them.

The real issue for me, on a day-to-day basis, was that I felt incredibly rough.

I was walking a tight rope with medication. A high dose caused mental health to worsen. A lower dose resulted in more narcolepsy symptoms. I had never particularly enjoyed the practical work in the lab anyway – spending days on end making a white powder from another white powder. I preferred learning about what the molecules did, rather than actually making them. Thankfully, this didn't stop me from completing the year, but it did severely narrow down my options for my fourth year masters project. I was told I would have to work in computational chemistry research, a subject I was even less keen on!

I decided that I would only stay for a fourth year if I could join a research project which would relate somehow to my other role as a creative entrepreneur. In the end, I managed to join a group in the engineering department, researching the environmental impacts associated with producing silver nanoparticles; silver particles which are one thousand times smaller than the width of a human hair. It was valuable experience, where I learnt how to take the manufacturing process and its impact on the environment into account at the design stage of a product. In this case, it was tiny silver particles with antibacterial properties, but the lessons can be applied to so many more things. I plan to map the environmental impacts of producing my silver lace jewellery, in order to minimise them when designing new pieces.

Although I enjoyed my research, I wasn't healthy enough to continue onto the next logical step of embarking on a PhD. It's something I imagined myself doing at a young age, but I'm glad that my path was diverted. Being an entrepreneur makes it easier to see the impact and tangible results of my work.

Back to business

After graduating in 2016, I found myself back on my entrepreneurial journey, where I formally launched 'Ruth Mary Jewellery'. The mental health struggles kept coming at me and so my sister generously offered to pay for me to see a therapist. I didn't really know where to start, until I remembered I had actually met a psychotherapist a year earlier, who turned out to be just what I needed. With the funds available, I gave her a call. That's when I found out I had post-traumatic stress disorder, triggered four years earlier: no wonder I had been finding everything a struggle since then.

With post-traumatic stress disorder worked through and out of the way – thanks to great therapy – I could finally focus on building my dream business and reaching new customers. Business networking has been a fantastic way of meeting some really interesting people and picking up private commissions. One of my favourite commissions to date has been a hair comb for a ballet dancer. As with my ready-to-wear collection, the main feature of the comb consists of silver lace, in this case silver lace flowers accented with pearls. The rest of the comb was cut from a piece of silver sheet. It was a joy to create something with a quality that is now usually just found in museums.

To date I have received a number of awards including being selected as one of the 'top one hundred small businesses' by The Guardian newspaper, which culminated in an invitation to Number Ten Downing Street. I also won the 'successful career from home award' from West Midlands-based Ladies First Network. This was a huge confidence boost, as it came one year after beginning treatment for post-traumatic stress disorder, and so brought encouraging closure to the most challenging chapter of my life to date.

Onwards and upwards

2018 has seen my work widely recognised within the jewellery industry. I was selected for a programme called 'Kickstart', alongside five other talented emerging designers, with whom I am exhibiting at 'International Jewellery London' – my debut at this prestigious industry show. I have also been shortlisted for the prize of 'top young designer under the age of thirty' by Professional Jeweller Magazine. It's an exciting time ahead and in a strange way, my health challenges have honed the resilience in me to move forward and grow 'Ruth Mary Jewellery' into an international brand. I'm now stocked in several jewellers across the United Kingdom and have customers from around the world.

I love sharing stories about my work, industry, and life – something I've had the privilege of doing as a keynote speaker on a number of occasions. So, I count my struggles as a blessing, because they have shaped me into who I am today.

My journey is best summed up by this quote:

In their hearts humans plan their course, but the Lord establishes their steps.

The Bible

Biography

I founded Ruth Mary Jewellery in 2016. I create couture lace designs that I hand stitch in silk thread and cast in precious metal; beautiful pieces inspired by what my grandma wore and that suggest a feeling of now, forever.

However, I wasn't always going to design jewellery for a living. I had set out to have a career in chemistry, when, during my time at Warwick University, illness caused an unplanned diversion. After being diagnosed with narcolepsy, my husband had to become my carer for three years, and although it was a challenging time, it turned out to be a springboard to my dream job.

Fuelled by my passion for luxury fashion, I developed my design skills and so the brand 'Ruth Mary Jewellery' began to evolve. I returned to finish my chemistry degree, but I had been enticed down an entrepreneurial path – one I became determined to take and develop.

www.ruthmary.com
www.narcolepsy.org.uk
www.citizensadvice.org.uk

Asha Ghosh

Asha's story was one of self-limiting belief, her inner voice often critical and negative. She felt she was never enough. After mapping out her career and her life, becoming pregnant changed everything – but not as much as she thought it would. The premature birth of her baby reinforced her innermost feelings of inadequacy until she found a way to reframe and empower herself to make changes which would benefit her tiny little daughter.

The stories we tell ourselves matter; they have an impact on how we feel and think, how we see ourselves and on our relationships with others, shaping how we make sense of our lives and ultimately deciding how our future plays out.

We have a strong bond with our stories even when they hold us back. But stories can be also transformative, especially when we choose to re-author the plot to help us to grow and develop. I had a moment where I realised an edit was required and with that decision I've found a freedom to begin to express my true self in a way that I've never been able to do before.

My unedited internal story was on constant repeat – its contents may sound familiar: it's an underlying silent inner chatter, speculation or assumption, often negative, often critical, often damaging. No matter the circumstance my internal narrator's perspective shaped all situations to prove why I was never enough and everyone was better than me; why they knew more, earned more, were happier, felt more fulfilled and had a better life plan. I was barely aware of it at the time. What I've now come to realise is those self-limiting beliefs had created an easy platform to draft a negative and dramatic story that I was well versed in telling others about myself. If you think about it, we explain ourselves to others through story; we may position ourselves as the victim of a wrongdoing, or that nothing goes well for us no matter how hard we try.

This underlying narrative can be difficult to re-write. Even when we've penned a new story, the legacy of this deep-rooted belief can be pervasive. On the day I went to hand in my notice I remember feeling like a hero. It was a perfect movie moment; I'm finally doing something for myself: cue music and a montage. The problem was there was a definite tinge of a negative subplot present, as within my hero montage there was no reference to all that I had achieved. My inner monologue was still subconsciously clinging to "I am not enough."

My new storyline was one of adventure. The plot overview was to work my three-months' notice, save a chunk of money, freelance in London and continue to save, enabling me to finish my MA dissertation without having to work long stressful hours. I was comfortable with the coherence of this version of life. My career change plot was mapped out. However, an unexpected twist and the addition of a new character appeared that weekend when I was hospitalised with a suspected ectopic pregnancy. A faint heart beat and a tiny wriggly dot on a screen announced that I was a few weeks pregnant.

My perspective of this news was warped by my belief that I was not enough. I had no job, limited maternity pay. Timelines and funds to finish my studies were shattered and I kept seeing my dream of starting my own business recede. The fear of not having, or being, 'enough' drove my decision to freelance in London anyway. The script I was using was that I was only pregnant, but the reality of trekking across London made me ill. Over the course of thee months I had three suspected miscarriages. A little heart beat would appear on screen again and again and this huge swell of pent up emotion would just pour out of me; it was like I was holding it in until the next time I saw the heart beat, not believing it was true.

At twenty-two weeks, struggling with blood pressure and unable to walk more than ten steps without verging on passing out, I'd lost trust in myself and my body and continued to hide my little bump. The mistrust left little capacity to think about birthing, nursery colours, baby names; pregnancy had become my untold story. After a period of six drama-free weeks it seemed a good time to tell people; baggy clothes were no longer disguising the realities of only having twelve weeks to go. Decision made: after a weekend away to celebrate our anniversary we'd start telling people. Deviation from the plan came when, sat in bed after returning home, my partner and I had a row. Triggered by my mistrust in my pregnancy I had not booked National Childbirth Trust or hypnobirthing classes and October and November dates were already full. Due date was Christmas Day, so we were now cutting it fine. How were we supposed to deal with childbirth if we didn't know anything about it?

At four am the next morning, we were soon to experience an alternative teaching method in childbirth.

There was a weird sense of calm between my partner and me. Although I awoke realising something was wrong, we knew the drill; this was our pregnancy norm. Ring the ambulance, inform the ward and run through case history with ambulance drivers and then off we'd go. The sense of urgency in the ambulance driver's voice when they were handing me over to the hospital indicated this time it was different. My next destination was the operating theatre. That hadn't happened before. My heavy eyelids refused to open but I could hear everything around me, starting with the slowing down of the baby's heartbeat. "Baby needs to come out now!" In my spaced-out state my protests were quashed by anesthetic and the next thing I remember it was daylight and my bump had gone.

As the anesthetic started to clear I found out I'd had tiny baby girl, all nine hundred and eighty-four grams of her (just over two pounds). At this point I had no understanding of my story. I was existing. Way too much to take in. I'd shut down. My first encounter of my skinny little baby was peering in the side of a covered incubator. The moments of parent bonding were not the priority here; she was wired up and there was a constant buzz of doctors and nurses checking and double-checking stats, bloods, breathing. I was watching all of this like a bystander.

Returning to a ward full of mums and babies, my interpretation of my situation was starting to be formed. A sense of incredible loss was filling my mind and body: loss of any decision-making on birthing, the excitement of telling people, showing off the bump. An invisible perpetrator had stolen the elation of being a new parent and left us with, well, nothing. As the realities of having a premature baby unfold you find there are very few facts you can cling to; they don't know if your baby will survive, how long she'll be in hospital, what complications we may face.

The basics of childcare seemed like an overwhelming obstacle. Breastfeeding was via 'Ivor the Engine', a noisy blue breast pump that sounded a bit like the 'Tardis' when it got going. My tiny baby could only be fed through a tube via her nose, initially two milliliters at a time, and I wasn't allowed to feed her. All those first experiences such as nappy change, washing her, touching her were all experienced within the confines of a plastic box, accompanied by wires, cables, constant beeps; all in a room that is hotter than the sun. Our inner voice can motivate, empower, encourage, inspire. Or it can tear us down, threaten and hurt us and my platform for drama was being set up, loss was moving into unjust, the unjustness of my situation was creating a whirling negative chatter.

Distracting myself, I flicked through my university reading list and a Carl Jung quote caught my attention: "I am not what happened to me,

I am what I choose to become." I was brought into the present moment, I began observing my thoughts, and realised I was dwelling on what I *didn't* have and fearful of what *could* happen. My internal tone of voice and the nature of my stories was destructive; I had the knowledge and understanding that what had happened was no one's fault, but it was omitted from the narrative I could hear – that I wasn't a proper mum.

How we arrange the key moments in the plot of our lives shape who we are and my anchor in my plot was I couldn't be 'a proper mum'. All my baby's primary care was delivered by the hospital staff and all the decisions made by them; what role could I play? So, my story actually starts here at the point when I realised that *I am what I choose to become*. And I chose to be a mother. As the choice sunk in I experienced hope in that moment; I was able to reframe my perspective of motherhood and my experience of motherhood, because it was my journey to experience.

Psychologists often refer to how sensitive children are to their parents' emotions and I learned that over stimulation can rewire premature babies brains and cause developmental issues. During pregnancies babies live all scrunched up, suspended in a dark place, comforted by their mother's heart and voice; not laying flat, under bright lights with a constant beeping, whilst adults prod and probe them every hour. I had an opportunity to become a calm oasis for my daughter; I recognised that dialing back my current emotional state, slowing down my thinking and my actions and becoming more present and mindful would benefit us both. My trigger was when I'd arrive each morning: I would place my hands on the side of the incubator and just slow down my breathing, focus on letting go of tension in my body and then just breathing. As time went on my daily routine extended to include a few minutes of meditation at home before setting off to visit my baby and again on returning from the hospital. Even though I could still hear the negative chitchat, I could now acknowledge it was there but have the ability to recognise that it was an old storyline.

Little by little I made further tiny and what on the outside seem insignificant changes to my thinking and behaviour. We shared a room with a mother who'd read aloud to her little one as research suggested it improved bonding and simulated what it would be like for a baby in the womb listening to their mother chat away. This seemed a good time to read the Harry Potter books. Our skin-to-skin time was my baby laid under my t-shirt on my chest, listening about Harry at Hogwarts and playing Quiddich. I slowly set about reclaiming my own natural smell so not to stimulate or expose my little one to unnecessary chemicals. I changed my washing powder, body lotions and cleaning products to non-fragrant. I tucked a little soft cloth into my bra in the morning and when leaving would slide it under her head so she could smell me whilst she slept.

Those simple touches made it easier to feel in control when I had tough days, such as when, out of the blue, doctors announced: "Your baby's hole in the heart isn't closing as expected," or "We're moving your baby to intensive care with suspected pneumonia," or "She has jaundice again," or "We want to discuss a possible operation." I'd empowered myself to make choices which were good for my little one and used those choices when I was experiencing stress from uncertainty. I could stay in the present with my little one and be a mum to her.

My experience showed me that re-authoring your story can redefine your sense of self and that your belief in what is possible totally improves. I didn't think I could be a 'proper' mum due to how my baby was born, but I found ways in which the nursing staff couldn't help her and these supported my little one emotionally.

My daughter is now eighteen months old; after bringing her home at thirty-seven weeks, still not full term and still only weighing four pounds, we started out on our new parenting journey a little earlier than others but we'd had plenty of practice in the hospital. She is now catching up developmentally and so far few we've had complications although many visits to the hospital and different clinics. However, the fears I'd set out with when I discovered I was pregnant are being slowly eroded. I've started my own business as a personal development and life coach and am now delivering workshops and running events about how even small changes can improve our lives. I have focused my dissertation on self-identity for women who are returning to work after childbirth and uncovering what support is needed to make the transition easier and more effective for them. We let great talent and key knowledge fall out of businesses as we don't give the right kind of support to women as they return to work; it's more than flexi-working, although that helps. And I am, of course, a mum.

I am enough.

We become the stories we tell ourselves and there is power in rewriting them, so please – tell a positive one.

Biography

As a personal development and life coach, Asha Ghosh is a big believer in the importance of stories as a way to transform not just ourselves but also the lives of the people who hear or read them. The inception of her business, 'The Honest Coach', is based on her personal values of integrity and authenticity, where Asha speaks openly and honestly about her own experiences so that she and those who witness her stories can move beyond limiting beliefs about themselves and their lives.

www.thehonestcoach.co.uk

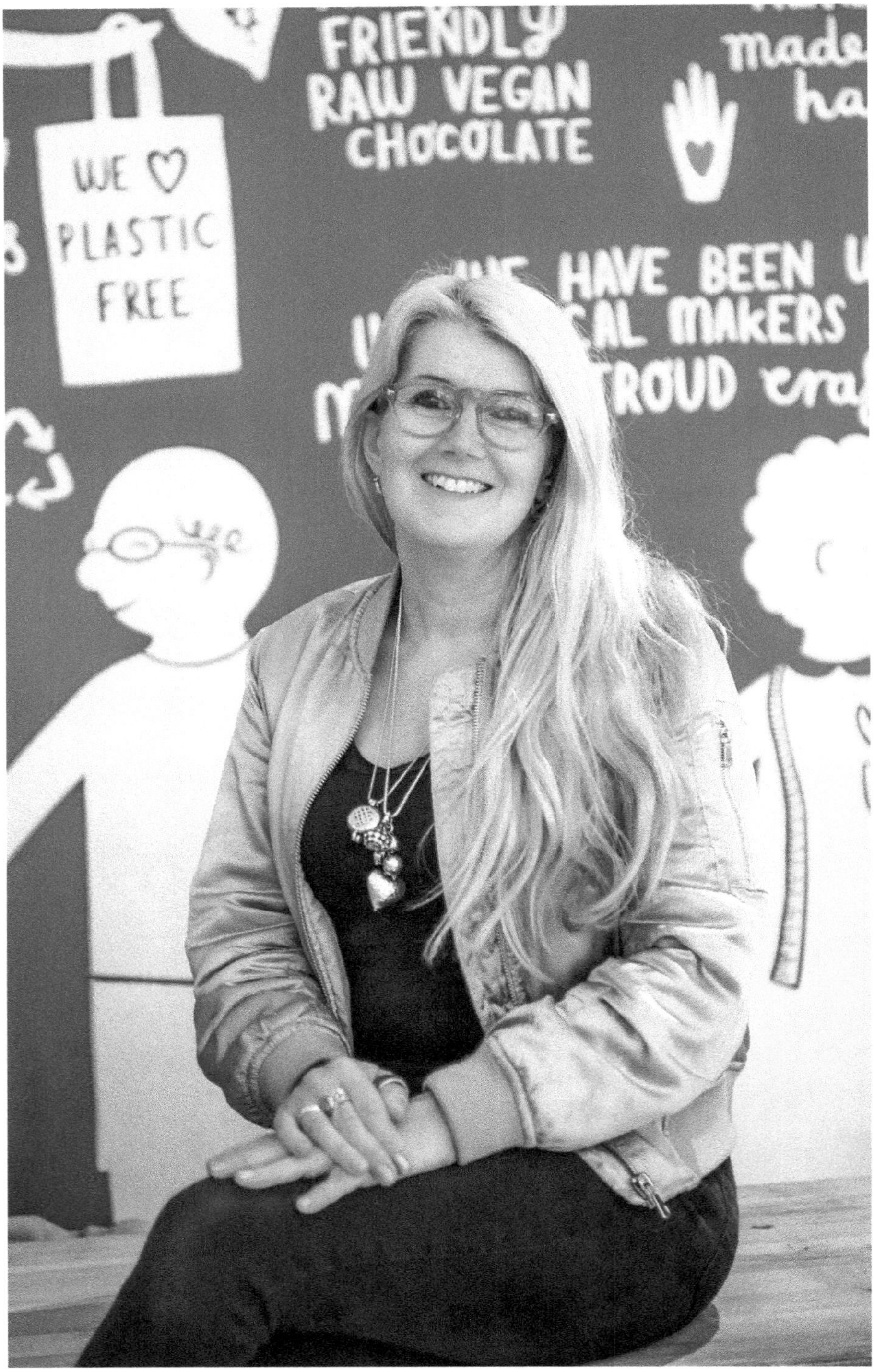
FRIENDLY
RAW VEGAN
CHOCOLATE
WE ♡
PLASTIC
FREE

Clare Honeyfield

Seeking the alternative and a thirst for learning led Clare to travel Europe with a freedom of attitude and enjoy adventures not many may experience. Her colourful descriptions of fruit picking, busking, cooking, intense heat, bitter cold and moonlight singing are pure joy. Back in England Clare used her experiences, together with a feisty attitude, to set up farmers' markets and tackle her local council's decidedly negative – even misanthropic – attitude. Naturally, she won.

> The secret of success is learning how to use pain and pleasure instead of having pain and pleasure use you. If you do that, you're in control of your life. If you don't, life controls you.
>
> Tony Robbins

I'VE ALWAYS BEEN A SEEKER. From my early teens I was always interested in the alternative, and was fiercely anti-corporation and anti-establishment. My business studies' dissertations were on renewable energy (quite ground breaking in the eighties) and on the global conduct of the pharmaceutical and food processing corporations. I always believed there was a better way of doing things, and found significance in my perceived difference.

At nineteen, I spent nine months travelling and working in Europe: a ski season in Switzerland, a month inter-railing around Scandinavia with a friend, a summer as an au pair around France. I loved the changing landscape, the new faces and the new skills I picked up along the way. But I never found what I was looking for. Not really.

When I returned I found a house for sale for a great price and approached the bank for a mortgage. I had saved a deposit, had a good job and thought it would be great to invest in property. The rather elderly bank manager looked at me over his half-moon glasses. "You, my dear, are far too young and far too pretty to be bothering your head about getting a mortgage" he said. At that moment, something inside me snapped. I had no words to express my anger, no means of addressing the injustice I felt. I never thought of myself as 'pretty' and really wanted to invest in property.

It seemed like a great opportunity. Looking back I could have gone to a different bank, spoken to a family member, tried another avenue. I think this experience confirmed everything I already felt about society at that time and I felt let down and defeated. To my grown up self now this feels like a massive over reaction: hindsight is a great thing.

At the age of twenty-two the birth of my first son changed everything for me. I had been working on a market stall and paying half my weekly wage on a mouldy bedsit in Gloucester, unsure of which direction to take in life. When my son was born I felt so full of love, so optimistic and so part of life again: he really was the most beautiful and perfect little being I had ever laid eyes on. His dad was unable to be what I needed and I moved to Stroud to get out of the poor housing situation in Gloucester. I rented a slightly damp cottage at the top of town with a friend, also a single mum. I studied Sociology, taking my baby to college with me on the train. He'd sit patiently in his pushchair during the lectures. I had a thirst for learning and a new direction in life.

Gradually we met people in Stroud and started socialising. Some nights we would trundle off in a converted pink fire engine to the Wiltshire Downs to protest about the nuclear weapon industry, going on 'Cruise Watch'. We'd conspicuously follow the Cruise missiles as they were taken out 'on exercise' by the military. There was a smallish space inside the fire engine which once stored the hose, and the carry-cot fitted here perfectly. My young son would sleep blissfully while we caused merry mayhem clogging up the roads with a convoy of brightly coloured vehicles, making noise and generally being a nuisance.

It was during this time that I met Fliss. Fliss had been living on a travellers' site on Vinegar Hill. Her 'bender' had burned down with all her belongings in it. She had a black bin liner of clothes, a badly behaved Lurcher dog and a small baby. "Move in with me." I offered. So she did. Fliss and I would go for long walks in the Slad Valley, laughing until we cried, hoping to be asked in to the big houses for 'lashings of lemonade and homemade cake'. That never happened, but with babies in slings we would walk for hours. We found our happiness again in each other's company and in fresh air and the beautiful landscape. Laughing again and being outside in nature was truly heartening. That winter it snowed and we spent long hours in the warm café in Slad Road, happily meeting new friends.

Fliss eventually moved on and I moved into the ground floor of a beautiful house on the side of a hill full of odd characters. I shared the garden flat with another single mum. The doors had beautiful etched coloured glass windows and the wood burner belched out smoke when we attempted to light it. When we repainted the kitchen walls, the paint ran down in streaks because there was so much condensation. We painted a bright yellow sun on our front door and I spent long summer days out at the back with my boy. The garden was wild and overlooked by the common, overgrown with grasses and wild flowers, and a wonderful suntrap.

This bliss was unexpectedly interrupted during my son's first birthday party, when a visit from the bailiffs informed us that the landlord was in arrears with the mortgage and we were unceremoniously evicted after the bank took possession of the property.

After many moves and two more blissful children, I wholeheartedly committed to a relationship and got married. We had three children under three and a half and moved often, always looking for the right long term let and eventually getting a great council house backing on to a playground. I learned to garden under the guidance of a neighbour, studied permaculture design, and made a lovely home. My hubby had been making wooden drums for some time and we'd travel around craft markets and events to sell them. I started running occasional craft markets and called them "Made in Stroud", running a vegan cafe at the events with a friend.

My wanderlust returned after we bought a rusty Mercedes camper van which we sanded down by hand and repainted with green tractor paint. One day I was sat in the van in the sun, having just dropped the boys off at kindergarten. I just felt like I wanted to see the world. No other way to describe it.

A month or so later we sold all our possessions and gave up our council home and drove off to France where we found work fruit picking. This was not the romantic notion I had imagined. The rows of Golden Delicious apples were covered in white powder where they'd be sprayed. When it rained, the water ran down the sleeves of my waterproof coat to my elbow, cold and unpleasant, soaking into the sleeves of my top. The rules about how and what to pick were very strict and the apples became heavy as the carrier around my neck filled up. I pretended to know what I was doing but clearly did not. We were paid by the hour and I was pulled up for being slow and not selective enough. "These apples are only suitable for jam!" I was told by the supervisor. The kids went to the local infant's school which was beautiful and way ahead of the education in England. Every day they had home cooked school dinners, the facilities were bright and clean – in the cloakroom, tiled with shiny primary coloured tiles, every child had a drinking tap and cup, and there were beautiful indoor climbing frames, toys and games. It was a joy. We lived on a campsite with other pickers, mainly from Poland. They would pick from six am to dusk every day, seven days a week, soaking up every opportunity to earn. At the weekends there were fires and singing and feasting but the focus of our Polish neighbours was always on work. "The first year you can buy a car," they'd say, "The second year a house and the third year a boat." They had their eyes on the prize and nothing was going to distract them from that. Money was their priority; I was always more interested in the experience.

While in France I noticed a job advertised in the back of 'Resurgence' magazine: 'Gardener and builder wanted to work for British family in Tuscany. September to February. Twenty hours a week in return for accommodation and all bills.'

Perfect! I called them from a telephone box in the next town and we set off a few weeks later, having just enough cash to get us there.

On the way to Tuscany we met a British couple in the north of Italy who stayed every winter in their camper van to busk for a few months and paid their annual mortgage from the income: this was a revelation in itself. They taught us how to busk, told us were to go, how to get permits and what to sing, how the Italians expect buskers to dress (smart and clean) and what music they like (The Beatles and other pop classics). We happened to have a Beatles songbook with us from my teenage guitar playing times. I played the tambourine and we studiously learned all the harmonies, my hubby using his classical guitar training to learn chords.

Tuscany was wonderful. We lived along a one kilometre long track on a small hill, Monte Verde, in a traditional Tuscan farmhouse. We had a small flat overlooking the garden, our own terrace and views over miles of stunning countryside. Here we planted olive groves, built herb gardens and converted outbuildings. I taught the owner, an artist, about mulching around the trees to keep the weeds down and the moisture in. Our three children played endlessly in the grounds, collecting porcupine quills and chasing pheasants, finding clutches of hens' eggs in the hedges and building dens. We would toast marshmallows on the fires we built to burn the brambles and years of undergrowth. I made lemon curd with fresh fruit from the trees and the chickens' eggs found by the kids. We went busking at the local markets three times a week to earn our food money. It was a good time with much laughter and even more red wine.

One winter's night on the highest mountain in Tuscany, a wonky wheel forced us to a halt, and our trusty old Mercedes gave up the ghost. It was minus fourteen degrees, far too cold to sleep in the van. An ornamental fountain stood frozen like an ice sculpture. It was Christmas week and everything was closed, so we knocked on the door of a local hotel. It was hard work, but we managed in broken Italian to persuade the family there to allow us to stay until the next morning. They showed us a cold room with one large bed, crisp white sheets, and many blankets. We all snuggled in there and were brought plates of cold foods and red wine. We slept so well and woke up the next morning to the task of taking our things out of the van and hitching back to our home on the farm where we worked. I remember having my big backpack on, (we had three children under six) and walking over the bridge which spanned a small river, the waterfall completely frozen and the morning sun pouring through the trees, the beauty of the fresh sunny morning, and the feeling of freedom: being in the world and knowing that literally 'anything could happen'. That is one of my favourite feelings in the world.

The job in Tuscany eventually came to an end and we packed up what belongings we could carry and travelled by train to the south of Spain in search of a mountain tipi community we'd heard about. Our busking endeavours had gone well and we had saved a million lira, so we had enough money to travel for a while without worrying about income. We were millionaires! We arrived in Spain in February and as our train crossed the Sierra Nevada and the Alpujarras, I wished I had packed more winter clothing. We found our way by bus and van to the tipi village and were welcomed and invited to sleep in the 'Big Lodge', the tipi version of the village hall, I guess. During our first week there it snowed. A bitter wind blew in under the tipi and we slept on the cold ground on sheepskins and blankets, piling everything we owned on top of us and huddling together to keep warm. We did our washing up in a freezing cold stream and drank out of jam jars as there were never enough mugs to go around. We wore all of our clothing at once, sitting around the central fire all evening singing together with everyone until the small hours. When everyone went off to bed we could go to bed at last, joining our children who'd been fast asleep by the fire for hours.

Spring came quite unexpectedly one day; the hedgerows started blooming, a twelve-year old boy started to build a vegetable garden, the sun became warm and golden, and rainbows played on the waterfall and surrounded me as I washed my hair.

Every two weeks we would build a 'sweat lodge' sauna and we would wash by jumping in the glacial melt pools which came down from the mountains. We still had ample cash from the winter's busking and walked every week to the weekly market in the local town, a couple of miles down the mountain, coming back with back packs full of fresh food for the week. On the way home we would stop at the spring fed pool, the midday sun drenching our backs with sweat, take our clothes off and dive into the cool clear water, before returning on our way up the mountain.

That spring we bought some canvas off the roll from some British tipi dwellers, borrowed a 'Singer' hand sewing machine and began stitching under an olive tree in the valley bottom. With help, this soon became a tipi cover with hand-sewn eyelets for the whittled sticks which would keep it in place. We borrowed a set of tipi poles and put up our new home by the river. In the evenings when the sun was low, the kids would scale the pine trees picking bags full of large cones. During story time they'd warm the cones on the fire stones to make them open with the heat, then they'd bash out the pine nuts, peeling and eating them warm tucked up in bed.

It was a summer of picking oranges and making marmalade over the fire, delivering wood-fired sourdough bread to the local health food shops, making pear compote with boxes of nearly perfect fruit which were being thrown away after the weekly market in the village, picking bramble tips and herbs to go on homemade breakfast japatis and of walking and swimming and moonlight singing. It put me in touch with the idea that there are many ways to live, many paths to tread and many people to meet.

We lived all summer off the money we'd made busking in Italy and eventually returned to the United Kingdom with just a rucksack each, a bedroll, a drum and a broken guitar. We sold the tipi canvas in France to pay for the ferry fare home, having busked, bussed and trained our way from Spain after a Volkswagen camper we'd been given broke down on the plains in forty-degree heat. We and our five passengers stayed in various squats, on beaches, on village greens and on trains as we somehow made our way north, dropping off a friend at the world surf championships in Biarritz en route. Here we were reprimanded by the lifeguards for swimming naked in the sea and sent back to our towels and bags to dress more suitably. On hot summer afternoons we would stop to find shade and while the children napped, would take it in turns to read 'The Celestine Prophecy', a profound journey in synchronicity.

Returning home to nothing, we gradually rebuilt our life. I worked for an indigo dyer hand stitching scarves for Shabori dying and helping with workshops, worked as a cleaner, cultivated gardens and made homes. I was an out-working hand sewer and an onion bhaji maker. My youngest son arrived and our family was complete. We found the perfect cottage and stayed there for ten years. Now having four sons at school, and having decided to discontinue my training as a 'Steiner' kindergarten teacher, I noticed that someone in town was getting funding for the 'Made in Stroud' idea. I was not happy. Didn't they know this was my idea? A friend suggested that if you're not happy about something then you have to do something about it: great advice and very timely. I arranged a meeting with the Leisure and Tourism Officer at the District Council and got permission to run a 'Made in Stroud' market at the Cornhill market place. "On condition that you include 'Food Links'." "I don't like farmers" I said, "I'm a vegetarian."

Stroud Valley's 'Artspace' helped me to write a business plan, budget and marketing strategy, local artist Vanessa Stopforth designed a logo and posters and Helen Brent Smith from 'Days Cottage Apple Juice' drove me around putting posters on lamp posts and in village shop windows.

I was given a desk in Stroud Valley Project office. SVP enabled me to get funding and helped me with policies and procedures and with planning: and so began the project to start the market. I had a volunteer who went through the Yellow Pages looking under 'F' for farmers and phoning them, mostly to no avail. I printed out press releases for the local press and spoke to the local branches of the National Farmers' Union, most of whom were not at all keen. After six months of meetings and many hours of work, the first market was launched by Isabella Blow and Jasper Conran. Isabella had been a long-time supporter of my work and we had previously tried to open a crafts barn at Hilles House, but couldn't get planning permission because of vehicle access issues. Jasper was working with my brother on Brazilian Fashion Week and offered to officially launch the event. This was so kind of them both and they were fabulous. Isabella wore an 'Alexander McQueen' lace dress with a wired hem in an extraordinary shade of mauve, a 'Philip Treacy' hat, and lots of red lipstick. Jasper wore a kilt and an un-buttoned crisp white shirt. At the time I was so camera shy I had to be persuaded to be in a press photograph.

I was invited to become a founder director of the 'National Association of Farmers' Markets' and bought myself a grey pinstripe suit from 'The Factory Shop'. At meetings I would ask, "What does that mean?" about every acronym and kept a list in the back of a large notebook.

Around this time I was invited to speak to 'Gloucestershire First' the Regional Development Agency funded business advice hub. After my presentation, the chair, a rather rotund man in pinstripe, said, "That's enough nice little stories about Stroud. What Clare's trying to do is to redirect a river upstream. Customers want to buy local produce from supermarkets." The Economic Development Officer from the County Council who'd invited me to speak looked embarrassed and asked if I was ok. "I'm fine," I said. And I was. This was my invitation to prove what I was capable of, and I did. I travelled to conferences and became an annual speaker at the farmers' market conference. The market took place twice monthly and eventually weekly. Again, I had to persuade the officers at the district council that this was a good idea, that people shop weekly, and that no, it wouldn't make the market any less special or less of an attraction. My husband now worked with me and we were invited to help set up markets in other towns. With others we set up 'Gloucestershire Food Links', helping farmers to diversify, and started working on helping schools and caterers in Gloucestershire to source better ingredients. We ran projects in schools and seminars for farmers, and won more awards than any other Farmers' Market in the United Kingdom. Being self-employed meant one of us could always be at home during the school holidays, and we soon bought a lovely family home which was always full of teenagers, trainers, cooking and noise of one sort or another.

After thirteen years of running markets we'd built the business and were running over one hundred and fifty markets a year. We also ran the 'Stroud Goodwill Evening', a late night shopping event on which we worked with other community members to make it more family focused, introducing a procession and family events when it was under threat of closure. It was with gratitude that I sold the markets business and moved on with my life, now a single woman once again. After a bit of trial and error I found my focus in 'The Made in Stroud Shop' and in a new sort of family life with grown up children, studying yoga in the 'Rishi Culture Ashtanga' tradition as taught by Yogamaharishi Dr Swami Gitananda Giri.

Through all of these adventures I have learned that there are no absolutes, that anything is possible and that if I want something in my life, hard work, focus and dedication will probably get me there. Wherever 'there' is. I believe that when we truly want to create something and when we focus on that thing, the universe conspires to get us there, because it is a universe of abundant creativity.

I am currently working with artisans and makers at the 'Made in Stroud Shop' and teaching yoga at Stroud Yoga Space. Studying has been a new challenge for me, and two years of practice, writing and reading has taught me more than I would ever have thought I could learn in that time. My passion is travelling and writing and I love working at music festivals during the summer, where I crew as a festival nanny. I'm in a cancan troupe and love our performances and walkabout gigs. These women are my soul mates and I love their beautiful energy and the wonderful snatched moments we have together throughout the year, making magic with music and dance. I'm a grandmother and love these little people very much. I also love to train at the gym. My current ambition is to get strong enough to put together an aerial trapeze routine to music. And to write a novel. Of course.

In my yoga practice I have found space within myself and I'm loving this adventure called 'life' with its constant unfolding and revealing little truths along the way. Sharing my yoga practice with others is a new joy and not something I imagined I'd be doing in my fifties.

One of my passions in life is encouraging others to follow their dreams, to believe in their projects and to use action as a tool for change.

I love my morning ritual of focus, meditation, movement and intention setting, and my aim is to keep the focus on creating a good life for myself. I sometimes lose this focus, but it's great to have the practice.

My four sons all tread their own paths and we meet often. They have grown up into wonderful humans and their partners and children bring joy and love into my life in a beautiful way I could never have anticipated. I love how completely individual they are, how they all have their own passions and how they fall back into being boisterous brothers whenever we meet up.

I recently saw a line from the poem 'The Summer Day' by Mary Oliver: "What are you going to do with your one wild and precious life" and I thought "Yes, what am I going to do with my one wild and precious life?!"

Biography

Clare grew up in a household where community events and working with the local media were 'just what happened at the weekend.' She was a member of the local Venture Scouts were she gained her Queen's Scout Award, Duke of Edinburgh Gold Award and became Chair of the Venture Scouts Unit. Clare started running overnight cross-country marathons in her teens and for many years held the women's record for the thirty-eight mile Cotswold Marathon.

After studying business and administrative skills, for a while Clare travelled and explored life, trying out various ways of living along the way. 'Made in Stroud' was born in 1991 when she set up an event of makers together with a vegan café, kid's area and a busker.

Founder of Stroud's award-winning farmers' market and co-founder of Gloucestershire Food Links, The Gloucestershire Association of Farmers Market, Made in Gloucestershire and The Made in Stroud Shop, Clare has worked with many hundreds of artisans overs the years, helping them to take their ideas from dreams to successful enterprises. From farmers to growers, food and drink businesses, craft makers, designers and artists, Clare believes that if you are passionate about your product and have great values, you will succeed. Her involvement in the emergence of the farmers' market movement as a founding director of the National Association of Farmers' Markets includes working with the National Farmers' Union, The Organic Association and others to write the criteria for farmers' markets in the United Kingdom, and writing the criteria for craft stalls and co-writing the Safe Food Policy for Farmers' Markets – all of which were all adopted as national policy.

Clare currently runs The Made in Stroud shop, is a yoga teacher, coach and public speaker. She is a raving fan of Tony Robbins and recently attended his London event, 'Unleash the Power Within', which she describes as "life changing". Her hobbies include spending time with her grandchildren, learning trapeze, aerial silks and dancing in a cancan troupe. Clare's favourite places to hang out are music and arts festivals in the summer and Goa in the winter, where she feels "truly at home."

www.madeinstroud.org

www.sva.org.uk

Juliet Robinson

A sensitive child, Juliet's childhood was made all the more difficult when, after her father was diagnosed with a terminal illness, her mother turned to alcohol. All Juliet wanted to do was escape. At sixteen she knew she wanted to become a nanny, loved her training and embarked on a successful career which took her all over the world. Her experiences, both personal and professional, are essential in her work as a family lifestyle coach.

I WAS BORN TO PARENTS FROM the north; mum was from Newcastle and my father from Sunderland. They met soon after my father graduated from Cambridge and were married in their early twenties; at this time my dad ran a pig farm and mum worked in a bank – their upbringings were as different as well. As I look back over my career and early childhood I have pieced things together and now use these realisations to help others see how they can overcome family challenges or personal difficulties.

My grandparents both worked at Guy's Hospital in London: one a gynecologist and the other a matron. Being working parents they had a nanny for my father and his two younger sisters until they were sent off to boarding school. In contrast, my mother had two older sisters and was quite spoilt. Her father was an officer in the navy and died when she was eight, leaving her mother much of the responsibility of bringing up the children on her own. They weren't wealthy, neither were they poor as they say in Newcastle. Over the years and through my work with families I now understand that what I experienced during my childhood, particularly with my mother and early relationships, unconsciously shaped my life, as is the case for us all. I'm proud of my parents and grandparents; they were inspirational and family orientated but for me, life as a child was not a particularly happy experience.

At the age of ten I recall standing in my bedroom when my mother came in and announced, "I have something to tell you." I don't know what I was expecting and didn't really give it much thought; the next sentence though, changed my childhood and life forever. I felt stunned and unable to fully comprehend what I had just been told. "Your father had been diagnosed with something called MS." Multiple Sclerosis is a degenerative disease that affects the nervous system. I remember the words, "There is no cure and dad may die in two, five, or ten years' time; the doctors don't know how long it might be."

I have an older sister and younger brother who my mum favoured: he was also quite spoilt. I reacted to her favouritism and was deemed 'the difficult one'. In reality I was a sensitive child and misunderstood – how those childhood labels stick and in turn we grow into them. I now have another view: although close in age my siblings and I were very different characters. I always felt much closer to my father; I loved his sense of fun, his humour, spontaneity and love of life. That was his gift, as well as educating and engaging us in activities.

As I think back to my childhood I don't recall much about my mum, except that she was a good cook and was always busying herself cleaning the house; it was always neat and tidy as she was very house-proud. She loved ironing – or so my father used to say, she even ironed our knickers and towels! It's strange how the three of us are all good at ironing too, the only thing is we haven't inherited her daily dose of house cleaning and hoovering. I now realise this was how she got rid of her nervous energy and fought her depression.

After receiving the news about my father, mum's response was to turn to alcohol. In our early teens not only were we living with a dying father but an alcoholic mother. My brother was lucky though – or so I thought. He was sent away to boarding school and absolutely hated it. I desperately wanted to go to escape from the awful life at home, but it was deemed more important for a boy to get 'an education'.

On Saturdays my sister and I would go into town with my mother; she would park in the pub car park and then sit at the bar whilst we went shopping for food. This was her escapism and if we were lucky, we would be treated to crisps and a fizzy drink. We got to town safely, but I absolutely used to dread the journey home; I literally lived with dread and fear in my stomach. I would sit in the back seat of the car and desperately pray there were no cars coming from the other direction.

We lived in the countryside and it was a six-mile trip to town with no markings on the windy road. The car would swerve well into the middle of the road and often veer across to the other side. How much my mum had to drink I will never know. I used to close my eyes when there was a vehicle on the other side and pray she wouldn't hit it and kill us all. Miraculously we made it home but the same feeling would arise the following week, when it was time to go into town food shopping again.

In many ways we were very lucky, we had a nice house in lovely countryside, went to school in the village and had lots of freedom. The hardest part was not telling anyone at secondary school. I became adept at retreating into a shell and keeping quiet. I hated any discussions about family life or anyone asking "What does your dad do?" I was so ashamed of what I had to deal with; I just wanted to hide when those conversations arose, in fact I became a quiet and shy child, instead of the gregarious, outgoing child I once was.

We had so much freedom because my dad was ill: on the other hand, we had to grow up fast and take on adult responsibilities. Gradually dad's memory worsened; he was becoming unstable on his feet and had to use a stick to walk with and would repeat things on television and in conversation – as teenagers we found this incredibly annoying. This was our life throughout our teenage years, living with an alcoholic mother who was embarrassing when drunk. On returning from school, we never knew what we were going to find. Would we have a meal on the table, what kind of mood would she be in? Would she start shouting at us or be fast asleep in bed? The dread came over me every day as I opened the front door. How I envied my brother Charlie, being away from all this.

Over time dad gradually got worse and ended up in a hospital for the last two years of his life. Mum continued to drink and we just accepted things as they were. Our relatives barely knew what we were going through, all the focus was on my dad and his MS. No one knew or understood how hard our lives were; I felt angry inside and also worried about my dad. I missed him being my dad, the parent to whom I felt closest; the one who supported me and got involved in anything we did – as long as rugby wasn't on television.

I missed his funny stories; the one where his father was driving along the road and went round a corner and dad fell out the car (they didn't have locks on doors in those days) and grandpa carried on driving – he hadn't even realised! My father could have died, but he survived. Another story he used to tell was one about his teacher at boarding school who said, "Robinson, if you try hard you might just manage to fail." 'Fayle' was my dad's middle name but this incident made dad even more determined; he not only passed, he made sure he came top of the class. He had so much spirit. He said to himself, "I'll show him." And he did – we receive lessons throughout our whole lives from those we love.

At sixteen I knew I wanted to be a nanny; I loved children and was completely fascinated by them. I used to take neighbours' children out for walks, volunteer in a youth team and babysit whenever I could. The summer before doing my NACMW (National Association for Maternal and Child Welfare) childcare training, I put an advertisement in 'The Lady' magazine and received over seventy calls with job offers; I was even offered a job in New York looking after three young children! At last I felt wanted and excited, I was going to do something that would give me the freedom to be myself! But sadly, it didn't, I still felt ashamed of my home life even though I chose a job looking after a young baby in London. I really could not wait to leave home and escape from all the fear, unpredictability and shouting from my mum – I hated home life and could barely have a conversation with her, she was always drunk. By this time my sister had left to be a nurse and my brother was due back home after his 'A' levels.

At eighteen my grandparents came to stay after one of their overseas trips, bringing us exciting gifts from India, Jamaica or wherever they had been. I told my grandmother about my summer job nannying and she questioned, "What are you going to do after that?" I had no idea and didn't care. I knew I loved kids and travel and it seemed the perfect job to me. After returning to London I had a couple of telephone calls to say my father had a fit and we had to get home quickly. This happened a few times and we were told to expect the worst, except dad was strong and kept defying the odds. He recovered but was set back further and his speech was now deteriorating. I used to travel home from London to visit him in hospital every weekend. It was hard to see him so ill; towards the end he could not walk and was pretty much bedridden. I will always remember how he took my hand and squeezed it shortly before he died and said, "I'm very proud of you." He died when I was twenty and we were told his death was 'a welcome relief'. I had no grief counselling or even read anything about death, I just got on with my life and accepted what had happened; it's what you do.

Shortly after this I went to work in Switzerland for a lawyer and his Italian wife who had a boy and a girl. I had twenty-four hour care of both children. The one-year old was described by his mother as being a 'really naughty' child, who woke four or five times every night and was very destructive. I love a challenge and reassured myself that I could always get on an aeroplane and come home if I didn't like it – after coping with death of someone close, nothing is ever that bad.

Within a week I had the 'problem child' sleeping through from seven in the evening and enjoying a two-hour lunchtime nap. His parents were over the moon as they had gone through so many nannies in a short space of time. This child was as good as gold, he was a bright toddler who had not been given much attention – this had all been focused on his sister, who had developed a shy nature. Steven even managed to get attention from his father who had largely ignored him before. Getting sleep changed their whole household and this is where my sleep training career began.

Back in London a few years later and after doing my 'Montessori' teacher training I was employed by an American banking family who had two children aged three and twenty months, then a new baby shortly after I started with them. One fateful lunchtime I went out with a friend who was visiting from Gloucestershire; I had never done this before. I left the new mother with her three children and was due to take the eldest to a party that afternoon. It was the first time that Annie had all three children to look after on her own. On returning two hours later, my boss screamed out – she had never, ever raised her voice before. I ran into the kitchen and found her holding her unconscious daughter Emmy, explaining that she had fallen out of her bedroom window on the third floor.

At times like this something inside you takes over and you jump into action. I remained calm but all I could think of was internal bleeding and the fact she had been moved. Emmy looked as if she was in a deep sleep and had a slight scratch on her head. I knew time was of the essence. I grabbed the car keys and raced down the road to the Royal Free Hospital with mother and child, leaving a friend who had never met the children before in charge of a newborn baby and a one-year old. When I returned to the house I had to make the call to her father who was on business in

New York and explain the terrible news: it was one of the worst calls I've ever had to make in my life. In situations like this you simply act, instinct kicks in and you take the lead, even when you have no idea what's going on around you.

The following day Emmy's respirator was turned off and I never saw her again. She was a very lively child, full of confidence and would chat to everyone in the high street. She lived in a 'yes' world and was not really made aware of boundaries and the word 'no'. It was a tantrum which took her to her bedroom. I felt guilty, even though I was not in the house at the time: I had meant to warn her parents that the bed should not be next to the window, I even sensed that something bad was going to happen. Sounds awful doesn't it? What was worse was when the press started printing comments that weren't true; it was so hurtful. Never believe everything you read in the papers. I had had previous experience of dealing with the press with another family, but this was so insensitive. I felt very angry but could not say anything. What was done was done, we cannot turn back the clock.

A few years earlier I was on holiday in India, and on arriving home there was a strange call on my answerphone. I immediately called my aunt and she said, "Oh, don't you know?" "Know what?" I asked. "Your mother has died, she had a heart attack." So I lost my father when I was twenty and my mother at thirty. I've had many experiences of death over the years with people who have left this world before their time. My father was fifty-one when he died and my mother fifty-six: I'm between these ages myself and it feels a bit surreal at times. What I've worked out as I look back over the years of my work as a child sleep and behaviour consultant is that I can now understand what my mother went through and what caused her behaviour when we were small.

"I had three under three," she often used to say. I realise that when she lost her father she was probably not given any help or support after his death, the same as the three of us. When she had my sister my parents were delighted, however within three months she was pregnant again with me. Between the time my sister and I were born she had lost her own mother. As I look back I now know that she was depressed for many years and never learned to cope with the loss, which explains her behaviour. I have seen similar situations with many of my clients, and this has given me deep insight to help heal the parents or children who are living in some kind of pain or fear.

When I get to the real truth about why a baby or child is not sleeping, I know that my childhood pain and suffering has not been in vain. In fact, it has strengthened me as a person and given me the perfect tools to do my job and support other families who are going through grief or challenging times with their children. I hope that my grandmother, who is also no longer with us, can now look down and smile and be proud of me for sticking to the career I chose and which has allowed me to work with some of the most amazing families – and live a jet-set life for many years.

Since moving to Cheltenham I've met many alternative therapists and fallen into the world of coaching which has allowed me to create my own programmes to support women after giving birth, or anyone who is struggling with sleep deprivation and emotional issues. In fact, it is through my work that I have been fortunate to meet lovely people like Susie and be able to help others heal family wounds or recover from a traumatic experience. Death, although hard at times to accept, does not define you: it makes you stronger, wiser and more compassionate.

Biography

I'm Juliet Robinson, otherwise known as the 'Sanity Nanny'. I originally trained to be a nursery nurse and I've managed to make a career out of travel, enjoying living the jet-set life working for many famous and wealthy families across the world. Later I became a Montessori Teacher, yet at heart I think I always wanted to be a child psychologist as I've always been interested in people, especially children. I'm passionate about helping families to establish secure parent/child relationships to prevent children from suffering in a way that most adults do not understand. Once we know what drives our own behaviour and beliefs, we can effect positive change and improve matters from one generation to the next.

After moving to Cheltenham in 2002 I began coaching and mentoring, which I love. I now work with busy and sleep deprived parents as a 'Family Lifestyle Coach' and am the author of the book 'Wits End to Wise Parent'. There will be more books to follow as I want to help many more families and assist in reducing the mental health crisis in the United Kingdom and across the world.

www.sanitynanny.co.uk

Jackie Howchin

Pain, both physical and emotional, has been present throughout most of Jackie's adult life. With true spirit and empathy, she has transformed her painful emotions and developed a deep passion to help others through her healing work. Her nature glows through her beautiful artwork – art which is infused with love and reiki healing energy.

I HAD THE BEST CHILDHOOD EVER – I just didn't realise it at the time.

I grew up on a small farm in a north Dorset hamlet. My dad was a herdsman and my mum a nurse. It was a wonderful time, when safety wasn't an issue, so my two brothers and I would disappear out to play all day and come home at teatime; they would be out on their bikes, and I would be in the woods day after day writing stories and drawing pictures of trees. But as I grew up, I felt a bit like the odd one out because my school friends all lived in the nearby town, in posh houses with central heating and colour televisions! They could walk to the shops and to each other's houses – and I was stuck out in the countryside with just my brothers and the farm animals for company. Little did I know at the time that my childhood was better than most. It wasn't until many years later that I discovered how much my friends really treasured those occasional weekends spending time with me on the farm – they were their happy memories.

I had a very strict childhood, and was certainly taught right from wrong in no uncertain way. But I had so much love and respect for my parents, and didn't know anything different, so my life was good. My dad worked incredibly hard on the farm, he loved his herd of cows and treated them with love and respect, calling them each by name. My mum was a wonderful carer; her nursing career was her true calling. Unfortunately she suffered with depression for a large part of her life, which made things quite tough for us all, especially dad.

From the age of five, whenever I was asked what I would like to do when I grew up, I would simply say, "I want to help people." I didn't really know what I meant by that, and thought perhaps I would be a nurse one day, just like my mum. But with my fear of needles I guessed that was really never going to be an option. I had been raised with the belief that "you must work hard for a living," so when I left school I went to Secretarial College, where I worked incredibly hard. I discovered a love for shorthand, and practised it every spare moment I could. My shorthand teacher was very kind, she saw my potential and wanted to push me even further, so she offered me free home tutoring every week. I was very proud when I left college with a shorthand speed of two hundred and ninety words per minute and was offered a prestigious job as a stenographer in the Courts; my parents were very proud of me. After seven years of such an intense career, hearing the horrors of murders and rapes repeated daily in the High Courts where I was now working, afraid of the dark and of walking alone on the streets caused by the terrible things I was listening to on a daily basis, I decided I had to leave for my own sanity and peace of mind.

I took a role as a personal assistant and worked my way up to being a manager at a language school. For the next twenty-eight years I worked very long hours for very little pay, but still had incredible loyalty for the company. Unfortunately I had no work/life balance and missed out on so much of my beautiful son's childhood because of my dedication to my career; something I truly regret. It had taken me many years to get pregnant as I struggled with lots of infertility issues, so when I found myself pregnant I felt truly blessed. But it wasn't to be a happy pregnancy – I was sick twenty-four hours a day, every day, for nine months. The birth was traumatic, and ended in an emergency caesarean. Then they realised that my epidural had been overdosed, and had blocked me up to my neck: I was unable to hold or feed my son when he was born and for two days after. Post-natal depression kicked in, and I struggled through darkness for three very long years, missing out on the first precious years with my son. I had given up my job permanently in order to be a mother, but unfortunately when my son was just six months' old my husband was made redundant and I had to go back to work to pay the bills. My boss was thrilled to offer me my job back, and was very understanding about my health, giving me the time off I needed to attend counselling sessions for my depression. My life felt like hell, constantly trudging through treacle, always conscious of the deep dark hole on which I was teetering every single day, waiting to swallow me up at any minute. So my life continued as a working mother and my marriage suffered because of it. I was just plodding through life, but little did I know that my life was about to change dramatically!

My world was rocked when my mum was diagnosed with cancer. After horrendous bowel surgery followed by radio- and chemotherapy, we tried our best to live a 'normal' life, but always with the fear of this evil disease hanging over our heads. Eighteen years ago, after a very long struggle, my mum finally lost her battle with cancer. I was fortunate to be with her when she passed, which was a traumatic experience at the time but is something I look back on as a blessing. At the time I was unable to contemplate how my lovely mum, who was a true earth angel, could have been taken so young and in such a horrible way. Little did I know that her passing was to change my life forever.

After mum died, I felt a desperate need to make sure that she was ok and free from pain, so my dad took me to a spiritual evening where a medium was giving psychic messages on stage. At the time I didn't believe in anything spiritual, and was reluctant to even go that night, but dad persuaded me with the promise that I could leave if I thought it was just 'hocus pocus'. When the medium came onto the stage and pointed straight at me, saying that my mum wanted to tell me something, I was stunned. She started telling me things about mum's funeral and about me that only my mum could ever know. I was shocked. Initially I accused my dad of giving her these details in advance, and insisted that he already knew this medium. Of course he didn't – and that was the day I started to believe in the spirit world.

I went home and devoured every book I could on mediumship, I was desperate to communicate with my mum whom I missed so much. I joined a Mediumship Development Group, and loved communicating with spirits. I also started to take an interest in reiki energy healing, having occasionally watched my dad healing at a local care home in Sherborne, not really understanding what he was doing but enjoying watching him 'work' with so much love and kindness. I researched everything I could about reiki and eventually signed up to take my Reiki Level One course. I didn't tell my dad because I didn't want to let him down if I failed the course, how silly was that? I *passed!* and went on to take my Level Two as soon as I could. Dad was so proud of me! This was the start of my new life, an exciting and wonderful path.

By this time I had left my career in the corporate world after realising that I really wasn't being valued by my employer. Redundancies were being made, and I was expected to take on the extra work. I started working for myself as a publisher of two community magazines in my local area, a pretty huge change of career but I was brave enough to give it a go and I'm still running my magazines today, twelve years later. I don't enjoy the 'selling' side to this work, as I'm probably the worst salesperson ever; I'm far too soft, and tend to give so much away, free adverts and huge discounts and am always owed money by people who choose not to pay for their advertising! I admit that I'm not particularly business-minded; I trust everyone until they prove me wrong! This is not helpful when you are supporting yourself financially and need to keep a roof over your head and food in the cupboard. But the beauty of working from home meant that I could also dedicate time to my healing work…although I can't really call it 'work' when I'm doing something I love so much.

A few years later I decided that I wanted to learn how to teach reiki to others so that I could share this wonderful gift. I knew that I wanted to create that wonderful ripple effect where I could teach others to use the gift of healing and they could all do the same. I chose my dad as my teacher for my final Master's Degree in healing, and feel so blessed that he is not only my best friend and mentor, but now also my Reiki Master.

My depression, coupled with the devastation of mum's passing, ended my marriage. The divorce was horrible, and I felt huge guilt for my lovely son who was caught in the middle of it all. I was not in a good place, and in my vulnerable state I fell into a very controlling relationship with a man who had anger issues. After seven years I was brave enough to end that relationship – just months before we were due to get married. This proved to be the best decision I ever made.

I transformed my painful emotions into positivity and developed a deep passion for my healing work, which is now the love of my life. It's been a long journey for me, full of very difficult lessons which have taught me so much about life. I'm very much an empath, picking up on peoples' feelings, pain and emotion, and the Universe has a wonderful way of bringing people into my life who are struggling with situations I've already experienced, such as divorce, depression, endometriosis, infertility. I'm a very open person and share my personal experiences with my clients, which leads to mutual trust; they see me as a 'real' person, not simply a therapist. I believe that healing with words is incredibly effective, so by encouraging people to open up and talk about their issues they are literally purging themselves of the negative energy that they have been experiencing and holding on to. I help them to understand how this negativity can manifest into physical 'dis-ease' in their body and how they can truly heal themselves by using reiki and changing their thoughts and actions. Teaching the 'Law of Attraction' is also a huge passion of mine, educating people to understand their energy, and how it affects not only them but everyone and everything around them.

Over the years I have helped so many wonderful people, and lots of animals too. It seemed that my life was pretty well perfect. And then disaster struck…

I was diagnosed with a herniated disc in my lower back, caused a few years before by an ice-skating accident. The pain was immense and I was told that spinal surgery was my only option. It was only during the operation that they discovered more than they were expecting: a little triangular piece of bone had been chipped off my spine during the accident and was embedded into my spinal cord. They had no choice but to remove it in order to prevent further damage and possible paralysis. Although the surgery left me with severe nerve damage in both hips and in my left leg and foot, I was relieved and incredibly grateful that I still had the use of both my legs. I was told to rest for eight weeks but I soon realised this wasn't going to be an option as I needed to keep my business going to pay the bills.

Unfortunately I undid all of the surgeon's good work, and six months later I was told my spine was now crumbling and further surgery was needed. I underwent a spinal fusion, and now have a rather impressive array of metalwork and screws in my back. The second surgery left me with even more nerve damage, which I was told would be with me for the rest of my life. I was left with severe numbness in both legs, bursitis in both hips and constant sciatica and lower back pain.

Once again I was told to rest, and it seemed I had no choice. The pain was excruciating, painkillers weren't helping and just made me feel like a zombie with nausea and dizziness. I couldn't do anything for myself. My partner had to help me shower and dress, even putting on my pants and tights. After four months' recuperation, where I was not able to work or earn any money, I was at my absolute lowest. I tried to be my usual positive self, focusing on all the wonderful things in my life, but a year later I realised that my life was now permanently limited – in my eyes anyway. I was no longer able to walk very far, go running, go to the gym and – more importantly for me – dance salsa! I couldn't even do my housework or ironing. I suddenly hit a wall and became very low and depressed. I had no reserves left and gave in to the pain. I simply couldn't see a way forward.

We don't plan for illness, injury or life-changing situations and this certainly caught me by surprise, dramatically changing my life in an instant. It was a stark realisation that I was no longer physically or mentally able to cope. To top it all, I had started to gain weight through lack of exercise and comfort eating.

A further life-changing event occurred when my partner of many years suddenly left me. He was not only my lover and best friend, but he had also become my 'carer' and had very kindly supported me financially whenever I needed help. I didn't think I could get any lower, but I did. I hit rock bottom and didn't want to continue with my horrible life of pain and heartbreak. My doctor gave me anti-depressants to help me get through the dark and lonely days, but I hated taking them. I was a healer for goodness sake, how could I show my weakness at not being able to heal myself!

And then the Universe brought into my life a lovely man who was a tetraplegic; he had come to me for reiki healing. A year ago he was a fit and healthy man, but one morning whilst getting dressed he caught his leg in his trousers and fell, hitting his head on the corner of the wardrobe. He was now permanently in a wheelchair having become paralysed from the waist down, incontinent and with limited use of both arms was unable to even feed himself.

That's when the lightbulb moment hit me... I realised that I was truly blessed and grateful for my wonderful life, because I was still able to walk! This wonderful man, with such a beautiful soul, brought me back to life again. Why was I relying on the doctors to help me with their drugs, simply trying to mask the pain, when I knew that the only person who could truly heal me was *me*, certainly mentally and emotionally. From that day onwards, I chose to accept that my life was amazing, just a bit different to what it had been before the surgery. I accepted that the metalwork in my back was permanent, and that the constant pain and inability to do all the things I loved was going to be a part of my new life.

Shortly after that my son Elliott came to spend the day with me. It had been really hard for him to see his mum so low and depressed. I shared my new vision with him, of my life of gratitude and love, and we had a wonderful day together. Then, for some reason unknown to me, I decided I wanted to try painting, so we went out and bought a canvas and some paints. Elliott was as surprised as I was, reminding me that I didn't actually know how to paint. I laughed and told him that I was so bad at painting that I had failed art miserably at school.

At that time I have no idea where this inspiration came from. However, by the end of the night, an abstract painting of the sea emerged onto the canvas. I connected into reiki healing energy whilst I was working to give me some pain relief and I experienced a huge sense of relief and wellbeing throughout the whole process, not to mention a massive feeling of pride at the end of the day. I was really surprised at what I'd achieved, and found the whole experience profoundly healing. Ten hours of pain-free painting!

By being truly in the moment, painting from my heart and soul and channeling reiki healing, I had found a way of healing the pain, emotional hurt and grief deep within me. Instead of waiting for my healing to occur, I now create the opportunity to heal myself through my art, and a positive outcome is achieved quickly and easily. My interaction with art now provides me with a break from the pain and stress of daily life: it allows me to create an exciting adventure full of release and dissolves my pain, rather than allowing it to overwhelm me and destroy my sense of self.

The most incredible part was when I realised that people were actually feeling the healing energy from my paintings. They would want to touch them as they walked past them on the walls in my apartment. I had channeled reiki healing energy through me and into my paintings – and so the magic of my healing art was born.

My passion for life and for helping others then expanded, and I found myself not only working with my reiki and life guidance, but also through healing art – allowing others to experience art and self-expression as a wonderful source of self-healing.

I started running Healing Art Workshops and Healing Collage Workshops to support and encourage emotional healing through art and creative self-expression for those living with pain, grief, fear, frustration, anger, anxiety, self-limiting beliefs, stress and so much more. Although I had no formal art qualifications, I found that I was able to create a loving and safe space where people could truly be themselves. It's not always easy for people to talk about their deepest pain and fear, so I helped them to use colour, shape and texture to voice their emotions without words.

Eventually I even learned to accept my new title of 'Healing Artist'.

I love producing inspirational channeled art, infused with love and reiki energy healing. My art is proving very popular, because it continues to provide healing to the people viewing it, or to the home in which it is displayed. I am being asked to paint special commissions, which are personalised to balance peoples' specific energies, or to lift and invigorate the energy in their homes. How exciting is that?!

More recently I was brought right out of my comfort zone when I was asked to talk about my life and my experiences at a local 'Positive Living Group'. With my nerves jangling and several visits to the loo, I was brave enough to stand up and speak from my heart; I was able to give people hope, to show them that there is light at the end of the dark tunnel – and to teach people that we all have a choice! Whatever situation we are in, however dark and scary and painful it may be, we can choose to try and find something positive on which to focus. I love teaching people about the 'Law of Attraction', and how our thoughts become things, helping them to understand how they can attract abundance into every area of their life just by changing the way they think and speak. I have since spoken at many events, helping to share the gift of hope, positivity and love. No more fear, just excitement and joy.

Being more in the public eye, I realised that I had another big issue that needed my attention – I was really conscious of my body and my appearance. My weight had gone up by four stone from lack of exercise following my surgery; I had started to hate the look of my body in the mirror, all the blubber and cellulite, my fat face and double chin and my tummy hanging over the top of my caesarean scar – just horrible. I stupidly told myself I was ugly and fat on a daily basis, reinforcing it over and over again. It's incredible how as teachers of positive energy and the 'Law of Attraction', we don't always practice what we teach! I self-sabotaged by eating unhealthy food and chose not to push past the pain to walk a little bit further! But I then realised that we have to go through these things, before we can realise what's happening, and simply wait for that light-bulb moment to occur again. My sensible head has now kicked in, with a realisation that my body is absolutely fine just as it is, right now. I'm learning to love my body again, as it is, lumps and all. I'm starting to accept my body's appearance, with gratitude that I still have all my limbs and organs, and can function normally. I've chosen to call my blubber my 'deliciously sexy curves', and am starting to truly love myself again. I know that I can't expect anyone else to love me until I truly love myself, so my life is still a work in progress, and that's my current project!

I now look back and realise that the tough challenges I faced throughout my life happened for a reason: they were all huge life lessons which helped me to grow into the person I am today. They gave me a choice: I could either remain 'stuck' in the darkness, or I could celebrate my life with positivity and love. I chose to change my lenses; I took off the dark glasses and focused on everything that is right in the world, instead of what is wrong. I chose to see a world full of possibility and to fall in love with life all over again. I chose to turn my obstacles into opportunities and to celebrate my wonderful new life with joy and wonder.

I have now truly arrived… I am at home in my heart, doing what I love, living an authentic life and helping so many people along the way. Loving what I do…loving life…!

Biography

Working with reiki for many years has created a deep passion for my healing work – now the love of my life. In addition to my reiki energy healing, I also believe that healing with words is incredibly effective, and my therapy therefore includes an element of 'life guidance': educating people to understand their energy, and how it affects them and everyone around them, is crucial if they have a desire to truly heal themselves in every aspect of their lives.

I am also a 'healing artist', producing inspirational channeled art, infused with love and reiki energy healing. My art has proven very popular as it continues to provide healing to the people viewing it or to the home in which it is displayed.

My Healing Art Workshops, and Healing Collage Workshops, are aimed at supporting and encouraging emotional healing through reiki, positive energy, art and creative self-expression for those living with pain, grief, fear, frustration, anger, anxiety, self-limiting beliefs, stress and so much more.

I now also run beautiful spiritual retreats, incorporating mindfulness, healing, stillness and reflection. These special adventures provide a totally immersive experience, allowing you to get out of your head and into your heart, bringing people together in a loving, safe space in order to heal, learn and grow.

www.jackiehowchin.com

Liz Clegg

When Liz saw the refugee crisis in Calais she knew she had to act. Thinking she could just go and deliver tents, blankets and first aid, she never thought she would end up staying. Opening the 'unofficial women and children's centre' was the next step in this incredible woman's work with asylum seekers and refugees. She is a true champion of these people, a feisty humanitarian who stands up to the system and makes a massive difference to many.

WHAT'S THE NAME OF THE POLITICIAN who died? Tessa Jowell. She was the first to visit Calais. It was hell back then; you remember what it was like. Anyway, she wants to come and visit the women and children's centre and I'm thinking, great. Come and have a look. See what your government is ignoring. It was a big deal. A turning point really, when people like her started to take notice.

Of course on the day Mohammad, Ghazan and Izat are hanging around the centre. These little Afghan boys are all twelve years old and unaccompanied. Great kids but volatile as you can imagine. So I'm thinking to myself, oh god, this could go either way. So I say to the boys, don't act too crazy. "Little crazy, not big crazy." This is 'important lady' I tell them. "Yes Liz. No big crazy Liz." The three of them nod along like angels. I think oh dear, that's not a good sign. But we have a no exclusion policy so that's just how it is. And anyway this is the jungle. Where am I going to tell them to go?

Tessa arrives with her entourage and we go inside to talk. A couple of the women are warming themselves by the fire. Nice Syrian ladies, very polite. Articulate. They tell their stories. Horrible. Emotional. The kind of stories politicians and journalists are open to hearing. Well, I hear a banging noise outside and I already know it's over. Mohammad is climbing up the outside of the centre shouting "Puck you!" I'm trying to keep a straight face and Tessa is looking at me thinking, is this ok? Well, there's a twelve year old on the roof having a tantrum so not quite. Soon the boys are tearing apart the building. I say building; it's really a tent. The illusion of safety. You forget that sometimes. Canvas plonked on mud. The whole camp was made out of sticks and stones and sewage and there are unaccompanied children living here going out of their minds. Mohammad is kicking off because he hasn't eaten in a while or someone's stolen his sleeping bag or some other factor that equates to horror in a place like this. So we evacuate. Tessa Jowell's in shock but nothing shocks me anymore. And I think I must be crazy. I've bloody lost it. We all lost it by the end. The refugees and the volunteers. Only difference is, we could leave.

I had the perfect storm of life skills to respond the crisis: I'm a trained firefighter, I lived on a traveller site, I'd worked with children. Troubled children. I think I had vaguely heard about Calais in the news but not to the full extent. I hadn't had a telly in god knows how long. But I saw this magazine when I was at Glastonbury festival working on the biggest litter pick on the planet. It had pictures of the church in the jungle. And I just thought I could go there and help. Just go and deliver stuff. And it's only in Calais. How far is that?

I Googled it and found out who was working there. I rang round. Found a French charity. They had started to take donations and they were overwhelmed. I thought I would just sort out the donations and get them back on track. I took wellies, I think. And then first aid. Anything in the shed at Glastonbury. Rob and Emily and people said "Yeah yeah, help yourself." And we started. They gave us loads of the old crew t-shirts to sell. So that's what kind of made me go. Without ever thinking I was going to stay.

The living conditions were horrendous. They had a few marquees up for mass sleeping. But the numbers were way over, and were going up and up and up and we were headed towards winter. People weren't getting enough food. They didn't have enough showers. They didn't have sleeping accommodation. And the official women's centre wasn't fully being used because people were fearful. Everyone thought you had to give your fingerprints, so women weren't accessing that facility. That winter…the number of people turning up: it was insanity. Every night, huge numbers of refugees arriving with nothing. You couldn't walk away; I'd been there about two months when I thought I needed to do something more permanent. Around September 2015 we opened the 'unofficial women and children's centre'. From there we distributed clothes and essentials. Created a drop-in centre for the little kids – a bit of respite for the mums. We became a jungle staple.

When I first met Sarbaz he was in a ditch having a fight. I fed him. I just remember feeding him. He was like a rabid dog. Watching with one eye, but stuffing his face. He ate way too much chicken rice. I said, "No, you're going to hurt yourself" because he was skinny. So skinny. Still is skinny. He came with me. I brought him food and it was gob-smacking watching him. He was just so hungry. You just watched him and go wow that's not right, the way he was. He was just watching you like a dog. A wild dog you give meat to. Everyone hated him. Gave me grief. Why do you help him? He's no good. It wasn't that he was no good; he was so little, too little to be living this crazy life. He was like a wild animal; he slept anywhere.

When Sarbaz first got to the United Kingdom I stayed with him for a few weeks to get him into social care. I was going back and forth to Calais to manage the women's centre. But he couldn't cope. I don't think any of us really thought it through, what it would be like for the littlies arriving, getting out of the back of a lorry, and just finding themselves here? None of us thought that through, did we? There was a sense of community in Calais, a sense of belonging; so many of them were there for nearly a year. Many of the younger Afghan kids were there for a considerable amount of time and it doesn't take long for children to create a community and a sense of everything around them and obviously they had us, didn't they? That's when I first became aware of the asylum system here, especially for kids and I realised how cruel it was. And then I knew that the work didn't stop in Calais.

We opened the Meena Centre in Birmingham to respond to the practical needs of asylum seekers and refugees. We connect them to local support networks. Direct them towards advocacy and professional legal advice. Provide emotional and psychological support. We're busy round the clock. Somebody said, "Oh my god, how can you run a whole building? This that and the other…" and I kind of go, "Well, to be honest, you know… I was trained to walk up to a building and manage something and that building was on fire." This place is not on fire. Yet.

The Geneva Convention, which is what asylum seeking is based on, is about allowing people to arrive in a country and claim protection. And yet we've named that whole process hostile. A 'hostile environment'. It's not rocket science to see how that doesn't work. We know the damage this causes to people on arrival. There has to be some kind of compassion here to greet people who are suffering trauma, as opposed to using this against people, discrediting people on every mistake they make in very stressful interviews and processes which are used against them to undermine their entire claim, as opposed to recognizing some really basic notions about the traumatised mind. Every psychologist, every mental health service provider, recognizes that the traumatised mind has difficulty talking and expressing any kind of linear or logical experience. Recall and memory is seriously impaired. It's very difficult to verbalize what's gone on, so you're not going to get a particularly good interview from the most needy. The system is actually prejudiced against the most vulnerable, because obviously the ones who are less traumatized, who have suffered less, are probably capable of getting through an interview without making any tiny little mistake – which month or exactly where or when or what something happened, because their minds functioning better.

Young people arrive here and often get 'age accessed'. If they are judged over eighteen they're put into adult accommodation. Many appeal and win their age dispute. In the meantime they've just spent however long out of education and living with adult males in G4S (a security services company) run accommodation. Who would you trust as an accommodation provider for people fleeing from torture and horrendous loses and journeys and conflict? When did G4S ever win a compassion award? So the young people just disengage completely. They react to the 'hostile environment'. And the Home Office is saying, "Well they won't engage." Why's that then? Tortured, you know. Abandoned. Exploited. Aggressively age assessed. Start drinking. Self-medicating. It's second on the list of symptoms of post-traumatic stress: self-medicating. So why's that a surprise? And why is it being used against young people? We're not providing mental health care. And we're not providing a trauma recovery setting. We're proving a hostile environment. Why are we surprised people are self-medicating? Or, worst-case scenario, committing suicide…like Alex. He won his age dispute, too late.

You don't become a fully-fledged competent adult at eighteen. They recognize that in the Children's Act. We would like that paralleled within the asylum process to safeguard young people, particularly borderline age-assessed young people. Recognize how many of them are winning their age assessments for god's sake. But outside of that, statistically eighteen to twenty-five year old males across the board are amongst highest risk of suicide in a lot of countries. Why the hell would you try to integrate when you're not welcome? When you're not supported. You are treated with distrust as a second-class kind of hostile 'thing'. How are we going to enable genuine integration and positive settlement here if we treat people like this and don't support them? What we want to see is the asylum process come in line with the Children's Act. Eighteen to twenty-five year olds seeking asylum should receive additional support and safeguarding.

We would like to see a young person's welfare officer in all initial accommodation alongside more willingness from local authorities to step in if a 'young person' is potentially a child. But nine out of ten times they go, "Not our problem." And the young person faces a drawn out court battle. The Home Office is the lead: the one thing throughout the whole situation that these young people have is that they are under immigration control. In my opinion the Home Office officials are the ones who have to lead the situation to provide meaningful safeguarding. Documenting this and that. Making it public is a part of what we try to do.

We have destitute women turning up. Literally destitute. Many don't speak English. Some also quite elderly: one last week, she looked about sixty-five. That was awful. Turned up drenched and we just put her to sleep on the sofa, gave her a cup of tea, dried her clothes off. We got a translator and started asking questions. Gently. Does she have any chance of any kind of fresh claim? Then it's onto the various charities that will house destitute women. You have a good chance of getting a claim in they can help. Failing that, you're stuffed. It's community hosting.

At the moment we limit the use of the building for children and young people unaccompanied and we do a lot of outreach. Relentless. Just one case takes forever; many hours to support one person. And then there are the 'randoms' who you find on the street. Found one young person who'd been sleeping for two months on the street. Says he's sixteen, ended up in adult accommodation. God knows what went on but G4S kicked him out. No safeguarding. No. We're shutting the door in your face even though you look really young, really confused. We're just going to shut the door in your face. And he ended up two months on the street. We spent days going to social services, trying to find a route through for him. Find a host. He didn't have a clue. He's sleeping rough on the street going, "I'm waiting for my interview." And you're going, well where was your letter? How are you going to find out about your interview? "Oh, they're going to send a letter." "But where to? You're sleeping on the street." He was just out of it all and the home officer shut his case, had him down as absconding. What happened was G4S had kicked him out and so he was oblivious. And he was really young. Worryingly young. Supporting them and documenting it all and trying to go through procedures that we know don't work just so we can document it – that takes weeks.

I was with one lady – she just rang up and went "I'm sick." She was destitute. G4S had kicked her out. Shouldn't have done, it was illegal. Onto the street three days before she gives birth. I was delivering baby stuff to that hostel, she was there and they were kicking her out. "Where are you going?" "Oh, they're going to send me here." "They can't send you there, that's the homeless place. You can't do that. They won't house you." So we spent four hours in children's services, going "She's about to give birth," and they said "Well come back when she does," and kicked us out. Eventually we got her into a charity home and then she rang me as she went into labour. It all went wrong. No heartbeat. They rushed her into theatre and it was horrible and she was terrified, I couldn't leave. Suddenly I'm putting on scrubs thinking "Dead babies. I don't want to do that. Oh my god." And the baby was born and he was all right. For some reason they thought I was her mother; someone said "Granny, hold the baby."

The entire system is disjointed. You can look at these ridiculous departments and processes and there's no cohesion, no staff who know what they're talking about so the top politicians, *they* produce the hostile environment. As you filter through various parts of that organization there are so many mixed messages. 'Drive to integrate.' 'British values', that kind of thing. They are really pushing that but in another department 'HOSTILE' and in another department '18 = ADULT. Do it yourself.' There are a lot of mixed messages from many different departments all pushing for different agendas that don't co-ordinate. And it's not rocket science to sit down and say "Perhaps you want to co-ordinate yourselves and come up with a holistic approach to this? The current situation doesn't work, you know?"

When people arrive in the United Kingdom they become invisible. Back in Calais there was public interest. Here, you think they're in the process so they're ok, but in reality, it's very different. People are held inside a very abusive process in incredibly poor accommodation with very little support. The only support they're really getting is from non-government officials scattered across the country, trying to highlight that women are being indefinitely detained or being made destitute, when we could offer a fair, dignified process that safeguards women or people in a meaningful way.

Life's difficult enough for British people. Imagine arriving here to an unrecognizable culture, not speaking the language or understanding the processes, not realising the poverty experienced even by British people. The struggle is about everyone, not just asylum seekers. We should be fighting for meaningful health: extra health services for the British people – and fight against homelessness. Better education: that is an on-going struggle, an on-going political fight. We have to recognize that asylum seekers are part of that struggle and we have to include them in it.

The kids from Calais who made it here are scattered all over. Some of them are alright. Well, none of them are really alright. We forget, don't we?

There's a real hippy poem called 'On children' by Kahlil Gibran, which begins:

'Your children are not your children' and part of a verse says:

> You may give them your love but not your thoughts,
> For they have their own thoughts.
> You may house their bodies but not their souls,
> For their souls dwell in the house of tomorrow.

I've thought that with my own kids – that they're nothing to do with me. What a child needs is kind of some kind of foundation. What you give your kids is roots and wings. That's what you do, isn't it? Psychologically and emotionally, you give them a sense of loyalty, a sense that there is an anchor, which then gives them the freedom to fly. Loyalty. It doesn't have to be over-emotional. It's something that's quite functional isn't it? To give somebody that sense of loyalty, then by default they will feel some kind of value. Which psychologically is quite important.

It was very distressing witnessing Sarbaz in the care system. Really. Profoundly. So I agreed to take him on. Got the house. And here we are. I thought I'd be retired on a beach in Thailand by now. Instead I'm living in Birmingham fostering an Afghan teenager with issues. Still, he made me a cup of tea this morning.

You have to laugh.

www.meenacentre.org

Sali Green

A quirky little girl whose parents broke up when she was just two and a half, Sali has always felt loved, however security and stability were sadly missing in her childhood. Constant anxiety developed into panic attacks and phobias. Lack of self-esteem and frequent self-sabotage led Sali to experiment with many means of self-help from dream therapy to booze before she finally found a diagnosis and a therapist who has enabled Sali to thrive and live a stable, joyful life.

I'M A CREATURE OF CONTRADICTIONS AND extremes. I love luxury and simplicity, indulgence and frugality, minimalism and possessions, town and country, natural and glamorous; I've lived in a manor and also in a squat and a fifty-pound caravan…you get the picture.

I've spent most of my life in Gloucestershire, peppered with a decade of living in London. My career has been unconventional, including pot-washer, glass-collector, waitress, sign-writer, cloakroom attendant, market stall-holder, retail assistant, DJ, blogger, project secretary, director's secretary, a few bursts of multi-level marketing, human resources administrator, office manager, medical secretary, charity fundraiser, graphic designer, events co-coordinator, social media content creator, carer for my Nanna and magazine and newspaper columnist, which all led to where I am now. I've also done a spot of modeling and have a huge love for music. My main hobbies are dancing, cooking, social media, art, literature, films, long walks with dogs, and I am partial to festivals and street food.

These days I'm self-employed and run an online directory; a brand ambassador for over one hundred independent businesses and an over forties blogger. Does reading that introduction make you feel as weary as it does me? Well take a breath, grab a coffee (or juice if you are into healthier choices) or push the boat out with a nice glass of wine or a refreshing gin and tonic and get comfortable for my brief contribution to 'Women of Spirit'.

I feel honoured to be included among such accomplished, brave and magnificent women and I hope that you find something within my story too that reminds you how far you yourself have come and what good things are in store for you. I also hope that you will find comfort in my progress with anxiety and that if you're struggling yourself, you'll feel assured that it's going to get better for you. I write as I would speak from one friend to another – it's not super-intellectual or cultural, but it's written with love and good intention. Susie Mackie is a wonderful, gentle and approachable woman with her own inspiring story, and I am thankful that she's bringing us together in this way to help inspire more women.

Roots

I was born in Cheltenham in 1969 to two baby-boomers: my father was from Birmingham and my mother from Nottingham. Dad's father

Horace was in the rag trade and Mum's father, known as Bill, was a Major in the army, with both their mothers being housewives, or to use the more modern term, 'stay-at-home mums'. Dad's dad did very well with his ladies' clothing shop in King's Heath.

Mum's Cornish grandparents were mild and understated people who lived a quiet and simple life. Gampy was a talented pen and ink artist and many years ago he set up a community centre for war veterans and out-of-work chaps to visit instead of drowning their sorrows in the pub. His drop-in centre provided tea and friendship to men who would otherwise be tearing their hair out if they stayed home feeling useless. In his garden he grew peonies and roses and he was a kind soul who bore an uncanny resemblance to Stan Laurel of Laurel and Hardy. All I remember of Nanny is that she gave me my first bowl of Coco Pops and I liked hanging out in her bedroom sitting at her dressing table looking at strings of beads and old perfume bottles. The dressing table has been a longstanding tradition our family, with Nanna and mum enjoying theirs too and always taking pride in their appearances. Mum says that 'Make-up is to enhance your natural beauty'.

Mum's other grandparents where snooty, aloof and well-to-do, with lashings of craziness, or to use more politically correct terminology: we have a history of mental health issues from our lineage on that side. They also invented Crouch Cars, which was one of the first ever makes of car. My Nanna (mum's mum) Marjorie Crouch was the essence of love, but only to family or a very select few people whom she liked. She suffered from things that were never diagnosed or spoken of in those days, namely agoraphobia and anxiety. I know she did, because I have experienced those unpleasant ailments myself and I know the behaviour exhibited.

Childhood

My parents split when I was about two and a half. Each claims that the other was unfaithful. I'm not going to side with either of them or pass judgement. They both know how I feel, which is that I absolutely adore them, so there's no need for having to choose a side. Not that you realise that when you're little. As a child from a 'broken home' you are constantly torn and wracked with guilt about loving or favouring either one or enjoying their company. What I've learned over the years is that people do the best with what they have at the time, and everything, and I mean *everything*, is about intentions. What lasts the longest is love, while other memories fade away, and I always felt loved. However, and there is no blame or bitterness here, I didn't feel the security required to grow into a stable child. I felt that nothing was in my control, and from here my anxieties, fears and phobias began to set in. When I was on form, though, I was really on form. A quirky, funny little girl who loved to write stories, do accents and impressions, act the fool and show off, and pretend to interview people with an old-fashioned tape recorder. I also loved animals. I felt like I didn't really fit in anywhere, but in the company of animals this was never a concern. Dogs understand our emotions better than we might give them credit for, I think.

The break-up was neither smooth nor easy; in fact it was decidedly rocky. My dad is a very highly-strung person and mum very sensitive. The heady combination of nature and nurture took me on a scary spiral during which I felt out of control and adopted a victim mentality. I had problems with food, socialising, school, shops (particularly supermarkets), restaurants, travel and basically everything. I developed a case of anxiety so severe that it didn't stop at meltdowns and panic attacks. It was all encompassing, covering fears, phobias, weird behaviour and obsessive-compulsive disorder. I've had agoraphobia, emetophobia and social phobia, and generally my panics would manifest in tears streaming down my face, getting very hot, and either heaving or actually throwing up, which is not a good look, especially when in public. The vomiting thing is why I became, for a while, addicted to travel tablets as a child. When I say addicted, I didn't take tons of them, I just had to have one every day in order to venture into the outside world and particularly onto the school bus. By the time I got to my teenage years and it was all so overwhelming for me, my mum and I started exploring counselling and therapies. So began my journey of self-development.

During my childhood mum and I returned to live with my grandparents a few times because in the early years mum was unfortunate enough to meet some unsuitable suitors and it took a while to find where we belonged. Well actually only one was horribly unpleasant: he cheated on her and was harsh and mean with me. Dead now. (We didn't kill him.) We moved around a fair bit. My folks did everything they could to give me a good education and spend quality time with me. I have loads of good memories. Mum had to work long hours and Nanna was always there to be my 'extra mummy'. I was incredibly loved and I'm thankful. My mother is beautiful: she attracted men like wasps around lemonade, and it was only when she got together with Michael that she discovered what consistency and loyalty is all about. Michael represents home. Michael has been her rock since they got together in the 1980s and they've thrived together all the way from there and watched the family grow. He is warm, fair and supportive. They now have nine grandchildren from my siblings and their partners. (I don't generally use the terms 'step' or 'half' unless asked where and how we all fit in.)

Dad met Vicky in the 1970s when I was five. I remember their first date, because I was on it too. Vicky's hair was swept up into a bun with a few wisps falling freely down her neck and she had a big German Shepherd dog, Zorba, with whom I bonded. On a summer's evening Dad took us to a pub by a river near Tewkesbury and I questioned Vicky the whole time; he hardly got a word in. The relationship blossomed and she swiftly became one of the main female role models and influences in my life along with mum and Nanna; I know I can turn to her too. Dad and Vicky have three more children, all now grown and accomplished, and two grandchildren.

To this day my parents still intensely dislike each other, but thankfully now that I'm a grown-up there is hardly any cause for their worlds to collide or overlap.

Off the Rails

So now I've set the scene here's what I did next: I went off the rails. I had a series of chaotic, turbulent and damaging relationships, a rollercoaster of a social life, enough heartbreak to write a book about and two near rape misses because of my unwise decisions and naivety. But another thing I've learned over the years is to focus on the *now*, and to put good things in place for the future. Writing about our woes can be therapeutic yet it's also not for dwelling on too long. I think I was a very broken person for a very long time and was always searching and often lonely even when in company. I always had people who loved me yet still I had this huge emptiness and lack of self-esteem. I'd get glimpses of confidence, fabulous opportunities, meaningful friendships, and usually I'd fuck them all up by sabotaging them. I still have best friends from school and I can't tell you how much I bloody well appreciate them. My parents and step-parents were always supportive but it was hard for them to understand what was going on because the grey and dark periods were so intense and hard to articulate and explain.

One such period was the time I got pregnant. An awful predicament presented itself. I was with a man to whom I felt very close, however had a sense deep down that we weren't going to be each other's long term soul mates. I had to decide whether to keep the baby despite all my fears and mental health issues, and be an unmarried mum with who-knows-what ahead, or to give myself a clean slate and fresh start and find my direction on my own before committing to bringing another human into the world. I chose the first option no matter how scary it was going to be. It was a baby boy. His dad Pete is a great, hands-on dad, and our son Joe is a joy to many people; he's intelligent and humorous and loves animals, particularly dogs. He is a treasure with a beautiful personality and he's definitely my greatest achievement, and will no doubt do special things and bring something positive and meaningful to the world whatever he chooses to do.

The Journey

During my darker days I grasped at anything I thought would ease my anxiety and help me learn to live a 'normal' life. I've tried so many things it's hard to remember them all, so here's a list off the top of my head:

- Jungian dream therapy
- NHS counselling
- NLP (Neuro Linguistic Programming)
- Private counselling
- Valium
- Booze
- Self-help books
- Christianity (Born Again, of course!)
- Hypnotherapy
- Holistic therapies
- Meditation

- Mindfulness
- Martial Arts
- Yoga

I've always felt a curiosity and fondness for words of wisdom and a gradual awakening to energy, signs and intuition. Somewhere along that path a wonderful thing happened: I woke up. I realised that everything happens in its own time and flow, and things don't need to be as hard as we are making them. Everything we do in the way of self-care becomes part of the jigsaw puzzle of our lives. We know when we've found something that fits right, and we need all sorts of different pieces to make the full picture emerge.

At a point where I got together with someone really special, Mark, I realised I was going to have to get a handle on all this shit and my ridiculous behaviour. The desperate times of anxiety or depression whose sinewy grasp I would fall in and out of like a damn rollercoaster were crippling and confining like a prison. First step, I got a medical diagnosis. Turns out I had 'Generalised Anxiety Disorder'. I was so pleased to finally be able to define it I almost felt excited that it was actually *something*, and better still, something that might be able to be treated either with medication or therapy. I had a choice whether to get a prescription of 'happy pills' from the doctor, or go the long and hard way round and get therapy with a psychologist. I rang a therapist whom I'd had the good fortune to meet through my business, and asked if she could help me. She said I should give it two sessions of therapy before I made the decision whether or not to go on the drugs, and she assured me we would be able to make progress and see the light at the end of the tunnel. Her words were: "Don't go on medication. Give me two weeks!" So I signed up for mindset coaching. By the time I'd decided to go for it, the appointment couldn't come soon enough. I virtually crawled there.

I have never looked back and I didn't go on medication. You have to work hard and do as the therapist instructs, and really commit to learning the tools and techniques for dealing with and overcoming anxiety, but it is highly possible. For me anyway, it has been successful beyond my wildest dreams. My newfound confidence filters down into every area of my life – relationships, work and self-development. I'm thriving in a way that surprises and excites me and I want to share it.

Of course, my partner attributes my recovery to being with *him*, and I have to admit that's a very big part of it. Just as my mum found her warm, dependable Cancerian, I found mine too. The story is still unfolding, and I will continue to write about it in my blog www.saligreen.co.uk/blog. I write about anxiety, confidence, love, positivity, mindset, lifestyle and business and I do videos on YouTube. Menopause next – oh joy! I rarely write about parenting because I feel I still have so much to learn, but my son and my partner's kids, and our unofficial foster son, are undoubtedly all going to feature at some point. And anyway, in the words of my son, "You're a terrible parent!"

I've also learnt to practise gratitude, accept compliments and believe in myself. I'm loving, empathetic, determined and creative and I have lots still to say and do. I have my directory and blog and have brought out my own organic skincare range. I'm also writing a book and run some large groups on Facebook. I've crowd funded enough money to successfully put four more people through therapy. These things never cease to amaze me, when I consider the fearful, nervous little girl and awkward woman I used to be.

Thank you so much for reading. I encourage you to explore your strengths, increase your good habits and skills, and to open up and communicate as you walk your own unique path, because we are stronger together.

Love Sal xxx

www.saligreen.co.uk
www.saligreenskincare.co.uk
www.iwork4uglos.co.uk
My therapist is Lorna Mumford 'The Mindset Coach'
www.yourmindsetcoach.co.uk

Sandra K Clarke

A rebel and a tomboy, Sandra felt she didn't fit in at school, seeing herself as an outsider, leading to feelings of disempowerment. Challenged with the concept of 'power' for much of her life, Sandra has discovered the greatest power of all – that of 'true power' within herself, which she sees as acting with integrity and passion, and sharing from the heart. She now works on strengthening this and on helping others do the same.

I RECENTLY TURNED FIFTY AND, AT about the same time, was invited to contribute to this amazing book, '*Women of Spirit*'. These two occurrences made me question how I came to be where I am today, and what has driven me here. As I look back over my life, I find there are two common themes: 'perseverance' and 'power'.

I spent the early years of my life rebelling against power, or what I perceived it to be. In my thirties, my understanding of power changed; I started to embrace my personal, feminine power and began using it to my best abilities.

My first experience of power was when I was about ten or eleven years old at secondary school. During my first term there, I found myself only mixing with the boys. Girls and boys categorically did not speak to each other *at all*, so, consequently, I didn't really get to know the girls. I admit I was always a tomboy, but I normally got on with girls too. In hindsight, I suspect that I sensed something was off with the girls but wasn't consciously aware of it. By the second term, I did everything I could to fit in with the girls and make friends with them. It wasn't easy; they allowed me into their group, but they often teased me during sports lessons and ditched me on the way home. I suppose today we'd call this bullying and although I'd never say it was serious bullying, it was certainly uncomfortable. To me, it was further confirmation that I didn't belong or fit in.

As it happened, I was Jewish, which was still an issue in Austria in the 1970s. The first time I felt detached from others was in primary school, and this feeling was provoked by a number of different circumstances. The priest who taught religion, for example, told me I was a 'nobody' because I hadn't been baptised and that because of this, my first name didn't really count. I always associated feelings of detachment and discomfort with power. School, teachers and the majority had the power and I felt suppressed and pushed aside by them: I felt like a 'nobody', an outsider, someone who was different and didn't belong. So at the beginning of secondary school when I was experiencing these same feelings, I automatically associated them with having a lack of power which I believed stemmed from being Jewish. I'm not sure now whether that had anything to do with it, but I was certainly different to those girls – they definitely held power over me, and this was a form of power I did not like. Interestingly, my grades slipped during that time, but neither my parents nor I ever thought that the two might be related. I don't think my parents even knew what was going on. I didn't think much of it; that's just what they were like, and you just had to get on with it.

The Austrian school system was a very authoritarian one in those days so the other power I rebelled against was the teachers. My parents taught me that the teachers were always right because they controlled your grades and if you didn't play the game, stay quiet and agree with them, it would affect your grades. I don't think it will surprise you to learn that I also got into trouble with them, as I always asked questions and wanted to understand *why* things worked in a certain way. They didn't approve of the constant questions and it left me feeling awkward, out of step with my surroundings, and powerless.

However, in the summer of 1979 my parents sent me to England for four weeks to live with an English family and learn English. My mother was born in London, and my father grew up in Cheltenham, so speaking English properly was very important to them both. Before I left, they started discussing sending my younger brother and me to the International School in Vienna. At first, I had vehemently refused to leave my school, yet once I came back from England, I changed my mind and asked them whether they could make the school change happen. Again, I wouldn't have been able to say why at the time, but I think that I found the long holiday in England liberating; I grew my independence (being away from your family when you're eleven for that length of time is a big step) and I had fun! I seemed to be accepted and was liked without judgement. It opened up the possibility that there could be a different life. I found English easy to learn; not surprisingly, I suppose, as I had been hearing it at home from a young age.

So, two days before the beginning of the new term, my parents moved us to the Vienna International School, a private school in part funded by the United Nations. While it was a private school, it was very different to the private schools here in the United Kingdom. The vast majority of children did not come from wealthy families, but from UN employees, other diplomatic staff or ex-pat families where the businesses paid for the school. There were around fifty different nationalities and there was no single majority: this meant that there was no power base and there was no 'normal'. The school's environment was so refreshing and inspirational, and the memories I made there have stayed with me my whole life. I've even kept in touch with the majority of my friends; it has always held a special place in our hearts. For the next six years, I had a wonderful time learning. I opened my mind and broadened my experiences. The school encouraged us to ask 'why', and to *understand* what we were being taught rather than to just regurgitate it.

We had times when we argued passionately against certain school rules; I remember walking into the headmaster's office with great purpose to argue against some new rule that had been imposed. He listened carefully to me, asked me to clarify my position further and took me seriously. In the end, the rule remained in place, but the simple fact that he treated me with respect and took my viewpoint seriously was enough for me. It never was about winning, but always about being treated as an equal and with respect. This school largely did that and it gave me an insight into how life can work when we treat each other as equals, no matter where we come from. I didn't realise it then, but many years later, when I began to consciously step into my power, I brought my experiences from that time back into my life and used them as a benchmark for my own conduct.

There was another form of power to which I was exposed, and which I rejected: the complacency and arrogance which comes with status and money. I associated power with (generally white) men who were complacent, had a degree of arrogance, or at the very least a sense of superiority (even if they claimed they didn't). I rebelled against all of that. I swore I wouldn't get married, and most certainly not to one of the sons of these people. As a result, I had some 'interesting' relationships that were never going to go anywhere far. I didn't want to fit into that world: sit back comfortably with a wealthy husband in a city where everybody seemed to know each other, where I was the 'daughter of...' and would end up being the 'wife of...' I rebelled against the system as a whole. I started a degree in architecture but didn't get very far with it. The intention was to use architecture to get into interior design, but once again I felt very similar to the way I did in my first secondary school – I didn't really understand how the other students thought and worked. Two years in, I acknowledged defeat, gave up and kept looking for the right thing to do. Eventually, my parents put their foot down (seeing as they were paying for all of this) and insisted I needed to either knuckle down with a degree and do it properly or get a job. I was torn at the time. I had an idea of what I wanted to do but couldn't quite find the right route to get me there. I decided I just needed to do *something*. I really wanted to study interior design but couldn't find the right course, so I decided to shelve my dreams and be practical. For some reason, I chose to do an apprenticeship as a beauty therapist as this was still a fairly creative profession. I liked the idea of doing make-up and, during my time there, I came up with a few interesting directions I could take it to make it more exciting for me.

However, I still ended up rebelling against 'power'. The power in this case came from my family and close friends who all told me that I would never complete the apprenticeship as I was incapable of sticking to anything. Their attitudes need to be explained a bit more as they might sound quite harsh and uncaring. My parents both came from families with very little money and they worked incredibly hard to give us the lifestyle and education we had been enjoying. They were worried that I had become spoilt and was one of those children that would never work properly, so their fairly harsh statement came from that fear. I understand that now, but obviously couldn't see it at the time: back then, their lack of faith in me hurt. I come from a very loving and close-knit family, so all our issues and experiences were discussed openly amongst us – something that's horrendous for a teenager trying to find their own space and independence. It also meant that 'the family' had a lot of power, at least in my perception, as it felt to me as if they were all successful and on-track and I was the odd one out, the one who was lost. I couldn't get my feelings across at the time as they weren't that clear. Despite this, my family tried to help me the way they thought was best and that was to put pressure on me. And it worked: once again I rebelled – they said I'd never finish it, so needless to say I did.

During those two years, I had some truly mind-shifting conversations with people who inspired me, which taught me a few things. First, I needed to leave Vienna as I felt suffocated and stuck in this close-knit, comfortable and complacent environment (again things I associated with power) and second, I could turn anything into something exciting and interesting by taking it in a direction which suited me. As my family thought I was never going to finish the apprenticeship, I used this as a bargaining chip. I knew what needed to change, so I got my father to agree that if I finished my apprenticeship, I would be allowed to study abroad should I find a university that would take me.

Here is where perseverance began to emerge as a strength I didn't know I had: for the first year of my apprenticeship, I was still very much holding on to my student lifestyle. I went out a lot, met up with my friends and also enjoyed the freedom of not having to spend my evenings studying. But, by the beginning of my second year, I'd made this deal with my father, so I decided to set myself a very disciplined schedule where I would give myself one evening and one weekend-day off per week. The rest of the time, I would stay home and work on my portfolio – and so I did just that. When it was completed, I sent it to four universities in the United States, United Kingdom and Switzerland, and was accepted into three of them: I ended up picking Goldsmiths College in London. It was another lesson to follow my heart, to do what I believed in, not listen to the 'powers' and to get to where I wanted to go. I was encouraged to go to New York by many, as that was the school with the highest reputation, but Goldsmiths offered a new course that was different and ground-breaking and it turned out to be the right decision for me. My real friends stuck by me and were really proud of me and the effort I had put into it. The rest just dropped away, as they never had been real friends anyway. They felt that me prioritising my work and education was me snubbing and rejecting them. My family was incredibly proud and really rallied around me. Their criticism before was not something they held onto; it was a response to where I was and, with hindsight, I have to thank them because if they hadn't upset me as much as they did at the time, I never would have stepped out of my comfort zone and knuckled down the way I did.

In 1990 I moved to London and my world opened. I felt truly liberated and explored attitudes and beliefs that were completely new to me; they were so different to the environment of complacency and power in which I had grown up. Unexpectedly, I stayed on after my degree and settled in London. I'd always assumed it would just be a stepping stone to Paris or New York, but I fell in love with London and spent my twenties there, having the time of my life. The design degree had clarified where my strengths lay, so I shifted from interior design to branding, then again to account management. I worked on perseverance during those years, committing to my journey and focusing on a goal. When I came out of university with my design degree, I rang almost all of the top one hundred design agencies in London, found out to whom to write, and sent in my curriculum vitae. I always followed up with telephone calls and got in touch with all the relevant recruitment agencies for that industry sector. It took about six months of freelancing and filling-in before I got my first job in a branding agency. I kept pushing and persevering until I was at a salary and management level I felt was right for me, which took about three years.

However, I was still battling against my perception of power. I played along with those in power and kept looking for another lifestyle, to see different values in action. Some might say I was naive or innocent, but I found the mercenary side of the industry quite frustrating. Using the language I now use, I would say the lack of authenticity and genuineness in branding and marketing was what put me off. One way or another, this brought me to Australia. My partner at the time and I went there to explore it for a while, with the intention of settling down (he was Australian and I could have settled with him as his common-law wife). But I was looking for a different lifestyle, one that wasn't controlled by big, powerful corporations. I explored, experienced and did a whole range of different things throughout the year I was in Australia. My partner left me within the first three months and moved to the United States, so I was there on my own, trying to work out what to do next. I'd only bought a one-way ticket and had just a few weeks' worth of money left, so I found myself some work and spent the remaining nine months seeing Australia as I worked my way around it. I deliberately chose a job completely outside my comfort zone and ended up as a groom for polo ponies, which I thoroughly enjoyed; it allowed me the time to completely review my own priorities and where I was going. The other thing that this allowed me to do was become a lot more self-aware. I embarked on a spiritual and personal development journey in earnest, something I had cautiously dipped a toe into before and is a journey I've been on ever since. I also began to change the way I thought about concepts such as 'power'. Working with horses is always a very grounding experience, and power is a big element of that relationship. They are such powerful beings and when we work with them, we need to embrace that power and engage them to collaborate with us, as force alone doesn't work. This is where I realised that collaboration, mutual love and respect can engage power in a very different way.

Once back in the United Kingdom at the end of that year, I took those experiences and decided to set up my own business – again to step away from the 'power' and work with people who were passionate and believed in what they were doing rather than those driven by status and money. I also continued to immerse myself in my spiritual and personal development; this was where I started making peace with power. During my personal development training, I began to realise that I'd always viewed power in a negative light. I started to understand that it could in fact be something very beautiful and compassionate. What I now call 'true power' is born out of respect and love for others. It's about being authentic and honest about your values, and who you are as a person. True power is acting with integrity and passion, sharing from the heart. Since then, I have been pursuing this form of power within myself: I'm working on strengthening it and becoming more and more powerful every day.

This form of power is also born out of a desire to help others and give them the power to achieve and do more; this has dominated my life for the last eighteen years. Initially, I used my marketing and branding business to do this and a few years in, changed and evolved my career path and bought into a multilevel marketing business, a business which focuses on giving power to people who don't necessarily feel they have any, whether that's because of a lack of health and energy, money or spare time in their lives. It is filled with highly successful people earning huge amounts of money, and who use this money and the time they have to volunteer, pay it forward and generally help others have a better life. This has truly changed my life at its very core, as putting all those things into practice in my own life has changed my way of seeing the world and working with others around me. Once again, perseverance comes into my story: everybody who has ever succeeded in a multilevel marketing business has shown immense perseverance. It takes time, focus, energy and patience to achieve your goals and it is something I admire in others and something I wish to strengthen and continue to grow in myself.

There have already been many ups and downs along the way; people attacking me for my choice to work within the industry of multilevel marketing, people questioning my decision to promote supplements, failures and rejections – consistently and continuously. Equally, people have come into my life with problems who have then improved their situation due to our collaboration. They went away healthier, stronger, with a clearer vision for their future, with more money and the knowledge that they have choices and options. That is the most powerful thing of all – knowing that others are one step closer to the lives they wish to have.

My journey is a long way from being over. There is so much more I've yet to do and so many people I have yet to reach. I'm still excited and still looking forward, aiming to change the world, one person at a time! When Susie first invited me to contribute to this book, I was hesitant as I haven't had any particular hardships in my life that I needed to overcome. So many of the other women featured have done such amazing things that I felt I might not have much of a story to share. Nevertheless, Susie encouraged me and reminded me what I *have* achieved and what I *have* done, so I agreed to write about it here.

There is no one moment in my life, no one turning point that changed my story from a negative into a positive. However, it has been a consistent, step-by-step development away from one form of power to another; one which I now proudly own and display wherever I can. I am powerful and I am proud to share this power with others and invite them to learn from me and from my experiences. Growth comes in many different forms and in many types of journeys. It has been quite a journey so far and I can't wait for what the next phase will bring.

Biography

Sandra Kanfer Clarke has spent more than twenty-five years in healthcare research and learned that the future for our health lies in prevention. She is passionate about educating people to help them make the right choices for themselves and their families.

She simultaneously worked in marketing and branding and this business background and experiences in both employment, freelance and self-employment led her to research different types of income streams that are compatible with a quality lifestyle. Network marketing, and USANA Health Sciences came out on top and Sandra now spends her time showing others how to create their ideal lives. Her mission is to change the world one person at a time and to show people that they are entitled and able to be and have the very best.

Recently, she began running health and wellness programmes that consist of workshops, one-on-one coaching and exercise and so provide people with all-round, holistic health support as well as vision and confidence building workshops. Sandra realises that you need confidence to embrace your vision to then take the steps you need to get you to your best life.

www.smadar.co.uk
www.smadarhealth.usana.com

Diana Brown

I am comforted by Diana's sympathetic but straight-talking thoughts on motherhood. Having sometimes said that 'a mother's guilt is born with the baby', I agree with Diana that the pressure put upon us by the media and our own unrealistic expectations can be tough to deal with.

Motherhood and failure.

Most 'failures' in life turn out not to matter. They cause momentary embarrassment or disappointment but in the grand scheme of things fade surprisingly quickly and often turn out to be blessings in disguise; they lead on to better things.

In old age, the time of reflection, true failures and successes are more obvious and for many women being a success as a mother matters most. Many of us consider ourselves to have made mistakes, got some of it right yet even with the phrase 'we've done our best' it was not good enough. We are not trained for motherhood, and neither are our children who ultimately become the judge and manifestation of our success or failure. It is, however, a partnership.

Designer babies don't exist even when the odds on sex, hair colour or sporting ability may now be selected. Children and circumstances are mainly a lottery and the hand we are dealt is happenchance. Nature is clever and we love our babies unconditionally when they arrive and promise ourselves that we will do our best to nurture and protect them come what may.

Each mother and baby is unique and presents an ever changing dynamic. The psychologists tell us that even children from the same family present different reactions and consequences. Thus those born 'special', needing more attention, energy or love than the majority, present challenges most of us wish not to or cannot imagine.

Those mums with sick or disabled children are dealt a heavy hand. It seems society does not want to involve themselves with other than perfect children, in case the malady rubs off on their own, which is an illogical yet instinctive response. Disability, however described is considered taboo, a dark secret before either the mother or child has begun the journey. I include fathers who take on the role of 'mother' in this instance because some have excellent nurturing instincts too.

All mothers want to be good mothers and there is a wealth of advice, too much in fact – enough to always prove you're wrong. For most of us, the well meant advice is enough to give us feelings of misgiving; only the super self-confident overcome this feeling of inadequacy.

As old age creeps up on me the idea of what's important in life changes – and with it my idea of failure. As a grandmother I reflect on the patterns of my behaviour. Although living in the moment, I can mull over past events without any need to change them. I see the snowball effect of the paths I chose.

Such a simple event as the trauma of a stillbirth at the age of twenty-one still has its memories for me despite being buried by time and common sense.

We can seldom do much about the big failures in our life because they are out of our control. I did not become the ballet dancer I trained to be, my husband left me, I never wrote that book, I failed an interview. Yes we can work on self-development exercises, but it's the ordinary everyday failures of things that we took for granted that other people seem to find easy or outwardly overcome that eat into our self-esteem. These failures reinforce our belief system and gather like flotsam in the wind. Before you know it you are a terrible cook, no good with children, especially other people's kids, no good at organising anything because it's bound to go wrong. Why do we buy into the myths of today that a perfect mum or child exists?

Mothers feel guilty all the time because we are surrounded by media telling us 'how to be a perfect mother' or about super mums who work in high powered jobs while looking after kids, cleaning the house, shopping and cooking nutritious food for all.

NO THEY DON'T! It's mission impossible except with loads of help. Most of us have to muddle through as best we can and remain calm and sweet tempered. And for most it's a twenty-four/seven role with no sick leave.

An example:

I always wanted to be a mum and have children but I got pregnant when young, before my life had really begun. Too soon, I thought, but lets get on with it. My, was I naive.

I was very healthy and so was the developing baby but at the beginning of the ninth month I woke up in the morning and didn't feel pregnant. "The baby is dead." I found myself telling the doctor. "That is a usual fear towards the end, since there is no room for the baby to move, but everything is fine," said the doctor at the teaching hospital.

Three weeks later contractions signaled the birth: and as I'd anticipated a dead baby girl was born/died. My Victoria was not to be. Starved of oxygen they said. It was better that she never was, since she would have been severely disabled or sick. I had no time to get to know her, because she was whisked away as she emerged into the world, never to be seen. I was removed to a remote part of the hospital in case I was infectious, where other misfits were placed. "What's wrong with you?" I was asked by a doctor.

Somehow the word stillbirth did not surface. Or was it also a live death? Silly things confused the issue. Do you register a birth and then a death? (Yes, you do register both). I received a letter in the post reminding me that it was a civil offence if I did not register the death. I felt an instant failure. I seemed to embarrass friends and neighbours alike, not knowing what to say. There are congratulation and welcome baby cards but somehow nothing for sorrow and death. It was easier for others to ignore me and avoid the issue.

Along with the shock came guilt: was it my fault? Was it divine justice, did I not deserve to be a mother? What to do with the presents, cot, pram, etcetera, now littering up the small flat. Deep sadness and sorrow took over from the excitement and the positive anticipation of before.

As they say, there is no book of instructions for the depression that consumed me. After about six months, my father, a silent but educated and wise man opened his hand to reveal a couple of pills. "If life is so hard take these pills…and if not it's time to just get on with life." I had not realised how numb I'd become but the obviousness of the alternatives presented made sense.

Now I am old, I reflect on the stillbirth and am angry at a society which does not have words to recognise the dilemma, neither the practical nor the emotional difficulties that occur. I was lucky that I had two children later but my subsequent pregnancies were full of fear that something would go wrong again or that they would die through my neglect.

I am apprehensive about my children. I also realise that I find myself apprehensive about anyone's pregnancies at a time when they are full of joy. It's difficult to be enthusiastic especially if they are unaware that things can go wrong. I am socially inept at such times. Reason has buried the dead as no longer relevant but my emotional memory never fades. Emotional isolation, and bereavement for someone I never knew shouldn't be dismissed as rationalisation takes over and life carries on. Yet my pregnancy was not an illness and so no medical discussion took place.

I felt I had failed my first daughter, that it was all my fault. I wanted reasons but my Victoria was not meant to be and nobody knew why.

I love being with kids, especially my grandchildren and cherish their very existence, treating each as a wonderful piece of magic.

I was lucky and went on to have two lively children and had 'a successful life' but that early failure always haunted me. I metaphorically held my breath waiting for my kids to be taken from me and while I wrote this account I burnt the soup. Was my subconscious telling me something?

It was forty-five years later when my grandson developed juvenile arthritis at the age of three. Irrationally I wondered if it was my bad fortune happening again but I will let my daughter tell you how she felt about the diagnosis and if my experience had affected her in any way.

I am currently writing a book 'The Creative Jungle' to share the insights and knowledge gained from a career as a University lecturer in Art and Design.

As a retired Art/Design University lecturer I have a special interest in the psychology of learning and creative thinking experienced in a practical setting – learning through doing. Teachers can only be catalysts to their students since we each perceive the world in our own unique way.

My mantra is that art (craft and design) and science are intertwined equally using our imagination and have a powerful social and cultural effect on each other. I hate the arbitrary divide society and education gives to our interests that naturally transcend the labels that identify them. Leonardo Da Vinci is my mentor where curiosity through the senses feeds the imagination.

Everyone is born creative as demonstrated in buckets by our children, but this is driven out of us by school where we are encouraged to conform. As adults we have much to learn from the young and especially from those who do not have an easy ride.

Becoming involved with 'PanickyParent.com' and sick children who spend a lot of time on their own and in hostile environments I have noticed how much more their imagination and self-reliance develops over their peers.

Retirement brings with it a reflective view on the way life impacts on our thoughts.

Biography

Diana Brown studied at London's Central School of Arts and Craft, and postgraduate level at the Royal College of Art. Her teaching career started as a part-time lecturer in the Foundation teaching 3D Design at Kingston University. This was combined with co-directorship of Glass Concepts, a design and make business in architectural glass murals.

As a full time educator Diana became a Senior Lecturer in Engineering Product Design BSc and MSc, devising and running the first creative art 'Special Effects BSc' at South Bank University, London. She later taught basic principles of Art and Design to architectural students.

Diana's qualifications as a grandma are two children, one boy and one girl (Panicky Parent's founder) who have gifted her with four grandchildren.

Diana Brown will be contributing regularly as a Panicky Parent guest blogger.

Annabel Lagasse

Sometimes life doesn't always go according to plan, and deals some totally unexpected challenges. When Annabel's little boy was struck with a rare disease, it threw their lives into turmoil and Annabel found them confined to the sick bed; endless hospital visits, tests and more tests, and isolation. Her response? To set up a website to help other parents and carers of children know that they are not alone; a place to express, share and learn.

I CAME TO MOTHERHOOD LATE. YOU'D say, I was 'knocking on a bit' to start thinking seriously of having kids. Maturity hadn't brought wisdom. But I was ready to give it a go, as ready as one ever is.

My child self knew nothing of my adult ambivalence, as I'd jaunted about the garden pushing dolly in a mini pram, roleplaying as Michelle Obama quipped 'mum-in-chief'. Then it had seemed a breeze.

When I received lovely news of an affirmed pregnancy after two uncertain years waiting, next came the cliché dread and panic: might something go wrong? Was I ready? Did I deserve this? My mother's first child was stillborn. This past shadow told me that joyous news assured no guarantee. I didn't rush to tune-up my diet, buy baby stuff or make plans. I daren't expect. The gods might be mocking. But the three-month scan was positive, the pregnancy rolled out in a textbook perfect manner. We got lucky. Suddenly we were (shock alert) a family!

For the tightly wound, superstitiously minded mum that I was, there were provocative portents. A well-meaning midwife threw out our pretty Moses basket during a home visit, saying bed linen was a *known cot death risk*! Trouble with baby feeds meant two in-patient stays in hospital in the first month. Concluding what I'd anticipated – I was a *terrible* parent.

Mercifully, the storm was followed by calm. My husband and I settled in to our domestic roles, perhaps reveling in night feeds and nappy changes, as any 'late to parenthood' with their first-born might. A few months in came the inevitable revelation – this 'parenting game' is full on, the disruption to our lives the new norm. We didn't know the bigger surprises to come. There were tired, noisy squabbles aplenty from clashes in parenting style, insecurities and all the typical pressures of modern life. Our minor struggles felt unique, to us they mattered but they were commonplace.

Young children are incredibly vulnerable. They come out too soon: unable to see, walk, or feed themselves. We're wired to be hyper-vigilant, our nerves on edge. We sense the accident about to happen, the better to save them.

One day, around his third birthday, my curious and cheerful boy fell sick. He wouldn't eat the 'hotchie doggies' (Brit speak: hot dogs) provided by our celebratory Hungarian/American neighbour Kathleen. His symptoms of lethargy and discomfort intensified, unable to sit, stand or move without screaming. This new malady erased his exuberant nature and consumed him. It persisted throughout trips to the doctor and later Accident and Emergency. I chose to trivialise them, unchallenged by any diagnosis. I was from a medical family and we were all healthy, it would pass. But inside me his rude cries were troubling. His desperation draining me and dragging me down. Did I think I could *will* him to turn the corner? Did I know he was gravely ill, on some level choosing not to care? Survivor's instinct? My husband's insistence and time passing pushed us back to hospital. Not too soon my guilty conscience would now remind me, and in days ahead. A new phase of our life began: with a diagnosis of juvenile arthritis, our vocabulary suddenly including unfamiliar words like autoimmune, pill diary and dexa scan.

Mother's guilt. Family guilt...could it be something we'd done? Angry, I searched for a thing to blame, or someone. But who should be blamed in this challenge – if I, his mother, didn't step up?!

So we carried the burden of our child's illness, along with worry about his heavily medicated future of steroids, methotrexate, iron...we would grow to acquire a self-consciously casual air about the difficulty, harbouring our sickness gremlin half secretively for the benefit of others and for ourselves.

But we had hope. Hope coming not from fake pride but gratitude for living in a country with free and good healthcare. For living now, close to 2020. Hope coming from each medical or emotional triumph gained along the way. And from a care team who genuinely cared. "These drugs seem to be working better," we mused, "he's getting less scared by shots".

Up and down, up and down we now ride the rollercoaster of a chronic condition. Never quite sure what we're dealing with. Like the joke weather we have in the United Kingdom. Will it be cold today? Put your anorak on or take your cardigan off? Will it be windy, warm or wet? Often, in Great Britain, it's everything in a single day. The only sure thing is an eventual and sometimes depressing return to grey.

Our 'eternal grey' in early days, was the clinical threat of 'MAS' (macrophage activation syndrome). This is a medical complication occurring typically in Systemic Juvenile Arthritis which my son has. It is characterised (in layman's terms – don't quote me) by all over body inflammation and dramatic changes in blood caused by an uncontrolled immune response. It's potentially fatal but it's also thankfully rare, though it was all I thought of. It was also a preoccupation of the medics. Because

MAS is hard to diagnose, occurring in many clinical manifestations, hence the ever-watchful eye. It could be triggered by an ordinary infection.

So we began a new phase of life with hope but trepidation. A case that highlights this strange duality of gratitude and angst is the childhood milestone: chickenpox. You have to 'be chicken' to fuss about chicken pox – right? Yet for us it's no ordinary hiccup and it tipped me into a state of paranoia. My chronically ill son was tossed from *contagion filled* school to hospital and back again in a never-ending cycle. Words like 'he'll be fine', 'it's nothing', 'no need to miss school', contrasted with 'come in for immediate intravenous acyclovir therapy' playing on repeat: a kind of clinical 'gaslighting' for a nervous mum.

Eventually we confronted our personal dilemma and investigated a safe administration of the chickenpox vaccine. Since my husband is French and we were clueless to private healthcare, we rang a consultant in France. He was more than helpful; it was arranged and then ironically my son caught chickenpox at his routine hospital check. Many precautions had been taken. He was fine. A triumph for the medical team, but we are now aware it can return for anyone immune compromised.

I often mused in early days of my son's troubles, how things would have been ten, fifty, a hundred years before. These strange mind games still soothe me. This sombre thinking acts as a 'downward comparison', renewing my gratitude. For him, so many drugs are new. Newly discovered, newly tested, newly implemented, newly approved. What happened before? Would he have been lucky? Would he have been in a wheelchair? Would he have faded away? Time machine back to early pediatrics and he'd most certainly be outside mainstream, convalescing throughout childhood – in obscurity. Too ill to physically engage.

But roll forward to 2020 and feel the power of modern treatments. Our drugs are often administered at home, maintaining well-being, alleviating symptoms, making illness almost invisible reducing me (in external eyes) to a *fussy mum* making me glad yet still insecure. Why? Because my experience doesn't conform to the norm, because medicine, busy doing its clever, demanding job has no space for a mother's ambiguous, messy feelings. Often, it seems, nor does society. We are perhaps too hung up on a myth of success to be able to accept less, however ridiculous. The seemingly well but arthritic child, for some a contradiction too far.

A recent trip to our nurse specialist addressed the old, tired issue of chickenpox again. We're told my son has plenty of antibodies but to treat him as if he has none. What alien-speak is this? I'm left to ask for clarification and risk looking stupid, appearing over-concerned or greedy for time.

I give up trying to understand. The more I learn the more I'm blind. It can't be dumbed down for the likes of me. And it seems even the professionals don't always know.

Fears about immunity have in the past triggered me into an obsessive Lady Macbeth phase. Bottles of antiseptic gel sat in the house, as ubiquitous as house dust. I endlessly washed my hands to 'out the damned spot', until, having worn away my skin, I developed urticaria. Such greater attention to hygiene revolutionised early medicine. But now we have counter theories like the 'hygiene hypothesis', warning us we may get sick because we don't handle dirt. We're told to cultivate our dwindling bacteria by feeding our gut. Keep away from bug-blasting antibiotics they say, which spoil merry cohabitation. It's giddying.

Always I'm left wondering if I've done it wrong – highlighted when I'm asked by a doctor, does my son have siblings or pets? Have we ever smoked? Was he born by natural birth, given formula milk or breastfed?

How does all this affect my son? Does he soak up my unease? Where does it leave him? Sometimes it leaves him dreaming in the dark about zombies. They chase him through the night hours, trying to 'infect' him and turn him into one of the living dead. What relaxes him? Jokes and – paradoxically – carnage. Some of his best therapy has been days spent with 'Grammy', knocking down Jenga towers populated by imaginary victims. As a staunch Star Wars fan, these victims are often fantasy droids. But sometimes the targets are significant: men, families, hospital buildings and homes.

He enjoys his imagination. And it's a great escape from illness. He likes to make armies and forts, spaceships and robots. With paper and Lego he creates characters and worlds. Sometimes these last just a moment or a day before being crushed, 'blown-up', or recycled. It's a good outlet for his frustrations and also pure fun. Other times his creations (if storable) are embraced as a family heirloom – such is their charm. But he also forces dubious artworks on us that we're really itching to bin.

My son's enthusiasms and obsessions are strong enough that they can influence friends and small people alike, though not the dirt averse or squeamish. He loves nature and is very tactile, whether handling bugs or earth. He can appreciate the beauty of nature, its destructive power, and endless transformation. He's known to be followed around a park 'Pied Piper' like as he 'digs for treasure', finds crawling things, or feeds spiders. Little children excitedly discover creeping creatures make 'pets' to take home in crisp packets, and spiders magic themselves on webs, by a caught and well-aimed bug. If you can tear yourself away from adult concerns and recapture your eight-year-old self, it's fun.

In our home we're not fearing spiders. Our concerns are for the drugs my son takes that squash his overactive immune system. This is fine when there's nothing wrong but any real threat leaves him vulnerable. We question what medicine to give and usually need to call for advice.

And there's more. A significant change in treatment can trigger MAS. A suspicion of it has already put us in hospital once.

With physical threats come emotional threats, physical decline can lead to emotional decline. However with my son it's more a case of coasting. I suppose I should be grateful for that. At school he neither engages in athletics (too challenging) nor engages much in class. Nothing tops the intensity of free play and he's not inside 'the group'. It's partly his nature and partly the nature of school that rewards extreme conformity. It's hard to challenge him when he's unwell. And we're not the sort to push. Yet I feel guilty; have I let him down? He is of course already challenged by the frequent medical checks and by days spent at home getting better, also by pain and fear and a premature awareness of his fragility. By being different.

Yet an independent spirit (sprung from nature or circumstance) can be an aid to life. If we have confidence in who we are, that's valuable. Our troubles can even help us better understand ourselves. It's the social stigma which comes from difficulty and difference that's tough. Our collective allergy to 'failure'. As if success is guaranteed, untainted by chance, or of unquestionable value.

So in my life I find myself asking: is it certain if something's a win – or a loss?

Biography

Annabel Lagasse is a Londoner, former teacher, writer and founder of the site panickyparent.com, a site for carers of kids, or kids themselves, wrestling with health issues, educational challenges, emotional concerns or life aspirations. Her site gives tips and insights and is a place to share.

Annabel, once a mum of a lively toddler, was completing a humanities PhD on the psychology of human movement (body language) and its expression in animated film. In an ironic twist of fate her son on his third birthday was struck by a severe arthritis confining them both to the sick bed, narrowing their opportunities and literally isolating them. Yet the journey has proved interesting. The site panickyparent.com is a response to their dilemma.

But who is Annabel really? She hates fixed definitions: she's a free spirit and a typical repressed middle-class Brit. She's an Olympic daydreamer and a middle-aged cynic.

She's someone discovering more than she ever expected (or perhaps wanted to) about child psychology, homeschooling, projectile vomit, trauma, nutrition, camping with a sharps bin and Lego builds...

If you've ever had a scare about your child's rash, mysterious fever, sleepless nights with a child in pain, anxiety over diagnoses or tests, or simply some heart-warming or hysterical moments with kids, you'll know what she's about.

www.panickyparent.com

Judith Humphreys

So often the challenges of childhood, especially where there is mental illness or alcohol involved, have a huge effect on a child. Judith worked hard at school, went on to achieve a degree and became a teacher. Sadly the pressure of unrealistic workloads and lack of support over the years led to a complete breakdown – but little did Judith know that this would ultimately lead her to a rewarding new career.

Teacher to therapist

My daughter once asked why I never talked about my past. My answer was that I don't like to dwell on it, I like to think about the here and now and plan for the future. I believe I've done quite a good job of burying past events but sometimes they jump up out of distant memories to give you a jolt.

My mum often said I was the quiet one, the one with my nose always stuck in a book. My childhood was turbulent; the story goes that I was the result of the last chance to build my parents' marriage. Apparently my father was bi-polar, but mental illness was not discussed in those days as it is today. My dad was a charming public school boy from a millionaire background and a successful entrepreneur. He bowled over my nineteen-year old working class northern mum when his rugby team descended on the little hotel where she was working. They had a whirlwind romance, quickly married and had my brother and sister. My mum blamed a near death car crash on my dad's mental instability but perhaps it was an excuse or catalyst for events spiraling out of control. He would go off on binges, have affairs and even sold the house they were living in. Debts racked up and he was made redundant. All the while his doting mother bailed him out of trouble because she kept him tied to her apron strings – with money.

Mum did try to leave and managed to get herself a housemistress job at a small private boys' school in Somerset, leaving my siblings with my grandparents. It must have been terribly hard for her, she had just scraped enough money together to secure a cottage and school places for my brother and sister when my grandfather asked her to give dad another chance. He had bought them a house in Horsham and promised that dad had changed and wanted reconciliation. My mum succumbed, gave up her job and relocated. However when I was born my dad didn't want the responsibility. The story goes that he never actually lived in that house in Horsham; he drove past, throwing a mattress on the front lawn and disappeared, minus his family!

I believe my dad broke mum's heart. I realise that she too was on an emotional roller coaster and maybe a little unstable. Living with her was all highs and lows; exciting but unstable. She was funny, beautiful and strong but there always seemed to be a drama or crisis.

I admire her because she managed to bring the three of us up on her own when money was tight and times were tough. Her parents moved to be near and help; my dad's parents splashed cash when it suited them, but it was all a bit Dickensian to be honest. They were the 'nobs' with the money, our benefactors to whom we had to grovel. At times they deigned to include us in family events. As I grew up I began to hate seeing them, when I was old enough I refused to have anything to do with them. I rarely saw my father: he sank into alcoholism and eked out his days in a grim little flat in Worthing. When he died I didn't attend his funeral, to me he was a stranger!

When I was eleven years old my mum remarried. Her second husband was called Mike. No surprise that he was another public school type, on paper a good catch: he worked for the Bank of England. He bought the family a big suburban family house, wooed my brother with driving lessons and a new car and promised holidays for the family.

I do have a lasting memory of when my mum said she was marrying Mike: I ran sobbing to my best friend's house. I didn't want a new dad. Mike was a cold character and my mum was different when she was with him; we felt shut out. My brother was my father figure! There was a lot of late-night drinking and whispered conversations; no wonder I sought escape in a paperback book. This turned out to be in my favour – my addiction to reading led me later in life to doing a degree in English and becoming an English teacher.

My siblings didn't hang around to see the ink dry on the marriage certificate and left home just as soon as they could. They did look out for me and I spent most weekends with them in their various abodes and towns, it was exciting getting on trains and buses to dip into their grown up lives. I too wanted to leave home.

Sadly Mike too was an alcoholic, a mean and manipulative man, and my beautiful and vivacious mother was kept in a gilded cage. I remember tense Christmas days with endless rows and moods. Time and time again my mum would put me in the car to look at new houses, find out about jobs or just disappear for a day to seek a little adventure. She would scour 'The Lady' magazine for housekeeping jobs and shared her daydreams of a different life with the only one left at home: me!

Mum felt she couldn't admit to another failed marriage; she liked living in a big house and having a husband who gave her status, never mind that she was miserable. What a waste!

I worked hard at school. I never felt very clever compared to my friends but I was determined to go on to further education: I passed all my exams and ended up at college in Cheltenham. I loved my three years partying hard, working hard and achieving a degree in English Literature. I spent an exciting few years travelling and working: I was a nanny in New York, I worked on a kibbutz in Israel, and worked in London as a personal assistant during the 'yuppy' years, loving every minute. I decided to go back to college and train to be a teacher, doing a PGCE (Postgraduate Certificate in Education) in Bristol which was where I met a tall bearded gentleman named Hugh and 'reader, I married him' – a quote from Jane Eyre, one of my favourite novels.

We bought a beautiful little cottage in Winchcombe. I was teaching in Worcester and Hugh was a Quantity Surveyor working in Bristol and later Oxford; all was well, we were happy and we reached the stage in life when we decided to start a family. This was the first marital challenge, one which caused me the first bout of depression; what a heart-breaking business is infertility. Everywhere you look you see pregnant women, babies, toddlers! My friends began to dread telling me they were pregnant. I began to avoid christenings. We spent five years undergoing tests to be told we had less than one percent chance of conceiving naturally. When we investigated adoption we were told some horror stories about the circumstances of the children available for adoption. There were no babies available in Gloucestershire. I would have to give up work and when

I discussed the idea of adopting a child from abroad the prejudice from my family was shocking.

IVF (in vitro fertilisation) was a costly business but Hugh's mum helped; we were the only chance of her having a grandchild and in spite of her old-fashioned outlook on aspects of life this was something she considered a natural step and an obvious solution. I managed to conceive and our son William was born on the twenty-seventh of February 1996, soon to be followed by James and then our little miracle daughter Abby, who has just turned seventeen. Looking at us, people would never imagine we had infertility problems!

I carried on teaching: full-time, part-time, supply teaching, exam marking, drama moderating and covering maternity leave. I juggled work with being a mother. I spent a great deal of time taxiing children around: managing childminders, after school activities and having fun. I used to thank heaven for holidays and weekends but as the demands of teaching grew these breaks seemed to dwindle. I spent so long working, planning and marking that I felt I hardly saw my family.

Then, seven years ago, my husband was diagnosed with bowel cancer. Thankfully he is now fully recovered although it was horrendous; he had to undergo surgery and have part of his bowel removed, for a while using a stoma bag but fortunately further successful surgery meant he no longer had to use it. I believe this crisis in my life began a spate of depression which I didn't really acknowledge at the time: I remember walking round our village over the Christmas period, the roads thick with snow and I felt like a Dickensian character, peeping through other peoples' windows, thinking everyone else was having a jolly time, yet I felt miserable. I was given some time off work but felt guilty; in teaching there is always so much to do and I felt terrible that I was letting down pupils and colleagues.

The next episode in my life was a breakdown caused by the stress of teaching: my workload was horrendous. Schools so desire an outstanding 'Ofsted' (Office for Standards in Education, Children's Services and Skills) rating that they put enormous pressure on their staff. Exercise books were scrutinised, I was teaching over one hundred pupils a week and each would have four English lessons a week – you can imagine the piles of marking: on average I would mark for three hours in an evening and five hours at the weekend. I had four GCSE (General Certificate of Secondary

Education) exam groups and two Key Stage Three groups being groomed for their SATS (Statutory Assessment Tests). It was incredibly draining and all too easy to fall behind: those work demands are simply not sustainable.

Schools are under huge pressure to achieve a standard of excellence and are under constant scrutiny. As a core subject, English has always been under the magnifying glass. Teaching the subject became joyless because of shifting curriculums and ever-changing exams. Teachers at primary and secondary level became robots coaching children to pass their SATS and GCSES. I loved teaching and working with children but as the requirements within the classroom became focused on academic success I became more and more unhappy. My lesson observations were never given the necessary 'good', I was accused of underperforming and finally I felt such a lack of confidence I dreaded going to school. It was no longer a rewarding job and became a job that made me miserable, stressed and anxious.

The final nail in the coffin came when I was requested to attend a meeting with the head of the school. When I arrived there was a panel of about six people sitting behind a desk. I broke down; my body failed me and I had a panic attack. I was taken home and ended up having six months off work. I barely left the house, I couldn't read or enjoy my hobbies but spent a lot of time with migraines and crying; my poor family didn't know how to deal with this shadow of their mum. At first I believed that this breakdown was a result of the traumatic meeting but of course looking back it was a build up of stress over the last few years.

My Teacher's Union was fantastic and made me understand that I was not alone: teachers all over the country were leaving the profession in droves and I believe they still are. The pressure on teachers is phenomenal with unrealistic workloads and horrendous accountability hoops through which to jump. There are no rewards for hard work. Parents and the public are quick to criticise, with little understanding of what it is like at the chalk face.

It just so happens that at this point in our family life my bright son James was being stressed at school. He was the brightest boy in his year and the teachers, being under pressure to achieve results, put immense strain on him to achieve. He just shut down and became school phobic: he could be found lying on his bedroom floor sobbing. I could understand!

We managed to get him to sit his exams and he left school with reasonable GCSEs thanks to a very empathetic head and a couple of dedicated members of staff. I am happy to report he is now doing an apprenticeship in welding and loves the creativity and opportunities he is being offered – this may not be academic, he may not have gone to university, but he is happy and fulfilled!

So what happened next?

I was signed off work for six months with constant migraines and little sleep. I was tearful and terrified and realised that I would not be able to carry on teaching: my confidence was shattered and there was no way I could step back into a class room, so I began to consider what else I could do. When I had migraines I used to have regular reflexology. A dear friend, my guru, suggested I retrain and become a reflexologist. I thought I couldn't possibly go back to college, nor run my own business; I was full of self-doubt and low self-esteem. However she fanned the flame of my interest in therapy and sent me information on courses – above all she had faith and could see my potential so I went to college to find out more. My husband had to take me, as I was still agoraphobic and couldn't drive. As soon as I walked into the college and met the tutor a weight lifted from my shoulders and I saw the opportunity for a different career.

It wasn't easy. I did briefly go back to teaching because I wanted to prove to the school that I was better, so had to make the effort: I worked my notice and as I was leaving had no more lesson observations and no extra responsibilities. It was a strange hiatus, a bit of a limbo. I went to night school, studied hard, completed ten case studies and practised treatments on one hundred people. In May 2014 I qualified as a reflexologist and a new career and lifestyle ensued.

During this year of change my darling mother was diagnosed with lung cancer and rapidly deteriorated. When she was in a hospice she held my hand and told me I only had one life and that I should follow my dream; it was if she gave me her blessing. I can imagine her looking at what I am doing now and saying, "Darling I am so proud of you." Actually, I am quite proud of me!

I am passionate about reflexology because it's a nurturing therapy which brings the body back into balance: I love seeing the power it has in making my clients feel relaxed and happy. Many are stressed working in difficult jobs or experiencing anxiety because of family life. I am empathetic and gentle: when people come to me they are unhappy and fraught, when they leave they are relaxed and recharged.

I've gone on to qualify in other therapies and can offer bespoke treatments tailored to the needs of my clients. Last year we had a beautiful therapy room built at our Cotswold home, which looks out into our pretty garden.

My teaching skills now come into use as I do talks and demonstrations on how holistic therapies can help with stress and anxiety, poor sleep, digestive and dietary problems and a host of common ailments. I have been involved in and organised wellbeing days and pamper evenings to raise money for charities such as Maggie's Cancer Charity, in commemoration of my mum and thanks for the survival of my husband. My confidence is back and I love my new life as a holistic therapist: the power of human touch cannot be underestimated.

I could have given up, I could have retired but I didn't because I would not be defeated, knowing I had a lot to offer. Clients say I have "magic hands" – one recently wrote a testimonial which stated my treatment was one of the most pleasurable experiences of his life!

I am proud that as a reflexologist and therapist I can benefit individuals by healing, reducing stress, inducing deep relaxation, balancing the body and revitalising them. I feel a deep sense of satisfaction and gratitude in the knowledge that I am helping others.

My advice to anyone who is stuck in a stressful job, an unhappy marriage or a bad place is to be kind to yourself. I was once taught to treat yourself as your best friend: this has stood me in good stead. I still have my moments of self-doubt, my days of feeling low and life still throws curve balls at me – but I look around and count my blessings.

In memory of my mum Jean Hook Sinclair.

Biography

I am utterly passionate about reflexology and other holistic therapies — anything that can make someone feel fantastic after a treatment.

It wasn't always that way: for twenty-five years I was a secondary school English teacher. Although rewarding, it was a job that left me feeling stressed and exhausted. I knew that I could not go on in such a state and so started to look for a new direction in life.

I was drawn towards holistic therapies and started my training at the Cotswold Academy. In 2014, I gained my ITEC Level Three in reflexology and then went on to qualify in Swedish massage, Indian head massage, and Hopi ear candling. Following my training, I continued to build up experience working in a spa and various salons, before deciding to start my own business. I love learning and developing my skills and regularly attend training courses to keep up with new treatments and products.

My home is in Alderton, north Cotswolds, and that is where I have my therapy room. Situated in a purpose-built extension, it overlooks the beautiful garden and is, I think, the perfect place to receive a treatment. I share my home with my husband, three children and two cats and they are often delighted to be the guinea pigs for when I try out a new cookbook recipe — well, the humans are anyway!

When I'm not giving treatments, I enjoy anything to do with fitness and nutrition, and especially love Zumba, tennis, cycling and walking. I'm up for any challenge: I have already climbed Snowdon, and this year I aim to conquer Ben Nevis. Of course, not all my interests are so energetic! To relax, I read and go to the theatre and cinema. Oh, and I think I've already mentioned cooking!

Another of my passions is to raise money for charity. I always take part in the Race for Life, and frequently arrange pamper evenings to raise funds for the cancer charity Maggie's.

www.judithhumphreys.co.uk

Three

Death Does Not Define Me

If you realize that all things change, there is nothing you will try to hold on to.
If you are not afraid of dying, there is nothing you cannot achieve.

Lao Tzu

Charlie Mitchell

Charlie was so happy she felt she simply could not wish for more. The shock of losing her partner so suddenly and inexplicably seemed impossible for her to understand. Yet with a mother's strength she knew she had to find a way to function for her children. This poignant account of love, loss and pain, to making a conscious decision to take good care of herself, step by tiny step, motivated Charlie to build a relationship with herself, properly, for the first time in her life.

MAY 2016 WAS A FABULOUS MONTH: it felt like there was simply no stopping me. My soul mate and best friend Jason had proposed and of course I said yes! I became pregnant within a month of trying. My two other children from my previous relationship were enjoying our life as a family of four, and were excited about the prospect of our new arrival. I was doing work I loved, facilitating workshops on leadership with young people. I couldn't ask for anything more; I loved every minute.
Little did I know that things were going to change so dramatically.

One June evening, I had difficulty getting to sleep because of a pain in my collarbone. It was so sore I went to the doctor the next day, but they couldn't find anything wrong. However, I got worse as the day went on and had another terrible night, so went back to the doctor. This time they asked me to go straight to hospital where I was admitted with pneumonia. I was devastated to be so unwell when I was just seven weeks pregnant, but there was nothing I could do. Knowing there was a risk I could lose the baby, I drew on everything I had to stay calm and found myself turning to something I've always loved: writing.

I started to write about surviving crises and living bravely, knowing that my desire to help others would also help me – amazingly, I was home five days later. While it took me months to recover, our baby had survived and that felt miraculous.

Fast forward to January 2017. Jason and I were having a meal about half an hour away from home when I realised I was in labour. I might have been calmer had I not been the one driving home! It was quite an experience, having a contraction every time I changed gear, which I realised at that point was quite often. I managed to drive back safely and just a few hours later Thomas was born at home as planned. We were delighted and Jason started phoning family and friends straight away to let them know our son had been born. He was an incredibly proud father! However, the midwife had concerns as Thomas was not latching on properly or maintaining his own temperature, so after our beautiful home birth, we transferred into hospital where we stayed for nearly three weeks.

It became clear quickly that Thomas has Down Syndrome. His little body was having difficulty getting started in the outside world, and we nearly lost him. The realisation he might not stay with us certainly put the Down Syndrome into perspective! I just wanted to be able to take our gorgeous little boy home. Thankfully, once his body got used to being in the world, he blossomed into a healthy and happy baby and we returned home to start our new lives together as a family of five: we were in our element!

It was obvious that Jason wasn't well during this time and I couldn't get to the bottom of what was going on. Juggling the needs of a newborn and my other children meant I didn't have a lot of time to focus on Jason. He said he had been for tests with the doctor but they hadn't found anything serious; they made a few recommendations about eating more healthily and getting more exercise, which all seemed sensible. Jason was helping me a lot with the day to day routine, and on Mothering Sunday in March 2017 he cooked a lovely meal for ten members of our family: it was a wonderful day full of love and laughter.

The next day, Jason had another appointment with the doctor and I wanted to go with him to find out more about his progress. He didn't want me to attend, which was unusual as he'd been quite happy for me to go to other appointments. I was certain something must be wrong. I even went to the doctors' surgery, and yet Jason would not let me go in with him. He slept for most of the rest of the day. I asked him if he was alright when he got up to go to the loo about midnight and he said he was. We went back to sleep.

At about two o'clock in the morning I heard his breathing change and I rolled over to see him take two more breaths, before he died. I tried to rouse him, but it was clear to me that he was no longer there. I called the ambulance who arrived within minutes and they tried for an hour to resuscitate him without success.

The shock was extreme. My brain simply could not process it. How could he have died? He had cooked for ten people yesterday. His son was just ten weeks old. He was my soul mate, the love of my life, my fiancé, my world. His toothbrush was still in the holder and his shirts in the wash.

Time stopped moving. Minutes felt like days. A day felt like a year. Thankfully, family moved in with me to help me with the children. I couldn't feel hunger, yet I was shaky and wound up tight like a spring. I knew I had to function: I was breastfeeding and expressing milk for our son and didn't want my kids to lose another parent. I had to get my act together.

I called everyone I could think of: the health visitor, a charity called 'Homestart' who help families in need, 'Winston's Wish' for bereavement support for the children, 'Cruse' bereavement counselling for me. People came with flowers, cakes, curry and baskets of food. The outpouring of support from friends, family and even people I had never met was incredible and made me feel very held during this horrific time.

Arranging the funeral was one of the most difficult tasks of my life. What would he have wanted? What snippets of conversations could I remember that might be relevant? I wrote down as many details as I could. The writing helped me notice things I hadn't pieced together before. Jason had told me in November 2016 that he did not think he would live to see November 2017. I thought he was feeling low and had organised some therapy for him, which seemed to help. I couldn't understand why he would think he was that unwell yet, with the benefit of hindsight, it was another piece of the jigsaw. He had sold some of his favourite belongings and had even bought me a memory box. It seemed strange at the time, yet I couldn't piece it all together. He had died suddenly, so a post mortem was required to explore his cause of death. I kept thinking, "I just want to know it was something outside of his control."

I did my best to ensure the funeral honoured him. It was as full and personal a celebration of his life as I could create, from the words the celebrant used to the drumming that had brought us together on our first date. It was poignant and heartbreaking, yet it was also a beautiful focus on the positives he had brought to the world. The children were able to take part in the way they wanted and we remembered the wonderful times he had brought to all our lives. After the funeral we developed our own new routine, with support from the services I'd enlisted. While it was exhausting and involved me dropping Ellie and Ali at nursery and school then coming home with Thomas to sleep and cry, it did work. And then the next bombshell arrived.

I had a call from the coroner who said that I should book an appointment with my doctor to discuss the results of the post mortem as there were details that I would find distressing. I eventually convinced him to send the post mortem to me and promised that I would also book a meeting with the doctor.

The results were devastating. Jason had not been having tests with the doctor. In fact, he hadn't been for several months, since an appointment I had last attended with him. He had a longstanding alcohol addiction that continued until his death and had led to his organs failing. The extent of the damage meant there was nothing anyone could have done by the time he died.

With Jason's death I lost our hopes and dreams for the future. We'd planned to get married, to have more children (Jason had wanted four), to both work part-time, to retire to Glastonbury. In the moment he died, all my hopes and dreams vanished, and it felt like a part of me died too. But at least I had our happy memories. Finding out his own actions had led to his death put a very different perspective on our past. Now, every detail was under my intense scrutiny. How had he managed to drink so much without me noticing? He always had a soft drink bottle with him, which probably contained the alcohol. Vodka doesn't smell and he had great oral hygiene – I just thought he liked mouthwash. He did all the shopping and would regularly pop out for extra ingredients when we ran out of things.

I didn't think anything of it at the time, and yet now it all seemed very different. Selling his favourite things was probably to get extra money, and even going to the shop to get biscuits for the midwife while I was in labour had a different perspective now.

His death had been incredibly traumatic for me, but to discover he knew his own actions were leading to his death and not do anything about it was a new low. I felt levels of guilt, blame and shame that I didn't realise were possible. How could I have not noticed? Why couldn't he tell me the truth? How am I going to be able to show my face? Honesty is so important to me, and yet I didn't even want to be honest with friends and family about the situation. Why couldn't he have just been hit by a bus?

Yet, this was not the first time alcohol had played a part in my life: my father had challenges with alcohol when I was a child, and I thought that would have meant that I would have seen the signs. Yet I didn't. I started to unpick our relationship and look for the evidence that I had missed. What I found surprised me.

I had seen the signs early on in our relationship and had actually asked him if he had been drinking one morning as I thought I smelt it. He had said no, laughing it off that he had something stuck in his teeth. In that moment, I later reflected, I trusted him over me. I had a feeling in my gut that something wasn't right, and yet I wanted his truth to be the real truth. I accepted what he said. In the months leading up to his death I continued to have these feelings that something was deeply wrong, yet I trusted his version of the truth which enabled him to carry on drinking until his body gave up.

There was a crossroads in front of me. Having been a professional coach for a number of years I could see the impact of my thinking on my behaviour: I could go in one of two directions. If I carried on with the guilt, blame and shame I knew I would end up with some really self-destructive behaviour.

"I'm hopeless. How could I not have realised? I am worthless."

These kinds of beliefs lead to a 'what's the point in any of it?' attitude which would have led in turn to me neglecting myself, probably drinking alcohol and letting my own life unravel – or I could do anything and everything within my power to create a different life. To stop blaming myself and start taking excellent care of myself every day. I read an article about breaking karma and was desperate to ensure the next forty years of my life could be different to the first forty years.

The message in the article was powerful: karma can be broken in a day. You just need to make sure any decisions you make are conscious decisions and you have considered your motivation. The author brought a Buddhist perspective with the core motivation of 'do no harm'. This spoke to me; I could see I was at risk of doing harm to myself with the level of negativity I was feeling. I decided to have 'do no harm to myself or others' as my motivation. How hard could that be?

I did a kind of self-CBT (cognitive behavioural therapy) and every time I felt myself getting into a negative loop I did some meditation using an app on my phone – at least twenty times a day to start with. It wasn't that I believed that I loved myself, or that I was worthy of taking care of, I just consistently kept taking the actions that I would have taken if I *did* have those positive beliefs.

I started to cook myself my favourite food: curry. Just simple meals with vegetables and a jar of curry sauce, yet it helped me to feel better. I started taking my supplements again, which always seem to have a positive impact on my mental health and looked for opportunities to do little bits of gentle exercise. Even just a few minutes of yoga or walking into town rather than driving made a difference.

I noticed how this made my day seem much longer. Each day I started to pay attention to little ways of taking care of myself. I realised that actually there are thousands of opportunities where I could either make a choice that supported me or one that was detrimental, even in a seemingly minor way; for example, I decided to stop drinking caffeine as I realised this wasn't helping me physically or mentally. However, when I went to see certain friends, I realised in the past I would have said "yes" to a cup of tea, even if I really didn't want one, just to be sociable, just to fit in with their usual routines.

I realised that these minor decisions were actually adding up and affecting how I was feeling about myself. Tiny, seemingly insignificant choices that were still a subtle form of self-sabotage. I noticed how much better I felt about myself and my life when I honoured my preferences in these moments. They added up during the day and could lead to me feeling generally energised or generally depleted. None of this was to do with the really big things going on in my life. None of it was life or death. Yet, I started to notice the cumulative effect: within a week I started to feel differently. I was still grieving and angry, still hurt and lost – yet there was also something fundamental that was starting to shift: I was building a relationship with myself, properly, for the first time in my life.

I was starting to listen to myself at a deep level. I was starting to respond to what I was hearing, even when that meant having difficult conversations with people. I noticed three separate occasions when

I would have previously said "yes" to something, and instead I chose "no." I noticed how hard this was. I noticed how I would have just said "yes" before and ended up with lots of unnecessary work that I would have done begrudgingly. I noticed how it made life simpler and slower; it took the rush out of life, and for the first time in my life I properly came to a stop.

A lot of shedding followed, getting rid of clothes and possessions that no longer served me. I took bag after bag to the charity shop or to the tip; carloads of stuff surplus to requirements in this new place of being present were disposed of. The physical release was mirroring my internal healing. It took months of diligently doing a little every day and I could feel myself slowly emerging like a butterfly from a chrysalis; finally taking full responsibility for all aspects of my life and making informed, considered decisions about what to do and when, was cathartic.

I lost weight simply by being more aware of what I was eating. I stuck to a fairly tight budget by bringing awareness to what I was spending. If I wasn't sure then "no" became my new default. Over time that has changed to a more tender and vulnerable place of "I'm not sure, I'll think about it." The "no" was a great protection for a while, and it was also extreme in its own way, a form of shutting down. "I'm not sure" feels more honest, it feels more open to possibility, to risk, to opportunity. It took time and courage to get to that point.

I am finally forging a new relationship with myself, through the white-hot embers of my life. The past and future I thought I was living have been razed to the ground. I am not fully healed, I'm not over it and I haven't achieved closure. I am still on my own journey of self-exploration which I hope will never end and yet I feel I have everything I need to heal every day. I can ride the waves of my emotions without fear of being lost in them: I know they will rage through me and pass on.

Finding out the circumstances of Jason's death brought such a mixture of powerful emotions. I spent a good deal of time trying to work out what was going on for him, which is obviously an impossible task. I have found some peace in appreciating that he made his decisions about his life, and regardless of my thoughts about those decisions, they were his to make. His habitual behaviour had been in place for years before I met him. I felt I must have done something wrong in order for events to unfold as they did – and yet the truth is even more unsettling: that I had done everything to the best of my ability and events still unfolded as they did.

Blaming myself was almost a way of me trying to maintain the illusion of control in a situation over which I actually had very little influence. Pema Chodron refers to this true lack of control as 'groundlessness' in her book 'When Things Fall Apart':

> "If we're willing to give up hope that insecurity and pain can be exterminated, then we can have the courage to relax with the groundlessness of our situation."
>
> Pema Chodron

A lifetime of tiny self-sabotaging decisions had led to me prioritising Jason's perspective over my own. I had trusted him over myself and that had put me in a difficult situation where I was not in touch with my own intuition. By taking loving actions and consistently asking myself "How can I be even more loving in this situation?" I have rebuilt my relationship with myself and my intuition; I now trust my feelings and follow them and I will always be grateful to Jason for showing me the importance of my relationship with *myself* first.

I can finally look myself in the eye and smile. I can sleep at night knowing that while I may make different choices if I face similar circumstances again, I did the best I could with what I had at that time. I don't make myself wrong for the life I have led. I appreciate my journey and the details that have brought me to this place. Loving myself has enabled me to develop deeper relationships with my children and to honour their individual uniqueness in more tangible ways. I am more open to their superpowers and their particular needs than I have been before.

My journey continues and I am developing a book of creative healing resources for people who want to break negative patterns and live bravely. I explore how it is possible to come back from the abyss and recreate our lives, sometimes almost from scratch, no matter how bad things seem. I will continue to use my experiences to support others in any way I can.

Far from being the end of my story, this is the beginning of a new chapter.

Biography

Dedicated to supporting charities to work effectively, I set up the social enterprise 'Creating Space For You' (CIC) in 2010. We ran leadership development and coaching support for staff, volunteers and trustees, offering subsidised places to organisations who would not otherwise be able to afford it. We have worked with over three hundred organisations in the last eight years, providing over one hundred and sixty thousand pounds of workforce development to the sector. This work is currently evolving as I explore how I can share my unique approach to creative healing more widely.

I am planning online and face-to-face workshops and events where people can explore my 'LoveCreateHeal' process, with plans for an exhibition to display our creative healing journey at the end of 2019.

I adore each one of my three children. We prioritise family time together and really appreciate the special moments that happen regularly in everyday life. They remind me of the importance of the present moment, of being able to fully experience emotions and release them, while being able to laugh and cry at the same time.

We remember Jason regularly with trips to Slimbridge Wildfowl and Wetlands Trust, a place he adored, and by giving each other gifts. Jason was incredibly generous, always with a gift in hand for someone, so this is a lovely way to keep his memory alive.

While we have had such a tremendously difficult time, we are all closer as a result. We are all more able to express our feelings and we are all more able to listen. We create space for each other and have a very real appreciation of the need to value this moment in its entirety.

For further details, including a free online course and Facebook community that is exploring the 'LoveCreateHeal' process please visit:

www.charliemitchell.co.uk

www.creatingspace4u.net

Tracey McAtamney

It's impossible for most of us to imagine the shock of losing a loved one suddenly and unexpectedly, let alone when this happens when they are in another country. Tracey's strength of character came to the fore when she had to tell her sons their father was dead. When dealing with her late husband's business created another set of challenges, Tracey found that a new version of her self was born, a true 'woman of spirit'.

ON THE TWENTY-EIGHTH OF JUNE 2004 my life changed forever. In bed with my seven-year-old son Oliver sleeping next to me, I received the most devastating telephone call of my life.

The moment my mobile phone rang after midnight I knew instinctively that there was something wrong. My oldest son Anthony, then fifteen, was packing his suitcase in the bedroom next door with his friend John. Anthony had finished his final General Certificate of Secondary Education earlier that day and was going on holiday with John's family to celebrate. Oliver was sleeping with me, because that is what he did when his daddy was away. 'Daddy', my husband Tony, was away in Spain playing golf for the Law Society in an international competition. He was a sole-practitioner solicitor; his practice was in Coventry. I too worked at the office dealing with the accounts and general office management. In his absence we had a locum solicitor and excellent support staff at the helm ensuring that everything ran smoothly.

I scrambled from bed and answered the mobile in the en-suite bathroom, hoping not to wake Oliver. It took only one word, my name, to know what had happened. The voice at the other end of the phone was Brian, one of Tony's golfing companions. I recognised his voice immediately. With a pause, all Brian said was "Tracey." With that I responded, "He's dead, isn't he?" I cannot describe the pain when he replied, "Yes." I felt as though I had been physically punched in the stomach. I clearly remember dropping to the floor still clutching the mobile and telling Brian that I would call him back.

Panic was rapidly spreading through my body and I was having difficulty breathing. How on earth was I going to tell my boys? I crawled from the bathroom and through the bedroom desperately trying not to wake Oliver; I needed time to think. I met Anthony on the landing and had no choice but to blurt out that daddy was dead. At first no words would come out of my mouth but then they just came out. It was bizarre, neither of us were screaming or crying, we were just holding each other for support. Poor John was clearly in shock. The two boys were brilliant, we heard Oliver stir and they immediately offered to settle him down. Telling a seven-year-old that his daddy is not coming home was never going to be easy but especially at one o'clock in the morning.

My mum lived in the granny flat attached to our house and I knew I needed to get to her; it's amazing, it doesn't matter how old you are, you always need your mother. I didn't want to scare mum by waking her suddenly so I tapped the door quietly. She sat up immediately; her face was instantly full of worry. As the words tumbled out, her face disintegrated into tears: this was not really what I had expected, mum was the strongest person I knew, she never cried. She always believed you put a brave face on and your brightest lipstick and everything would be okay. Not this time. This was all too familiar to her; it obviously brought back memories of when my dad had died when I was only seven. Mum hadn't cried then, she had just gone into protection mode. She had coped then but seeing it happen all over again to her daughter and grandchildren was too much. I found myself hugging her and telling her everything would be fine.

I still didn't know the details of Tony's death so with trepidation I got back on the telephone to Brian. He was waiting for my call and the sadness in his voice was echoed with each word as he explained the events leading up to the telephone call. Brian had not been playing golf with Tony; he was playing a different golf course with a different team. Brian had been told by his golfing colleagues that Tony had suddenly excused himself, complaining of a backache and had seemed agitated. He had called a doctor to his room who had attended and could not find anything significant wrong; he had given Tony some anti-inflammatory pills and left. The golfers only realised that something was seriously wrong when they were having dinner and Tony did not appear; he was not answering his phone or the door. The hotel manager was called and when he opened the door, Tony was lying on the floor; he was dead. I gasped, feeling the familiar punch to the stomach; I had imagined that Tony had died on the golf course with other people around him, not by himself. So many questions: why had he not called me to let me know he felt ill? Why had the doctor not been able to save him? Had a priest been called?

The last conversation I had with Tony was two nights previously when he had told me what a fantastic practice day he had playing golf. He told me how beautiful the view was from his room and he told me he wished we were with him and finally that he loved me. How could he just die?

Brian assured me that a priest had been called; this was important to me because I knew how important Tony's faith was to him. My brain was hurting and I couldn't take in any more information; I promised to ring Brian the next day. I began to feel as if I was in some kind of nightmare; it was still only two o'clock in the morning, how would I get through the night? I found myself calling our closest friends, Lesley and Ray. They arrived at the house within minutes followed closely by Father Kevin, my priest friend.

Mum had gone into making tea mode and the situation felt surreal. Father Kevin told me that I would have some important decisions to make very quickly: was I going out to Spain to see Tony, as it would be the only chance I would get? My brain hurt too much.

When more friends arrived, I decided I needed to walk, to think and to breathe. My friend Robin took my arm and we walked and walked. I was terrified; I had the worst thing in the world to do when I got home, to tell my baby that his daddy was dead. His world would be shattered and there was nothing I could do to stop that. The birds were beginning to sing and daylight was appearing. I thought morning would ease the pain, but it didn't.

I can clearly see all the concerned faces as I head up the stairs to Oliver. I open the bedroom door and he is awake. He is smiling. The smile begins to disappear and he says, "Mummy you look sad." I climb into the bed and his small hands cover my eyes. "Mummy, don't cry, don't cry mummy." I hadn't realised that I had tears in my eyes but I knew immediately if the only thing I could do to help Oliver was not to cry, I would not cry. The speech I had been preparing in my head since the phone call began to spill out. I explained that daddy had gone to heaven;

he hadn't wanted to leave us but God had some very important work only he could do. Daddy would be with us, watching over us all the time and if we looked into the sky at night, daddy would be the brightest star. There, I had done it. I did not know how he was going to react. His little face was scrunching up and he was blinking with disbelief, but he wouldn't cry. I told him that it was okay to be sad and cry; he just shook his head. I held him tightly and then asked if there was anything he wanted to ask me. He thought for a moment and then asked "Do I have to go to school today?" I smiled and told him no he would not be going to school. Next question, "Can we go down stairs now?" That was easy. Finally, as I carried him downstairs, he whispered in my ear, "Mummy, will you help me find the brightest star tonight?"

Everyone downstairs seemed to be holding their breath as Oliver entered the room. Typical of a small child, he climbed onto Ray's knee and after a moment asked, "Can I watch the cartoons now?"

The house is full of people coming and going; it is strange, Anthony is quiet, his friend has gone home and Anthony will not be going on holiday with him. Oliver is acting like it is just any other day. I have never felt so alone in all my life.

All the family had been informed, including my stepdaughter Helen. Helen had told Tony only the previous week that he was to be a granddad; he had been so excited. I was terrified the news would be bad for her unborn baby, but she had to be told. Although the shock in her voice was apparent she automatically wanted to know if the boys were okay and she also offered to break the news to my other two stepchildren, Victoria and Gerard, both holidaying in different parts of the world. I was very grateful.

The insurers had been contacted, the office had been called and the SRA (Solicitors' Regulation Authority) had been notified. The arrival of my accountant and solicitor friends highlighted other problems. Tony's Will could not be found at the office. This is crucial for a sole-practitioner, a Will must contain details of who will take over the practice until a sale is arranged; failure to produce a Will could result in an intervention by the SRA. This news was serious, serious enough that I knew immediately I would need to go straight to the office and search for the Will. I travelled to the office feeling like a zombie; thank goodness I was not driving. Facing the staff was hard, everyone was emotional and seeing Tony's empty chair was heart wrenching. The secretaries were struggling with the dictation tapes, listening to Tony's voice when they now know he is dead. The Will is still not found and I return home to face more decisions.

Tony's body needs to be repatriated: decision made, I confirm that I am going to Spain to bring Tony home. I know I need to see his body and say my goodbyes. A flight is arranged and Anthony is accompanying me, together with my friend Lesley and Tony's sister. We look like a strange bunch amongst all the happy holidaymakers. On the flight I try to talk to Anthony about his feelings, he has been so quiet. It is strange, I am unable to concentrate and Anthony seems engrossed in a book. I laugh to myself, before this happened the worse thing in my life was that Anthony was dyslexic and didn't read until he was thirteen; I longed for him to read and now he is reading! He suddenly responds, "Ok mummy, I don't like what's happened but there is nothing we can do about it. I promise I will not turn into a delinquent overnight." I am speechless. He then presses the buzzer for an airhostess and asks her to give me a glass of wine!

We arrive in Cadiz to be met by Brian who escorts us to a hotel; not the one Tony died in. I just feel numb. We arrange to meet Brian the next day to visit the morgue. I feel like everyone must be looking at us during breakfast. People are getting ready to spend the day by the pool or beach and we are going to see Tony's dead body. I keep my dark glasses on and give up on trying to swallow food. Will I ever know happiness again?

After spending forty-five minutes on a taxi journey which should have taken fifteen minutes, we realise that we have been ripped off. Good start. The morgue looks like it is undergoing major reconstruction works and there are workmen everywhere. We are ushered through some doors and into a corridor, I presume en route to a chapel of rest. Not so, Tony's body is presented to us on a trolley in the corridor. With gasps of horror Anthony is dragged back the way we had come; I am left staring at my husband. It is not very dignified; his eyes are wide open as is his mouth and he is wearing nothing but a white sheet. I kiss his cheek and tell him this was not part of the plan; he should be out on the golf course. Tony's sister returns with some holy water and I whisper my goodbyes to him. Anthony and Lesley are visibly shocked by what they had seen. I am upset that Anthony had seen his dad like that; I was going to decide whether it was appropriate. It wasn't, but I hadn't been given a choice. Anthony seems more concerned about me but I assure him that I am fine, just numb.

The funeral director then introduces himself; not what I was expecting, a man in tight black trousers and an open necked white shirt, showing a very hairy chest. A gold medallion is hanging around his neck. One problem: he speaks no English. Lesley starts to communicate with the help of a mobile phone and a Spanish friend on the other end. It seems to work and although all he is saying is "Sí, sí," we manage to make some arrangements. As we try to leave, Lesley looks uncomfortable when he refuses to let go of her hand which he is kissing – only in Spain can you get hit on by a funeral director! It makes us all laugh though.

Next stop is the hotel to pack Tony's case. I am relieved, it is exactly how Tony had described it on the phone and I sigh as I see his swimming trunks and towel still drying on the balcony. I am comforted as a golf ball appears to roll from under the bed, a sign perhaps. I pick it up and hold it tightly. Breathing starts to be a little easier. Case packed, I join the others.

Back at our hotel Anthony has a swim and reads his book; Tony's sister goes for a rest. I need to walk. Lesley and I walk fully clothed along the beautiful beach, my trousers completely soaked by the waves, but I don't care. We walk for miles and gradually I begin to talk. I can feel a hidden strength within me making me feel stronger. I will take control. I will arrange a celebration of life for Tony's funeral, with a garden party. I will sell the office and I will do everything in my power to take care of and protect my boys.

We arrived back at our hotel a bit singed from the sun but feeling more hopeful. We are met by Tony's sister who is in a panic, "Something terrible has happened; the SRA has frozen all your office and client bank accounts." I shrug my shoulders. "I will deal with them when I get home."

The new me is born. Tony had always dealt with solicitors, accountants and bank managers; it was part of his job. It was now my job to do this and I did. I gave Tony an amazing send off. I met with the SRA and against all odds they did not intervene. They took the unusual decision to allow me to take control with the help of a locum until the office was sold. I found a buyer and managed to wangle my way through masses of legal problems and major headaches. My boys have always been my priority and my hidden strength.

I met Phil when I was forty; Oliver chose him for me whilst he was doing some work at our house! Phil is also a scuba diver and underwater photographer; he captured Oliver's imagination with fascinating stories of sharks and shipwrecks – as well as my heart.

In 2014 mum was diagnosed with terminal cancer and I took some time out to be with her. I also set up an events company working mostly for charities, and following mum's death I jointly took over 'Ladies First Professional Development' a networking and lifestyle management company.

2018 has been a poignant year. Anthony celebrated his thirtieth birthday and his engagement to Tammie, and Oliver celebrated his twenty-first birthday and graduated from the University of Nottingham with a 2.1 in Politics and International Relations. I still miss Tony every day but we have survived and I couldn't be prouder.

2018 is also the year I first spoke publicly about my loss and dealing with grief and resilience. I have also been invited to write my story, which I am in the process of completing, the profit of which will be donated to helping to support children and young people coping with grief. In doing so I have opened boxes that were closed when things were too painful to deal with. I have cried, I have also laughed and I feel very privileged to be part of *Women of Spirit*.

Biography

I was born Tracey-Anne Lynch, daughter of Shirley and Tommy Lynch and younger sister to Tina Maria. When I was aged seven and my sister aged ten, our dad died suddenly in a fall, breaking his neck. We were raised by our amazing mother, who protected us like a lioness caring for her cubs.

At the age of twenty-two I married Tony; he was the sole-practitioner of a solicitor's firm in Coventry which we ran together; my role being in charge of the accounts and general office management. We had two sons, Anthony and Oliver. We were happy!

On the twenty-eighth of June 2004 my life was turned upside down when I was widowed at thirty-eight with two boys aged fifteen and seven. Devastated, I picked myself up and began the fight to save our business, home and most of all to protect my boys. I became a different person overnight. After selling the legal practice I set up my own recruitment agency, Warwickshire Legal Recruitment, working in association with Warwickshire Law Society. I did this for ten years together with being a locum legal cashier.

In 2014 I set up an events company, working mostly for charities, and I jointly took over Ladies First Professional Development, a networking and lifestyle management company.

The 'hidden inner strength' I found to cope following Tony's death is what has shaped my life and made me the person I am today.

www.ladiesfirstnetwork.co.uk

Sara Meredith

Only when her baby was placed in her arms did Sara know what she had been searching for: motherhood. Along with joy, tragedy has been part of her journey of motherhood. When I met Sara and saw her interact with her little son, I saw clearly how the magic of her love lit up both his world and hers. Her words, "Everyone has a right to *live loved*," came straight from her beautiful heart.

GROWING UP I WAS CONVINCED THAT I was from another planet, like a cuckoo egg left in the wrong nest. Forever being told I was too sensitive, too emotional, I just never felt whole, never complete. I survived by hiding away, never being true to myself, or self-medicating with alcohol or food. Even when I got married I waited for my husband to leave, never feeling good enough or worthy of him.

Then at twenty I gave birth to my daughter and as the midwife placed her in my arms I finally knew what my heart had been searching for: motherhood. This tiny wrinkled baby was the most beautiful thing I had ever seen; I was sure my heart would burst for the love I felt for her and for her three sisters who followed.

Being a mom fulfilled me in a way that I would never have expected, yet even in this joy, I self judged and found myself lacking. When my third daughter Olivia was four years old, I heard the words that broke and freed my heart all in one go: "I cannot promise you forever."

You see Olivia, better known as Livvy, entered this world on her own terms in May 1999. Alongside a dramatic labour, she struggled with feeding and severe reflux and I promise you she could vomit the distance of a table with a smile. She, like her sisters, was beautiful; she had the cutest blond hair whose curls twisted around my finger, a smile that could light up a room, she walked, she talked and developed normally until one day, she didn't. Around her second birthday Livvy disappeared into her own world, her communication stopped, the gift of hearing 'mama' lost to the universe. Then her seizures started, one turned into twenty-six, twenty-six turned into one hundred and six. No one had any answers, doctors judged me: I was too hysterical, too dramatic and one even suggested I wanted to believe something was wrong with my daughter.

I was scared, how could I protect her when the enemy is invisible? How could I keep her safe when I didn't know from what to hide her? Slowly and slowly my little girl disappeared into this unknown illness. My heart grieved for whom she had been, my soul scared for her future. Until that moment when I sat in the neurologist's office and he introduced me to 'Rett Syndrome': the answer to my questions. The thief had a name, but also had a great cost.

Like any parent hearing the words, 'severe disability' they have to ask the question they don't actually want answering, "Is this life limiting?"

The honesty of that doctor is something for which I am so thankful: "I cannot promise you forever."

Now this may sound the worst thing anyone could ever hear and yes it is a sentence that rips at your soul, but the truth is none of us really know how long we have left in this world. We spend our lives making plans for the future, what we want to do, what we dream of doing, that we actually forget to live life in the here and now. Hearing these words from the doctor highlighted to us that nothing, no time, was guaranteed. We needed to take life as it came and live in the here and now, in the present moment. This challenged me far more than I could ever imagine, the girl who preferred to live in the shadows was being thrust into the light. As a family we decided to make changes and create memories whenever we could.

I would love to say that life played fair from this point forward and that I had found my place in this world but it didn't. An innocent dog walk turned into an assault and physical damage that would change my life forever. This assault left me physically disabled, emotionally scared and finding myself on another journey of self-discovery. I was diagnosed with fibromyalgia and chronic pain due to spinal damage. My body changed, I put on weight and for a while I was bed-bound, all so very different from the life I had led as an active mom of four. I couldn't walk to the bathroom without help, couldn't lift my daughter and couldn't care for my girls alone. My husband had to leave his job and in my mind at this point I became the burden I had always believed I had been.

Again it was my children who wouldn't allow me to fall into the abyss. Whilst they understood I had been hurt, we had spared them the details. They knew mommy was hurting but they still needed me to be their mom. I had to find a new normal, find ways to still enjoy life even though I was in pain. Livvy would be my biggest inspiration here; she had never given up on life, so how could I? Yet even with an incredible role model I still struggled. I realised that I have always searched for my value in others; being a people pleaser I yearned to make everyone happy in the hope that they would like me, love me. Now in my weakened physical state I couldn't be that person again. I was dependent on others, something I wasn't used to or enjoyed. Asking for help nearly destroyed me, it began to confirm the lies I had told myself since childhood, "You are useless, you are worthless."

For a while I fell into deep despair, the physical pain was so intense and I was getting no relief. I started suffering blackouts which was frightening; one day finding myself at the bottom of the stairs when the last I had remembered was being at the top. Not knowing when these blackouts would happen left me more scared to go out, to be visible to the world. I just didn't recognise the person in the mirror anymore, I truly believed I had failed my husband but worse than that, I had failed my children.

My thinking stayed this dark place for a while until I attended a pain management clinic; here I was supposed to get my head into the place where I could live with my illness, but also receive a physical plan to help me with my pain. It was at this clinic that the doctors told me that my condition at the this point had no cure, that I had to find my new way of life and simply make the best of it. I was given a physical management plan which listed the amount of activity I was supposed to do; it seemed I should be limited to pegging a load of washing out each day. WHAT?!! I was a mom to four girls, a mom to a disabled child, how can I be this limited? I asked the specialist if I stuck to this plan would I get better? His answer was "No but you may be in less pain." I knew there and then that I had to make a decision. If I was going to be in pain anyway I may as well live life to the best that I could. Unfortunately this specialist didn't agree with my thinking and I was asked to leave the course. A journey between hospitals ensued until thankfully I came across a specialist who was more understanding and actually admired my desire to live to the full. Yes I may rattle from pain medications and yes some day's pain wins but I was finally finding a new sense of peace. Like all storms in life they have moments of rage and moments of quiet; I prayed and hoped that this was my family's time of peace.

As a family we slowly found our new normal, my husband helped care for me and my girls and Livvy's health allowed us to create some incredible moments. It took a new way of thinking for us all, 'slowly but surely' became our new pace. Ok I wasn't going to be teaching dance anymore but I had started finding comfort and fulfilment in blogging; sharing my journey and Livvy's with anybody who happened upon my site. I wanted to share that life may be a little different but it was still good. Livvy may have been disabled but she loved life; together as a family the girls rock climbed, ice skated and canoed. *Rett Syndrome was what Livvy had, not what defined her.*

Yet in the end it is what stole her from us. In November 2008 Rett Syndrome became the thief in the night and took my beautiful girl from me. Our family was shattered and the shock nearly killed me; there had been no warning, she went to bed laughing only never to awaken. My heart was broken, nine and a half years is never enough.

Grief is a nightmare from which you never seem to wake. Every moment of everyday my heart aches for my beautiful girl, yet in the darkness her sisters were always my light. I knew I couldn't allow them to be swallowed by the pain, I had to remind them that they had to laugh again, had to love again. They became my sole focus; in hindsight I may have driven them crazy with my constant pestering but they treated me with grace and together we tried to find our way again as a family. Losing a child is a pain I can never find the words to explain; I thought I had known pain but nothing prepared me for this. My mind tumbled into the old ways of self-hatred, self-disgust. I should have known. I should have stopped it. I should have saved her.

Again I had to find a way to stop the falling, yet I knew this time it had to be for myself, not just for others. Allowing myself to find my identity in others was not allowing myself to actually know *me*. I needed to find out who the person in the mirror was and actually find some peace with her.

It was the loss of Olivia that made me realise I was trying to hide from pain by being the people pleaser. By denying my own truth I was creating a numbness that wasn't reality. To grieve Livvy I had to allow myself to feel the pain and that scared me like crazy. Yet somehow I had finally come to realise that to love fearlessly you had to accept the risk of pain.

It is a weird revelation that to love is to risk pain.

Loving oneself feels a strange place to be. I felt that self-love was actually egotistic and vain, completely not realising the fact that it is a necessity of life.

Protecting oneself is an innate survival skill with which we are all born yet somehow, somewhere I had lost my way. I cannot remember the time I had ever sat down and made a decision based solely on what

I wanted; my decisions had all been based on the needs, wants of others. Now don't get me wrong, my loved ones are my heart, but how could I teach my girls to be true to themselves when all I am showing them is how to live a lie.

I found myself sitting at the dining room table writing a list of things I wanted to achieve for me. This list changed often as I finally found my truth and allowed my heart to admit its desires. I wanted to like the person I saw in the mirror; I was tired of hiding under baggy clothes and self-contempt. I attended a body-confidence day for plus-size women and it was a revelation. I was surrounded by incredible, confident and beautiful women who could not care less what the number on their label said! They loved fashion, beauty and life and really allowed me to view myself in a different light. I had spent too long punishing myself for not being a size eight that I was failing to see how beautiful I was right here and right now. I had always stopped buying myself new clothes under the concept of "I will buy them when I am slimmer," or "When I have lost a few stones." These women rocked my world and encouraged me to try styles in which I would have never imagined myself, but you know what, I looked pretty amazing if I do say so myself! I explored the world of plus-size fashion with excitement and a new sense of identity. My confidence soared when the next year I was asked to model at the event. I walked that catwalk scared silly but my goodness it was so liberating. I finally liked, no, loved who I could see in the mirror.

Still, my journey was far from all about how I looked, I needed to know my own heart and also see my own value. I knew I had amazing children, I knew my husband was a good man but what did I know about myself?

Have you ever sat down and tried to remember who you wanted to be before life got in the way? I had to travel back to the time when I was sitting in my grandad's lap asking him about what I had to be when I grew up. His answer was "Whatever you work to become." He saw no limits about me then and I needed to see none about myself now. Whilst I love my job as a foster carer, as I child I dreamed of attending university and the privilege of wearing the cap and gown after graduating. It may seem trivial to some but for this working-class girl university had always been something for the wealthy and out of my reach. Yet life does sometimes have a funny way of opening up doors that you believed were forever closed. A speech I gave at a therapeutic childcare conference impressed a lecturer so much that she encouraged me to apply for a place on her degree course. This girl who left school with only General Certificates of Secondary Education was finally able to achieve her heart-hidden dream: I graduated. Yet as I looked out into the audience on my graduation day my heart ached for the people I wanted to be there; those whose approval, whose love I craved. Newsflash: people will not love you the way you want them to. I am finally realising this is a fact of life; no matter how hard you try, or who you try to be, some are just unable to give you the love you need. You have to find it within yourself. Here I was, a body-confident graduate and still desperately seeking approval. Will I ever learn?! The answer is I don't know if I will; maybe it's an innate part of me to always want validation from others, yet what I am finally realising is how far I have come.

Learning to love myself has allowed me to become braver than I could ever have dreamed. After losing Livvy I could never have imagined I would have the strength to love fearlessly again, yet in June 2017 I became the proud mama to an adorable little boy named Daniel. My little man puts the 'complex' in complex needs and life is full of uncertainly and fear, but my goodness he is a such a blessing. Caring for him has filled my heart with such joy. The adoption process was hard, yet in every step my truth became my own. Why do you want to adopt? Why such a complex child? Why take such a risk? My answer is "Why not?!"

I am a woman who loves to love; this is me, I am emotional, empathic, sentimental and I cry at everything, but I love who I am. My heart beats strongly for those I care about. I am a woman who needs validation but even in my self-doubt I will find the strength to persevere. I am a woman who is anxious and fearful yet even in fear I will still say "yes", even when "no" is the safer way to go, even when the world believes I'm crazy. I know who I am: I am a tangled mess full of doubt, second-guessing and panic but while these emotions are part of me they no longer define me. I am Sara, I am a mother, a wife and a friend but most of all I am a woman of spirit, strength and courage and I am pretty amazing!

Biography

I'm a forty-two year old woman who simply loves life. I embrace each new day with a nice cup of tea and the philosophy of hoping to make someone's life a little brighter.

My life is a wonderful bag of chaos. I'm a mom to four incredible girls. They are twenty-two, twenty-one, seventeen and forever nine. I'm also a newly adoptive mom to a gorgeous four-year old boy with complex needs and to top this all off I also foster children with special needs.

I have been married to Alan for the last twenty-one years and he drives me completely insane, but I do love the bones of him. We keep promising ourselves more time for just the two of us then we go and do something crazy like adopting a four-year-old; obviously we just don't enjoy alone time.

Whilst I work full time as a foster carer I am passionate about writing and blog over at www.rebelwithkindess.com.

With my family I also run the charity endeavor 'Livvyssmile.co.uk' a memory making charity which we started in memory of our late daughter Livvy.

www.rebelwithkindess.com

www.livvyssmile.co.uk

Paramjit Oberoi

It is not simply that Paramjit and I share the same birthday which has created an affinity between us, we also share many values. When I first read her story it moved me to tears, tears of sadness and yet also of relief. What a rare gift is her ability to create something so beautiful out of something so many fear: death. Oh, and her smile could light up the darkest night!

Thank you daddy, I'm no longer afraid of dying

"Death is perched on your right shoulder." My father must have repeated this to me hundreds of times since I was aged about eight. I couldn't understand what he was saying, not until the fourteenth of October 2002.

Would you like to come on a little journey with me? Yes? Ok, let's start from here…

I arrived in England from India in 1954 with my parents and my older brother, when I was six months old. I'm in total gratitude to my parents who nurtured and instilled in me both Eastern and Western values. They brought up their seven children with rich spiritual and philosophical understandings of life and death. Spirituality is the essence of who I aim to be, and I'm continually learning at every step of my life.

Conversations about life and death

My father often talked to me about life and death; the conversations would go something like this:

"Paramjit, the ultimate fear is the fear of dying."

"Dying is a transformation. The body dies but the soul continues to live on."

"It's like changing a piece of worn out clothing."

"Death brings the experience of joy to the soul as it goes home to the ultimate maker. It's like the divine spark in the human person merging with the divine flame."

"The purpose of life is to attain union with the divine."

"Death is not an end of life but a moment of transition where the self, the soul leaves behind the body. This realisation comes through God knowledge. The Gian (God Knowledge) is given by a spiritual Guru."

"The atma (soul) which is eternal is never born and will never die."

"At the point of death the soul merges with Paramatma (the supreme soul or over soul)."

"It's important to live a life detached from the physical world."

These sayings were part of on-going conversations in our home which became part of my psyche from a young age.

Marriage and children

I was aged twenty-four on the day of my arranged marriage. My husband,

Harbhajan, twenty-nine, came from India. I was a little apprehensive as we'd never met, only having communicated by writing, but we settled happily into married life. Within ten years we had completed our family: we were blessed with two beautiful daughters Navneet and Sheenam and our charming son Amanpreet. We lived in Greenford, Middlesex, but purchased a ten bedroomed hotel in Derby eighteen months after our marriage. Harbhajan decorated the hotel while I stayed in London for three months, working as a Community Social Worker. Each Friday, I would complete the tiring three-hour drive home, and then return to London early Monday morning with our six months old little bundle of joy, Navneet.

We were a young couple trying to make ends meet, to make a life for ourselves. I remember coming home one Friday to find my husband standing on a chair, perched on a tall table, painting the ceiling of our old Victorian hotel. Horrified to see him in this dangerous position, I asked why he wasn't using a ladder. He replied "We have no money to buy a ladder!"

To support my husband I left my job in London when we opened the hotel. I also found work as a Community Relations Officer in Derby. Looking after two daughters, working full-time and running the hotel began to take its toll on us, and we felt it wasn't the right environment to bring up our two daughters. So in 1985, we sold the hotel, and purchased a grocery store and off-licence.

I was promoted to Principal Development Officer in the Social Services Department in Matlock. Finally we had our own home. The girls were contented; their school and nursery was nearby. We were grateful for a happy family life.

In October, I had a massive car accident, a head on collision with a lorry from Europe driving on the wrong side of the road. I'm truly blessed to be alive. My neck was in a brace for many months, we survived this ordeal by the *grace of God*.

Harbhajan was tired all the time. I was trying to hold down a responsible job, as well as looking after our children and helping in the shop. One day, we woke up to find a bus stop outside our shop. It was a free bus service to a supermarket, Sainsbury's, which had opened locally. Within a few weeks we were bankrupt.

We were devastated. We sold the shop and off-licence in the last week in March. Our baby was due early April: the girls were adamant they would send the baby back if it was a girl!

We didn't have a roof over our head, only my income to live on, with another mouth to feed. To try and salvage the financial situation we purchased a chewing-gum machine franchise. Unfortunately we were sold a business that didn't match up to its description, resulting in further financial debt. Blessed to have been brought up in families where we had faith in God, we remained optimistic. It was a very tough time to say the least, made worse by hubby's tiredness and sudden mood swings. Thinking he was going through depression after having to sell the shop, I encouraged him to go to the doctor.

We moved into our new home in Littleover, Derby, in July 1988. Harbhajan still suffered from exhaustion and mood swings. He decided to stay at home and recuperate whilst looking after our son and I continued working. Harbhajan's condition deteriorated further. His symptoms included lethargy and depression and I also noticed signs of restricted physical movements. Harbhajan's doctor put him through tests to find out what was wrong. I encouraged him to find a job to give him some routine routine, and in 1989 he found work as a trainee in the Education Department in Matlock.

A vision

One particular day I made hubby breakfast and sent him off to work. I had taken leave thinking friends from Kent were going to stay the night, but they decided not to stay. I decided to catch up with chores. Looking at the pile of ironing I thought "I really don't want to do this today." So I lay on my bed for a rest, and neither asleep nor fully awake, I had a vision.

I saw my husband laid out with flowers around him. My mum passed me a white scarf, which signifies widowhood. I didn't accept the scarf; instead I put my finger to the floor, covered my index finger in dust and put it on my forehead to make a bindi, denoting I was married. The vision was so vivid, even now when I close my eyes I can visualise the scene and smell the flowers around his coffin.

That split second the phone rang; it was hubby. "Are you alright?" I shouted down the phone, "Thank God you're alive!" Completely unaware of my vision, he told me he had been in a car accident. It turned out to be a blessed escape – he'd banged his head on the steering wheel and had just cuts and bruises.

Harbhajan is diagnosed

I'm glad Harbhajan had that accident; I'll explain why.

For the last few years, I had been worried about his driving and perceptual ability. I always offered to drive, especially when the children were in the car. I knew something was wrong and put it down to settling in a new country, depression, isolation from his family in India and the businesses not working out.

An MRI scan revealed atrophy in the brain.

After a few days in hospital professional after professional contacted us for appointments. Another brain scan was arranged in a specialist hospital in London. Blood tests were taken repeatedly. Family history was scrutinised for any major illnesses. Nobody told us what they suspected, it truly was a harrowing time. What got us through was our *faith*.

After the diagnosis our lives fell apart. I was in total disbelief and was also trying to support our three children, hubby and handle all the emotional upheaval that comes with hearing devastating news. I didn't accept the diagnosis. I wanted another opinion, another opinion and another…

We arranged a private consultation. Dr J's response: "After taking into account the family history, the blood results, brain scan and physical examination today I'm really sorry to say I've diagnosed your husband with Huntington's disease, which is terminal

I said "But aren't you terminal Dr J?" He replied, "I know you are in shock." I burst into tears. His response, "I'm sorry Mrs Oberoi, but this is the beginning of your tears."

I walked down his long stony drive holding tightly to hubby's hand, got into the car, put the windscreen wipers on then realised it wasn't raining. It was my tears.

Saying goodbye

Tenth of October 2002, I remember it well; it was my mum and dad's wedding anniversary. I had been feeling uncomfortable and sad all day but couldn't put my finger on why. I went to my friend Ranjit's home and started crying saying, "My heart is feeling very heavy but I don't know why." Taking a first sip of tea, my mobile rang. "I'm really sorry Mrs Oberoi but your husband has…" The phone disconnected, my battery dead. I rushed home, gathered the children and my phone charger. Ranjit offered to drive me to Sheffield to the specialist nursing home where my husband had been for the last few weeks. I told her she could accompany me, but I was driving. I needed to feel in control of this very uncontrollable situation. The children asked why we were rushing. I told them Daddy was unwell.

In my heart I felt he had died.

When the phone was charged I received another call. Hubby had been rushed to Sheffield General Hospital after choking on a 'Mars' bar. He suffered a massive heart attack and was in a critical condition. I can't remember the journey but I vividly remember saying to myself "Please God help me, I can't get through this by myself."

Harbhajan was in a coma.

The kind nurse's face looked sad. She told me things were not looking good; the next twenty-four hours were crucial. We sat by Harbhajan's bedside for four days and nights. He was wearing new pyjamas, surrounded by his favourite scent, flowers, scented candle, with spiritual songs playing and friends and family praying. His room was full of love supporting him on his onward journey to his ultimate home. I hope someone takes that much care, love and commitment when I go!

I would describe it as a time of sheer bliss, it was heaven on earth…

The children were witnessing a positive experience of transitioning to his ultimate home and the soul merging with the *oversoul*.

The nurses said the last sense to go was hearing. We were sure to be positive with our words. The nurse enquired if everyone had been to see him. I responded, "Yes, all family and friends have travelled from north and south." The staff at the hospital were incredibly supportive and compassionate, supplying us with endless refreshments. Although everyone had visited I felt something was still holding him back from letting go. Suddenly I realised he hadn't heard his mum's voice. I rushed to the nurses' station and asked to make a call to his mother, in India. I told his mum I was going to put the phone to her son's ear so he could hear her voice and that she needed to release him and let him go. This was the most difficult conversation I have had in my life. Little did I know my dad's teachings would be my saving grace forty years later. Fortunately she understood; I saw hubby's left eye flutter on hearing his mum's voice. It was so beautiful to observe and witness, I felt he had completed his journey and was ready to leave his mortal body and become forever immortal.

I explained to the children that daddy was going to his new home but we would feel his presence always. I reminded them daddy could still hear and they could say anything to their daddy. They were very brave and told him how much they loved him and would miss him. By fluttering his right eyelid he acknowledged his children.

It's a scene I will cherish forever.

Several hours later after the nurses had said "It won't be long," he was still struggling with his breathing. I noticed on a few occasions his breathing changed but as soon as Sheenam touched him he began breathing normally again. I witnessed this for at least half an hour. Something was going on between them at a deep cellular level. I asked the nurse to take the children out so that I could spend some quiet time with hubby. I held his hand and whispered into his ear "Thank you for our three beautiful children, I promise to look after them to the best of my ability. I now release you." I turned my back on him. I was detaching to enable him to detach and move on. A few minutes after I turned my back and without Sheenam in the room, his breathing changed. I asked the nurse to bring the children in. All four of us folded our hands over his chest and prayed.

The nurse stood in the corner of the room. I noticed she had opened the window slightly.

My husband's breathing pattern changed, all of a sudden there was complete silence, and a white cone shaped light left his mouth, going straight out of the window. Shaking the nurse, I uttered, "Did you see that, did you see that light leave his mouth?" Whether she did or didn't, her response will remain with me forever. She said "Mrs Oberoi you are a very blessed family. Not many get to witness this light." A few seconds later Sheenam went close to her dad and said "Thank you Daddy, I'm no longer afraid of dying."

What better gift could a father pass on to his child?

Anticipatory grief

Little did we know why the link between Sheenam and her daddy was so strong: the genetic link manifested the day after his funeral when, at the tender age of nineteen, Sheenam was diagnosed with Juvenile Huntington's Disease.

There was no time to grieve my husband's passing. We were now facing the challenge of anticipatory grief. The specialist's words echo in my mind. "The Juvenile form is far more aggressive, with a shorter life span of ten to fifteen years." My beliefs and faith were shaken to the core. Having nursed my husband I knew what might be coming. It made it harder but also I was more determined than ever not to be beaten by this disease. It would be untruthful to say that the diagnoses didn't affect me. I was devastated for my little girl, and for her brother and sister for what they would witness. The only saving grace was that our eldest daughter was clear of the disease, giving me solace and hope.

Sheenam's words at her daddy's deathbed on fourteenth of October 2002 still echo in my mind. "Thank you, daddy I'm no longer afraid of dying."

Those words were to become the foundations of the rest of her life.

Death brings life into focus

Sheenam is brave and courageous and has experienced some very low points in her life. There are two choices: to sink or to swim. Sinking was not an option. Why? Because she has me as her mother! So what has kept us afloat? Knowing that however much you love someone, you cannot die for them. These words by Rumi, a thirteenth century mystic poet, were now our reality:

"Birth and death are two sides of the same coin. Each event marks the end of one chapter and the renewal or beginning, of another." Rumi calls death "A wedding with eternity."

"Death has nothing to do with going away. The sun sets, the moon sets but they are not gone."

"Goodbyes are only for those who love with their eyes. For those who love with their soul there is no such thing as separation."

I was witnessing everything I'd been taught about death first-hand. I reflected on hubby passing and felt I hadn't really grieved. I analysed and questioned what was going on inside me, stopping me going through a grieving process; if indeed there is a grieving process. Maybe my steadfast spiritual faith meant I didn't need to go through this process as I had accepted and embraced death fully. Maybe I suppressed my grief knowing I needed the strength to cope with Sheenam's diagnosis. Maybe I grieved everyday whilst he was slowly dying. Maybe it is a combination of the above or none of the above.

What I can say with certainty is facing the reality of death helps me on a daily basis.

A day after hubby passed a very dear friend of mine had a stroke. I kept myself busy visiting my friend in hospital, supporting Sheenam, coming to terms with living as a widow and a single parent. Those labels are actually another story for another time…

My mother often said "Don't leave till tomorrow what you can do today, don't leave till later what you can do now." These words felt so poignant now. On a lighter note she also used to say "Always wear clean underwear when you go out, you never know when you might end up in hospital!"

I began to understand the fragility of life. We only have now.

Our lives are made up of a collection of memorable moments. Navneet had made a photo frame with a picture of our family; this takes pride of place on her dressing table. She had etched "My Forever Family." I went into her room after hubby passed. Even though a child had written "My Forever Family" it doesn't mean this will be forever true in this world. None of us will be here forever. It's with a dream-like innocence that we tell ourselves "the forever stories."

This dream-like state helps us to cope to a certain extent but ultimately we have to face the truth, "That which is born will die." Staying connected with this *supreme power*, this *essence*, which was never born and will never die, the *universal force, God* or whatever reverential name we wish to use, supports us at every step of our lives if we can learn to trust and connect. This thinking made me realise how death brings life into focus, giving me the power to truly live in the present moment.

How blessed we are as a family to no longer fear death. I'm not saying there isn't sadness around death – but there is no longer fear.

Within a six-year period I have recently witnessed the passing of my mother, a dear friend, my father and my mother-in-law and a number of other friends. Like Sheenam's dad gave her the gift of not being afraid of death, I thank my father for giving me the same gift.

Dying a good death

On fourteenth of October 2003 I was asked to speak at the National Health Service's 'End of Life' conference in Lancaster titled 'How to Die a Good Death.' I asked if I could bring a picture of my late husband to put on the stage – the day of the talk was the first anniversary of his death. My talk illustrated the components of a good death from my personal perspective and experience. I'm grateful we had the opportunity of doing these things owing to our particular circumstances. I am aware that this might not be possible for everyone:

- Facing the reality that the person is dying.
- Talking with the dying person in a kind, loving way, knowing that hearing is the last sense to go.
- Trying not to have any unfinished business.
- Staying with the dying person till their last breath.
- Detaching from the person dying supports the transition.
- Talking to the children about death.
- Letting everyone have the opportunity of saying goodbye.
- Giving everyone individual time with the dying person if they wish.
- Preparing the room as though it is heaven on earth with all their favourites.
- Letting them know you love them and you release them.
- Verbalising that you will take care of those left behind, especially children.
- Contentment in your heart knowing you've done everything possible.
- Having no regrets. I really didn't want to leave any opportunity to have to say "if only."
- The song "In the living years" by Mike and the Mechanics echoes in my head daily as a reminder… "It's too late when you die to admit you did not see eye to eye."

Sheenam

It's not an understatement to say our lives changed forever when Sheenam was diagnosed with Juvenile Huntington's Disease. We felt we would never recover from this devastating news. It was unbearable to see our child go through this painful diagnosis knowing the consequences of this devastating disease. Then we faced reality and chose to live life to the full despite the diagnosis. Sheenam completed her degree in International Tourism Management and travelled to nineteen different destinations. She has such an amazing spiritual strength. Whilst people of her age were planning their marriage she planned her Will, carefully naming who would get her prized possessions after her passing. Although it was a painful process to witness, I began to understand Sheenam's character and her deep understanding and acceptance of life and death.

My soul was touched

I wondered who would receive her most precious gift: the teddy bear her daddy hugged throughout his final days would be passed to her nephew Steven. I believe Sheenam and hubby came into my life to teach me life lessons for which I am eternally grateful. Sheenam is now in a wheelchair as she can no longer walk or talk and has a feeding tube in her stomach, yet her spirit is unbreakable. I have a saying when I talk about turning adversity into strength. "What is the gift wrapped in sandpaper?"

The gifts have been enormous, too many to include in this chapter.

Reframing our lives has enabled us to live a life full of peace and gratitude despite going through horrendous situations. Reflecting on the impact of this illness we have done more with our lives than we may otherwise have done without it. This illness has been a blessing reminding us not to waste time on negative contemplation. As a family we love more openly, share more vulnerably, feel the depth of sadness and pain intensely, value life so deeply, live less judgementally, forgive more easily, worry less frequently, surrender more easily, live more adventurously, act more resolutely, value relationships over material possessions, and live in the moment more often. We have developed incredible faith and courage, are more accepting of the things we cannot change and have the courage to change the things we can. The 'Serenity Prayer' hangs on my kitchen wall.

Through setting up Sheenam's charity, sheenamswish.co.uk,

kind-hearted souls have entered our lives; restoring our faith in humanity, enabling us to see 'the gift wrapped in sandpaper.' Our faith in the *almighty* is unshakeable. It has taught us the beauty of totally surrendering to the will of *God* and accepting "*His* will be done."

Peace is achieved by surrendering to the *Universal power* in full faith knowing that the best outcome will happen for us.

Death has not defined our family; however it has truly shaped our thinking.

We embrace this concept, value life and live it to the full.

We are learning so much and thank the *Ultimate power* for giving us the strength and courage to continue each day and live within the essence, which is limitless.

It is not how tragically we suffer but how miraculously we live.

Biography

When meeting Paramjit you will find an enthusiastic, experienced, creative, emotionally intelligent, self-motivated, spiritual, professional woman with whom you develop an instant rapport and connection at a deep level. She is an effective communicator with well-developed interpersonal skills and a commitment to bringing out the best in everyone she meets.

Paramjit's life has been dominated by caring responsibilities. It was an arranged marriage, and her family was unaware that Huntington's Disease ran in her husband's family. Now widowed after many years of caring for him, she cares for her daughter who has Juvenile Huntington's Disease.

Throwing herself into work as a businesswoman, managing teams of community development workers and later as a lecturer and life coach Paramjit achieved a variety of senior roles as well as raising three children. She used her experience as a carer to be a Non-Executive Director of Primary Care Trust for many years and now sits on the Board of Carers UK as a trustee.

Paramjit also supports the running of her daughter's charity sheenamswish.co.uk, set up to support other young people with Juvenile Huntington's Disease.

She spends as much time as she can on writing and is in the process of completing her book on miracles and her father's memoirs.

The love of her life is her grandson. She enjoys his company and continues to learn about the beauty and simplicity of life through the eyes of a child.

www.sheenamswish.co.uk

Sian Davies

Sian is one of so many women who say, "I'm nothing special." I beg to differ, as I see her as quintessentially pretty, with a light that shines from within. The grief of losing her husband invaded her whole being, including the loss of her identity. Counselling enabled her to see a way forward and eventually she embraced a new challenge which brings joy to not only Sian, but to all the many women she helps with her wonderful personal styling.

Susie has asked me to write about my grief experience! Really, can I go there? I am through all that now; do I want to go back and think about it all again?

Yet, to be part of this book would be wonderful. Am I a *'Woman of Spirit'*? I am just an ordinary woman who was widowed aged forty-eight and refused to let it ruin the rest of my life. My life is now a happy one so perhaps I should tell my story to give hope to others to know that it is possible to survive grief and come through it stronger and more resilient to a happier place. There is no denying grief is a terrible state to be in, but it does pass if you want it to, and you can grow from the experience. I will never get over losing my husband Hugh but I have come to terms with his loss and have built a happy and successful life since. I know he would be immensely proud of me for that.

We are such products of our upbringing. I emerged from mine rather lacking in confidence, an extrovert who was happiest at home and rather shy in the outside world. I am the eldest daughter of older parents, much loved from a happy home. When I was six we moved from Sheffield to Birmingham for my father's work. At my new school I didn't speak like the other children so was bullied. Academically I didn't take to school either; learning to read was a struggle. I now think I am slightly dyslexic but that sort of thing was not picked up then, you were just viewed as stupid, which undermined my confidence. I never really fitted in at school. I remember being a teenager and looking with envy at 'the cool girls,' beautiful creatures who found school work effortless, whilst I felt a million miles away.

School was a place to keep your head down and survive. If I worked hard I just about got by. I didn't do too badly at 'O'level stage but dipped my 'A'levels as the boyfriend was more important than doing revision. Failing my 'A'levels meant the planned university place was shelved so I went through clearing and got a place at Bristol Polytechnic on the Higher National Diploma in Business course. All student accommodation had gone and it was a matter of finding somewhere to stay. Talk about sliding doors moments...was it destiny that I found the last room in an all girls' student house? Next door but one was an all boys' house where I would meet my future husband! Student life was good, I loved the freedom and I was coping well with the course as I was actually interested in the subjects. I made friends and even had a nice boyfriend.

I first met Hugh at one of the visits to the boys' house. Hugh was twenty years old but seemed much older: he was already working in a bank, drove his own car, wore a suit every day and to my mind was so out of my league I never really gave him a second thought. Hugh offered to give my friend some driving practice in his car before she returned home for her test in the holidays, Yvonne asked me to come along as a chaperone and I happily agreed. The car lessons were fun and usually entailed Yvonne driving to south Wales. When we came across a country pub Hugh would declare the lesson over and we would all have a drink before Hugh drove us home. Fun times and instead of being my usual shy self I was very relaxed, safe in the knowledge that I was being a good chaperone for Yvonne, as clearly Hugh had designs on her. How wrong I was. When Yvonne left Bristol before the end of term to sit her driving test Hugh actually suggested I finish with my boyfriend and go out with him. I was amazed at his bare-faced arrogance and confidence! That was Hugh, as he often told me "You make your own luck in this world."

Hugh was a big character with tremendous energy; he loved life and lived it to the full. I had never quite met anyone with such a zest for life. I don't know whether I was flattered or just plain intrigued by this confident, charismatic young man who seemed to make things happen, so I did finish with my boyfriend and life with Hugh commenced.

By the end of my first year at Bristol I had sailed though all the exams except Management Accounts – which remain a mystery to me to this day. If I failed the accounts re-sit I could not continue into the second year...failure was not an option Hugh said so one traumatic weekend Hugh (the banker) taught me how to do balance sheets by rote. Many tears of exasperation but somehow I learned enough to get through the re-sit and remain on the course.

Life with Hugh was exciting, he had grand plans for his life and this now included me. He left the bank, went as a mature student to university and by aged twenty-four had set up in business as an independent financial advisor organising mortgages and pensions. We remained as boyfriend and girlfriend while we both developed our careers. I joined the National Health Service in a service improvement role. Our careers were blossoming with fun-packed weekends and holidays together. Our courtship was therefore a long one and I was twenty-six Hugh twenty-seven by the time we finally married.

The 1980s were good years; Hugh's business took off and we were more than comfortably off. Hugh worked very long hours and I provided the comfortable home environment, providing the stability to his mad life. He was a strong character and to keep the peace and maintain a happy marriage I bent around him on many issues, only digging my heels in when I really wanted something. He gave me confidence, love and a very exciting life. We were a great team and life was good.

Before too long our three gorgeous sons arrived; we both loved being parents and enjoyed a busy family life with Chris, James and Gareth. I continued to work in the National Health Service but now part-time – I needed the balance that work gave me where I wasn't just wife or mother. Working also made me more assertive to hold my own with Hugh. Busy, busy times, they were very happy years for me. As for my boys, they turned out to be remarkably 'cool boys' – the sort of children I had envied as a child: gorgeous looking, confident, self-assured, high achievers, seizing life. They are also loving and caring. I am of course rather biased.

In January 2004, life changed. Looking back Hugh hadn't been well for several months. He seemed to catch every bug going and was definitely under the weather. One Sunday, while carving the Sunday roast Hugh ate a piece of beef and started to choke. The meat was stuck in his throat and we ended up in Accident and Emergency. Finally it shifted and Hugh went to the doctor the following day and was referred for an endoscopy. He came back from the appointment saying, "Sian, you have done wonders with those waiting lists. They think they will see me within two weeks." I froze. "They said two weeks?" "Yes" he said, "Isn't that fantastic service?" I knew that a two-week wait referral meant the doctors suspected cancer. The next two weeks passed in a blur; Hugh blissfully unaware, me burying my head in the sand.

Two weeks later, with Hugh all drugged up from the sedation, my worst fears were realised: Hugh had oesophageal cancer. It is a bad cancer to get. They needed to see how big the tumour was to decide if it was even operable. I couldn't believe it and neither could Hugh, who of course refused to believe that nothing could be done. The next few months were hell. Hugh expected me to personally micro-manage his patient pathway. Knowing the National Health Service as I did I was on the case with every test result, speeding up the process by nagging and chasing. As Hugh predicted his tumour was operable but only just, he needed it to shrink through a course of chemotherapy before they could operate. The very risky operation was followed by a couple of days in intensive care followed by months of recovery. The great man that Hugh had been was debilitated and it was horrific to watch. In many ways he was a broken man and relied on me a great deal. Hugh was the worst patient, he hated being ill and was exasperated by his inability to do things. Family life went on as best it could but we had a new perspective on life. Things that once were important now were not.

Just a year after the big operation Hugh was in low spirits so we decided to take advantage of the good weather and booked a week in Salcombe. We had a share in a 'Boston Wailer' boat and Hugh loved blasting it around the bay at high speed. That sunny day in Salcombe is etched in my memory as we were almost carefree, but by nightfall Hugh was far from well and coughing up blood. I spent the night on the phone to the out of hour's doctor's. The nearest hospital was miles away so we agreed to wait till morning. The doctor took one look at Hugh and we were on our way to hospital. We hoped it was a pneumonia, which they could stabilise; sadly it was not to be. Hugh started haemorrhaging and we nearly lost him. Twelve days in intensive care and our worst fears were realised: the cancer was back. This time there was no more oesophagus to remove so surgery was not an option. Hugh was terminally ill.

Facing death when you know it is going to happen is a weird one. On one hand it gives you the chance to say things, but generally Hugh's approach was to have an unshakable belief that he would pull through so there was no point in saying anything. Something that I found impossible to understand was that Hugh believed I would spoil the boys rotten if he wasn't around (he wasn't wrong there) so he felt compelled to become an authoritarian father. Poor Chris, who was just eighteen at the time, bore the brunt of this. He had just left school, was driving, had a beautiful girlfriend was just starting out on life and I don't know if Hugh was jealous or what, but he was very hard on Chris.

Hugh started chemotherapy again and the hope was that even though they couldn't get rid of the cancer they could keep it at bay so Hugh could enjoy life. We holidayed in Scotland, we went to New York and sailed back on the Queen Mary 2; this was our new normal. We arrived back from holiday both with a cold bug. Barely recovered Hugh wanted to go to Cheltenham races for the November meet. He walked miles that Friday in the cold, he saw his friends and enjoyed the racing but of course overdid things. That night he was ill and we ended up back on the oncology ward. A few days of antibiotics and he was better; however I was exhausted and still not well. I got him home on the Tuesday and we had a wonderful day together. I even got him to agree to try a simpler life, as I wasn't putting up with mad behaviour when he wasn't well.

That night Hugh suggested I sleep in the spare room saying "Your cough is going to keep me awake all night, why don't you get a good night's sleep in the other room?" For once I felt ok to leave him. I dosed myself up and sloped off to bed.

In the morning I crept past our bedroom; unusually all was quiet. I went downstairs, emptied the dishwasher, tidied the kitchen, made Hugh a cup of tea and went up…he was totally still…he had gone, just slipped away in his sleep. It was the kindest way for him to leave this world but totally devastating for the rest of us.

The next few days were a blur. So many good friends and family, so much love numbed you from the reality of what had happened. Sleep eluded me. Yet on another level I was in control and organised all that had to be done. Time was distorted; it dragged yet passed very quickly. I remember that it had been the half-term holiday on the twenty-fourth of

October when we had happily boarded the Queen Mary 2 in New York, just a month later, the twenty-fourth of November was Hugh's funeral date and the twenty-fourth of December Christmas Eve.

By day I coped fairly well; I was slow, distracted, exhausted but functioning. It was the night when I was alone that I had space to process. Then I felt like an out of control computer processing, processing and trying to make sense of it all. I thought about Hugh's illness, had we made the right decisions, my marriage, our life together, how was I going to cope as a widow, how would the boys cope, would they be damaged, what could I do to help them? It felt as though my head was against the washing machine on full spin cycle with large trainers inside, clanging away. The noise in my head was deafening and the only solution was to get up, play music and busy myself.

Chris elected himself as the head of the household and was ordering everyone around, trying to be very practical. James was suffering from every symptom going, headache one day, stomach ache the next. My poor friend bought up an entire chemist shop before we conceded that nothing would make James feel better. Gareth became younger that his twelve years and if no one was around just wanted cuddles on the settee.

For me, I felt quite empty and could quite understand how those widows flung themselves on the funeral pyres. I felt half a person, so lost without Hugh, scared for the future and totally unsure of my ability to do anything. If I had had my way I would have built a six-foot fence around my house; I wanted to keep the boys and myself away from the world. I stopped watching the news; I couldn't cope with the troubles of the world. I found it difficult to concentrate on television of any kind; music was all I could cope with.

The weeks passed, by mid-January Chris left as planned on his gap year travels. On the one hand I wanted him to go so he could go back to being an eighteen-year old again, on the other hand I was worried about him going and we all missed him. We were now a family of three from the original five, empty nesting and grieving.

I went back to work, probably too early, but had made the decision that life had to continue as normal as I could make it. My boys had lost their father so at all costs they could not lose their mother too.

The lyrics of 'Whistle a Happy Tune' resonated.

"Whenever I feel afraid, I hold my head erect
And whistle a happy tune so no one will suspect I'm afraid.
The result of this deception is very strange to tell,
For when I fool the people, I fear I fool myself as well."

Rodgers and Hammerstein –'The King and I'.

I had to look the part: I would do my hair, makeup and dress well. It was like a mask that helped me cope and showed the boys primarily, but also the outside world that I was coping. I think it was also to fool myself. It was a struggle though; there were times I would hold it together and work well all day, get in the car to drive home, music on, but by the time I had driven to the top of Cleeve Hill I had to stop because my tears were flowing so it wasn't safe to drive. I would sort myself out, reapply the makeup and go home to the boys to cook the evening meal.

A widowed friend told me to be kind to myself and do something really nice at least once every month; this was good advice. When I realised Chris would be in Australia during the Easter holidays I decided to take the boys and my sister to go to meet him. We had a wonderful time and it was good to prove to the boys that life was different but we could, and should, have happy times ahead.

When Hugh was ill I had reduced my hours at work. I should now step up again and work more hours, but I didn't want to; I hated leaving the boys, my heart wasn't in it. Hugh had never been part of my work so why did I feel like this? Grief invades everything you do and that annoyed me. I took unpaid leave to cope with the summer holidays and a few months after that I took a whole year out.

As the months went on I seemed to be getting worse not better. I wasn't just dealing with the loss of my husband I was grieving for the loss of my identity too; I was no longer Mrs Hugh Davies. Certain invitations we went to every year didn't appear, the world had moved on. A few faithful friends kept ringing and inviting me out even though at times I wasn't much company. Other 'friends' fell by the wayside.

Grief, if you let it, is a growing experience. I have never thought about life so much, my values, my beliefs and what was important in life. These were the questions that filled my head. I went to Cruse Bereavement Care where a lovely lady listened to me every fortnight; they deserve a medal those lovely councillors. She helped me see things more clearly and made me less frightened, braver and more assertive. I wasn't a half, I was a whole who was coping; the boys were doing well, I was basically doing well. I had a mountain to climb but instead of always looking ahead at the impossible summit, I needed to turn around and look how far I had come. I pleaded with her to fast-forward me through grief, as I hated feeling like this. She wisely said, everyone's grief is different, some are short, some are long and you will get through it if you want to.

I met other widows and widowers…the club no one wants to join. I went on a Cruse weekend away which was the most humbling experience. I met there a gorgeous young woman who had been eight months pregnant with her first child when her husband committed suicide. I met many who were struggling financially or who had children who were being difficult and not coping at school. None of this applied to me. I really was lucky and should count my blessings. James had achieved a decent set of General Certificate of Secondary Education exams just months after his father died and the boys and I were closer than ever. No teenage angst, they just wouldn't do it to me. I knew I wasn't always a fully functioning parent; Chris's university application came back refusing him entry to his chosen university until they had more information about his 'criminal conviction'! He had ticked the wrong box on the application form, the sort of thing we both would have picked up normally.

The months turned into years and slowly the pain eased; I was coming to terms with Hugh's death and was beginning to look to my future and how I wanted it to look. During the year out I did a lot of thinking. The gift that grief gives you is that you realise your own mortality and suddenly life is more precious and should not be wasted. It felt as though I was dishonouring Hugh's memory if I wasted life by being miserable. I had to pull myself out of grief and get on living this precious life in a positive, productive way, as Hugh would have wanted.

I also thought about what *I* wanted; a new challenge in my career, a new partner, but he had to be the right man. It was safer to stay on my own than venture into a bad relationship so I was in no rush. I would have liked a new home, not the big family home Hugh and I had built together. I wouldn't do much about making this all happen until the boys had left home but as a precursor I did a lot of tidying that year. Way before I had ever heard of Marie Kondo and the 'The Life-Changing Magic of Tidying' I was sorting the garage, drawers and cupboards. It felt empowering; every tidy, organised drawer felt like my life was coming back together again.

Maggie's Cancer Charity also became part of this new life. Just before Hugh died we read about the proposed Maggie's Cancer Caring centre that would be built in Cheltenham if they could raise funds. Maggie's is a charitable organisation, a drop-in centre that provides emotional, psychological and practical support to all cancer sufferers, their friends and family. In the past cancer support has basically been palliative but thankfully so many more people are surviving cancer. It is always a huge trauma in your life and there was a growing need for support for cancer survivors. Hugh and I read about Maggie's in the paper weeks before his death and we both agreed that that sort of support was much needed and would have been helpful for us. The collection from Hugh's funeral went to Maggie's and it wasn't long before we started the Community Fundraising Board. Helping Maggie's felt positive, got me out to new events on my own and helped me make new friends. I am still part of it today and so proud of the fact that many thousands of visitors have been through the door since Maggie's Cheltenham opened in 2010.

How to start a new career was a whole new challenge, I had only ever worked for the National Health Service. Again I consulted a counsellor, not Cruse this time, as this wasn't a grief issue, but I had seen the benefit of talking problems through with a trained counsellor.

As a fiftieth birthday present a lovely friend paid for me to have my colours done with Jan from 'House of Colour'. The difference was profound. Women who are depressed want to appear invisible and research shows they dress in dark, neutral colours. Looking back the colour had gone out of my life and it was now time to embrace my fabulous 'winter palette' of clear, bright, cool-based colours. I followed the colour session with the style day where I learned how to dress for my body shape, to choose fabrics, shapes and styles of clothes that flattered; clothes that reflected my personality, clothes I loved. I had a major cull of my wardrobe and started wearing less frumpy clothes in my most flattering colours and shapes. It felt great. I looked younger and the effect was hugely confidence boosting. At the style day I told Jan I was at a turning point and wanted a new career and she said "Sian you could do this job if you wanted to."

Later her words kept going over and over in my head. Could I really desert the National Health Service, its final salary pension, the security of a paid job and run my own business? ...*yes I could!* Life is for living!

In 2010 I qualified as a 'House of Colour' consultant and not long after I bought the Gloucestershire franchise from Jan. The training wasn't easy and running your own business has many challenges but somehow I was coping, in fact more than coping. Running your own business means you can busy yourself twenty-four hours a day if you want to, and as I was learning so much I immersed myself in it all and life wasn't so lonely. It was a win-win situation. I was looking better as my personal style developed which gave me more confidence. Clients came to me happy and excited that they were going to have a lovely time with me and they left even happier. I could also work from home and was in control of my diary to work around the boys. Apart from the paperwork it is the best job in the world! I love meeting so many people and helping them in what is often a life-changing way.

It was meeting one of my clients that triggered the next change in my life. All the time the boys lived at home I didn't feel the need to pursue the idea of a new relationship seriously. If it had happened I would have been delighted but it didn't. I briefly 'went online' but nothing more than emails and the odd first meeting. Internet dating rather shocked me as I realised there are some very damaged men out there, men who had been badly hurt by women, not something I had ever come across. I found the process emotionally draining and hugely time consuming, which when you are busy with a business I didn't need.

Once Gareth left for his gap year travels, I was completely on my own and the need to find a partner became more important. A client came to have her colours analysed and over lunch I found out she was new to the area. She explained she had been widowed and had moved to this area when she married her new husband. I asked her how they had met and she said it was through internet dating. She had devoted an entire nine months to 'the project' as she called it. Signing up for many sites, she invested all her time and energy into it and after 'kissing many frogs' she had finally found her wonderful new husband and was blissfully happy. I thought of Hugh's mantra that you 'make your own luck in the world' and realised I had to prioritise this and make it happen. In fact I think that if Hugh could see me now, he probably wouldn't recognise the woman I've become – and he may well not be able to cope with her!

I rewrote my dating profile and signed up again and decided to have a more positive but light-hearted attitude to the whole ghastly process. My adventures online proved to be a source of amusement; my sister Dee loved hearing the latest instalments. After one disastrous meeting with a UK Independence Party candidate who looked nothing like his profile, my sister was still laughing when her friend Jilly called by, and she told her the whole sorry tale. That afternoon Jilly played golf with Hedley. Having been widowed and now divorced, Hedley asked her "Surely you have a nice friend I can meet, I've been on my own long enough?" Jilly put the two conversations together and by the end of the week Hedley had invited me out to dinner. We hit it off immediately. Both two lonely people looking for love. Hedley is a lovely man; we share the same values and want the same things from life and make each other laugh. We have both been through the mill and so value our relationship enormously. For me love second time around is very special.

It is now nearly twelve years since I was widowed and three years since I met Hedley. I have survived grief and come out the other side: I have finally reached my summit! Six months ago Hedley and I moved in together into our lovely new home. I am sixty years old this summer and really want to celebrate. Sixty is nothing for me to fear, I am grateful to be here, and happy to embrace my aging self – that is not to say I am letting things go. I believe in exercise, healthy eating, and of course making the best of your appearance; it is about your attitude to it all. I am at peace with myself and in a happier place than I have ever been. I am happy with Hedley, I enjoy my work and genuinely want to help others feel better about themselves. My experiences have molded me into a very content being, safe in the knowledge that if life isn't as you want it you can, and should, do something about it. It might take time but just keep going. I am realistic; ill health will hit one of us at some time in the future but I hope we can push back the bad times for many years yet. For my future? Well just more of the same…ooh and some grandchildren would be lovely!

Biography

Following the death of her husband, Sian's personal journey to peace has seen her reinvent herself. A new career, a new partner, a new home, a new life!

Sian is an award-winning Colour Analyst and Personal Stylist with House of Colour and believes that striving to be the very best version of you, both mentally and physically, is empowering. As her self-esteem and confidence grew she felt more able to deal with life. Sian now helps her clients realise their true potential through colour and style, believing that "everyone deserves their own personal stylist."

Sian is also a community fundraiser for Maggie's Cheltenham, a drop-in centre for those affected by cancer.

www.cruse.org.uk
www.maggiescentres.org
www.houseofcolour.co.uk
www.houseofcolour.co.uk/siandavies

Acknowledgements

Heartfelt thanks to the many who have contributed to this book, not least the incredible, generous-hearted women whose stories unfold in this, the second volume of '*Women of Spirit*' – for without you there would be no book! You are an inspiration and true life-enhancers.

Thank you to my mother Jill Grayston for your continued support and the time you spent editing these stories while being a full-time carer to my darling father – bravo you!

Tracey McAtamney, your gentle spirit touches many through Ladies First Professional Development, and with our collaboration, together we are surely stronger. I am so proud of my Ladies First special award 'Advocate for Women', thank you!

Henny Maltby, your absolute belief in '*Women of Spirit*' and your expertise in helping me 'get it out there' is hugely appreciated.

Amy Wright, you are such a talented young writer and your input helping me grow '*Women of Spirit*' across social media is truly valued.

Helen and Anna at SilverWood Books, thank you for your expertise and attention to detail during the publishing process. Here's to many more volumes of '*Women of Spirit*'!

Author's Note

How fortunate I am to have found my life's purpose in a way that leads me to meet so many amazing women! At the age of sixty I am in the best place ever, as living life with purpose is living life to the full. My mission? To enable as many women as the *Women of Spirit* books and movement can reach across the globe to live an authentic life, knowing their true value, and to thrive, not simply survive – and long before they reach sixty!

The word 'spirit' means 'the vital, animating essence of a person.' How very true that is, and exactly what I aim to capture in each woman's portrait.

For thousands of years, humans have been telling stories; they are now an intrinsic part of our society and culture – in fact storytelling is one of the many things that define and bind our humanity.

Stories inform people's emotional lives and we know that truth is sometimes stranger than fiction. Some of the stories in this book just couldn't be fabricated, so if fiction has the effect of increasing empathy towards others, how powerful might the stories in this book be?

It is my vision to share our stories with women who need support and inspiration. Through these stories, patterns, clues and signposts guide the reader towards inspiration, enlightenment and empowerment.

My aim is for women to know that they are not alone. And in this, I, and all the other women of spirit are working together – because as a team, we can achieve so much more. I invite you to join us via our website www.womenofspirit.co.uk

Mission Statement

To inspire and empower women to develop a healthy sense of self and to know their true worth.

Vision Statement

For women to lead a life full of confidence and strong self-worth, a world in which we inspire each other towards self-empowerment.

If You Enjoyed…

If you found this book worthwhile, please help us spread the word by popping onto Amazon.co.uk and writing a review. Thank you!

You are also very welcome to join our wonderful community on Facebook and Instagram – links via our website www.womenofspirit.co.uk.

Lightning Source UK Ltd.
Milton Keynes UK
UKHW051201030419
340402UK00002B/4/P

9 781781 328385